Research Highlights in Technology and Teacher Education 2013

Senior Book Editors

Leping Liu
David C. Gibson
Cleborne D. Maddux

Book Editors:

Victoria Brown
John Lee
Ron McBride
Paul Resta
Raymond Rose
David Slykhuis
Becky Sue Parton
Jeremy Wendt

Published by
AACE--Association for the Advancement of Computing in Education

Research Highlights in Technology and Teacher Education 2013
(ISBN: 978-1-939797-04-9) (ISSN: 2169-0839) is published by
AACE, PO Box 1545, Chesapeake, VA 23327-1545, USA
757-366-5606; Fax: 703-997-8760; E-mail: info@aace.org
© Copyright 2013 by AACE
www.aace.org

Available at http://www.aace.org/bookshelf.htm

Research Highlights in Technology and Teacher Education 2013

TABLE OF CONTENTS

Forward 5

Preface 7

Reviewers 12

PART 1 MOBILE LEARNING AND SOCIAL MEDIA

Revisioning Teacher Preparation for Mobility: Dual Imperatives 13
  Peter R. Albion, Romina Jamieson-Proctor, Wendy Fasso and Petrea Redmond (Australia)

The Role of Handheld Computing in Facilitating Teacher Resiliency through Problem Solving 23
  Irina Falls and Rita Hagevik (USA)

Knowledge and Practices Relating to Netbook Use: The Voices of Primary School Children in St. Vincent and the Grenadines 33
  Coreen J. Leacock, S. Joel Warrican and Andrea Veira (Barbados)

Is There Anybody Out There: Twitter as a Support Environment for First Year Teachers' Online Induction Workshop 41
  Yehuda Peled and Efrat Pieterse (Israel)

PART 2 ONLINE TEACHING AND LEARNING

Assessment Practices that Support Deeper Learning in Online Learning Communities 49
  David Gibson, Alexander Halavais, Nils Peterson (USA), Philipp Schmidt and Chloe Varelidi (South Africa and France)

Designing for Critical Thinking and Learning: Online Communication Platforms in Teacher Education 57
  Tina L. Heafner, Teresa M. Petty, Michelle Plaisance and Abiola Farinde (USA)

Students Being Teachers: Foucault's Eventalization in an Authentic E-Learning Hybrid Course 65
  Christopher Worthman (USA)

Parent Involvement and Student/Parent Satisfaction in Cyber Schools 73
  Dennis Beck, Robert Maranto and Wen Juo Lo (USA)

PART 3 TECHNOLOGY INTEGRATION IN PRESERVICE EDUCATION

Pre-Service Mathematics Teachers' Growth in Incorporating Technology into their Teaching Practices 81
 Barbara Ann Swartz and Joe Garofalo (USA)

The PBL-TECH Project: Web-Based Tools and Resources to Support Problem-Based Learning in Pre-Service Teacher Education 91
 Thomas Brush, Krista Glazewski, Anne Ottenbreit-Leftwich, John Saye, Zhizhen Zhang and Sungwon Shin (USA and China)

TPACK: Exploring a Secondary Pre-service Teachers' Context 101
 Petrea Redmond and Jennifer Lock (Australia and Canada)

Pen Casting in a Teacher Education Program 109
 Nancy B. Sardone and Barbara Cordasco (USA)

Aspects of an Emerging Digital Ethnicity 117
 Nan B. Adams and Thomas A. DeVaney (USA)

PART 4 IMPACT STUDIES

The Effects of Student Response Systems (SRSs) on Eighth Grade Pre-Algebra Students' Achievement and Engagement 125
 Lauren Happel, Sanghoon Park and Ron McBride (USA)

Do Gender and ADHD Affect Media Multitasking Attitudes and Behaviors? 135
 Lin Lin, David Bonner and Kim Nimon (USA)

Examining Factors Affecting Beginning Teachers' Transfer of Learning of ICT-Enhanced Learning Activities in Their Teaching Practice 141
 Douglas D. Agyei and Joke M. Voogt (Republic of Ghana and Netherlands)

PART 5 K-12 APPLICATION AND PROFESSIONAL DEVELOPMENT

How People, Tools and Rules Enhance or Inhibit Technology Use in the K-12 Classroom: A Design-Based Activity Systems Analysis 151
 John Cowan and Mayra Daniel (USA)

The Challenges and Supports of Teaching Geometry in a 1:1 Classroom 161
 Anthony Dove (USA)

Teachers Teaching Teachers Technology: An Innovative PK-12 Professional Development Program 169
 Mark W. Simpson and Sheila Bolduc-Simpson (USA)

Using Technology to Promote Mentoring and Reflection between Beginning and Experienced Math Teachers 179
 Denise Johnson, Farrah M. Jackson and Nancy Ruppert (USA)

FOREWORD

Research Highlights in Technology and Teacher Education is now in its fifth year of publication, and has become one of the most important journals for the *Society for Information Technology and Teacher Education* (SITE). This journal represents the best of the scholarship offered at the SITE international conference, this year held in New Orleans, and featuring nearly 1300 researchers and scholars from 62 countries!

Only a select set of articles, from the broad array of papers presented at the SITE conference, make it into the *Research Highlights* journal. To be considered for publication, a submission must first be accepted as a "full paper" and then designated for consideration as a potential article for the *Research Highlights* collection. At that point, an even more rigorous review commences. While still a "new" journal, *Research Highlights* is already one of the "most viewed" in the extensive holdings of the *AACE* digital library (EdITLib).

The articles in this edition are guided and nurtured by a strong team of editors, who frame the publication with an insightful preface. As I read the preface and the collection of articles in the journal, I am struck by the notion that I have a clearer sense of the current *state* of learning technologies, especially, as it relates to the field of teacher education. Moreover, it collectively represents an international perspective!

I am especially encouraged by the solid collection of articles that focus on "K-12 Application and Professional Development," as the 2013 SITE conference featured a prominent voice from K-12 education advocates. Through the commitment of LACUE (Louisiana's premier voice for K-12 educational technologists) and SITE leaders, an outstanding day of professional development, dedicated to the K-12 community, was offered as a pre-conference workshop.

This year's *Research Highlights in Technology and Teacher Education* is under the solid leadership of senior editors Leping Liu, David C. Gibson, and Cleborne D. Maddux. I cannot thank them enough for their steadfastness and professional dedication. As an organization, SITE is notably strengthened by their unyielding commitment and rigorous standards. In addition to their outstanding professionalism, the *Research Highlights* collection would not be possible without the dedication of the numerous book "editors" and "reviewers," who collectively did the tough editing and review work, necessary to bring this journal to fruition.

As you read this journal, I hope you consider ways that your voice can be represented in the future, first through a presentation at the SITE international conference and then through publication in *Research Highlights in Technology and Teacher Education*.

Regards,

Michael Searson, Ph.D.
President, SITE
Executive Director, School for Global Education & Innovation, Kean University

PREFACE

Research Highlights in Technology and Teacher Education is now in its fifth year of publication. Collections in this book series have presented a growing body of research, highlighted with contemporary trends and issues, creative methods, innovative ideas, theory and practice-based models, and effective use of traditional as well as new tools in the field of information technology and teacher education. This year, twenty chapters are organized into five themes: (a) mobile learning and social media, (b) online teaching and learning, (c) technology integration in preservice education, (d) impact studies, and (e) K-12 application and professional development.

MOBILE LEARNING AND SOCIAL MEDIA

Mobile learning has gradually become one of the top trends in learning technologies over the past decade. Mobile devices offer students from K-12 schools to universities a wide range of "on the go" opportunities to extend and enhance learning. Studies in this area have focused on effective ways to use mobile technologies in teaching and learning for teacher education students. Four chapters are included in this section.

In the first chapter "Revisioning Teacher Preparation for Mobility: Dual Imperatives," Peter Albion, Romina Jamieson-Proctor, Wendy Fasso and Petrea Redmond report a study conducted in two Australian universities in which participants used iPod Touch to access course materials and performed online activities in online courses that were designed to integrate the use of mobile devices. Differences are found between mean pretest and posttest attitudes toward using Information and Communication Technology (ICT), expected usefulness of iPod Touch for learning, frequency of using the iPod Touch for learning activities, and perceived desirability of a mobile device for study. The results indicate that obtaining the best outcomes from adoption of mobile technologies in teacher education will require adjustments to course design and to the behaviors of both preservice teachers and teacher educators.

Next, Irina Falls and Rita Hagevik present a study that explores "The Role of Handheld Computing in Facilitating Teacher Resiliency through Problem Solving." In this study, student teachers were instructed to use a mobile learning device (iPad2) and selected apps during their internship semester to cope with professional challenges and to develop resilience. Data were collected from three pretest and posttest surveys (*The Teacher Self-Efficacy Scale, The Resiliency Scale,* and *The Technology Use Survey*) and from weekly reflections. The authors provide suggestions concerning use of the strategies to develop resilience for pre-service teachers, and ways to use handheld devices to facilitate reflective problem solving during this resilience development.

Under a one-netbook-per-child policy, schools at all levels in St. Vincent and the Grenadines are gradually providing netbook computers to all students. To explore issues related to children's use of netbooks at home and school, interviews were conducted with 63 students in a sample of primary schools. In the third chapter "Knowledge and Practices Relating to Netbook Use: The Voices of Primary School Children in St. Vincent and the Grenadines," Coreen Leacock, S. Joel Warrican and Andrea Veira report the findings of the study. Children's knowledge relating to the technology, use of the machines, and misuse of this resource turned out to be the main issues when children started to use netbooks for their learning. These issues should be taken into consideration when initiating the use of any technology for children.

With social media applications, interactions take place in virtual communities and networks where people create, share and exchange information and ideas. In the fourth chapter, "Is There Anybody Out There: Twitter as a Support Environment for First Year Teachers' Online Induction Workshop," Yehuda Peled and Efrat Pieterse from Israel present a study that examines the benefits of Twitter as a support tool to enhance social interaction among 17 early-service teachers who participated in an online induction workshop. During the induction workshop, over two thousand tweets were posted, which provided constant monitoring of the participants' progress. Experiences and findings from this study could be of use to educators who are interested in using social media applications in their teaching and learning.

ONLINE TEACHING AND LEARNING

Online teaching and learning for teacher education has been studied for decades. At various times, research and practice have focused on areas such as: exploring the use of new platforms or tools to deliver online instruction, theories and practice of instructional design for online learning, means of communicating and collaborating in an online learning environment, assessment and evaluation for online..

Chapter five describes a framework for "Assessing Deeper Learning in Open Online Learning Communities," which consists of eight practices generated from a thorough examination of the literature by David Gibson, Alexander Halavais, and Nils Peterson from the United States, Philipp Schmidt from South Africa and Chloe Varelidi from France. The chapter begins by defining deeper learning and outlining a case for elevating formative, performance-based assessments over summative assessments; and then extends to the discussions on the eight practices that support deeper learning outcomes. This framework can serve as a research agenda for researchers in the field of teacher education.

Authored by Tina Heafner, Teresa Petty, Michelle Plaisance and Abiola Farinde, chapter six "Designing for Critical Thinking and Learning: Online Communication Platforms in Teacher Education" presents a qualitative study. The purpose of this study was to identify approaches that promote higher levels of engagement, learning, and dialogue in online learning environments. Multiple sources of data (such as individual interviews, asynchronous threaded discussions, archived logs of text chat, archives of both the synchronous and asynchronous sessions and candidates' submitted work) were collected from 30 preservice teacher candidates enrolled in online education classes. Five levels of analysis and a structured coding process were used to cross-validate data interpretations. Revised Bloom's Taxonomy (RBT) was also used as an evaluation tool to classify the level of cognitive development necessary for effective online learning to occur.

In chapter seven "Students Being Teachers: Foucault's Eventalization in an Authentic E-Learning Hybrid Course," Christopher Worthman describes the development and teaching of an authentic e-learning hybrid English language arts (ELA) methods course that illustrates Foucault's concept of *eventalization* and Gee's sociocultural theory of learning. In this self-study, the author analyzed blog entries and weekly discussion posts by preservice teachers enrolled in the course. Results show that the teachers demonstrated an understanding of the complexity and ambiguity that defines ELA as contextualized practice.

In the last chapter of this section "Parent Involvement and Student/Parent Satisfaction in Cyber Schools," Dennis Beck, Robert Maranto and Wen Juo Lo report on their investigation of parental involvement and school satisfaction in a cyber charter school, using a student (n=269) and parent (n=232) survey. Results show that increases in reported parent involvement are associated with higher levels of student school satisfaction. No statistically significant differences are found in school satisfaction across demographic groups. This study may provide implications for teacher education students when they prepare for their future teaching in a cyber school.

TECHNOLOGY INTEGRATION IN PRESERVICE EDUCATION

Technology integration is another key theme in the field of information technology in teacher education. This section features studies focusing on content area technology integration, and methods, strategies, or models used for technology integration. Five chapters are included in this section.

In chapter nine "Pre-Service Mathematics Teachers' Growth in Incorporating Technology into their Teaching Practices," Barbara Ann Swartz and Joe Garofalo document their study to investigate the improvement of preservice mathematics teachers' instructional practices through incorporation of technology. Data collection took place during a two-semester secondary mathematics pedagogy course consistent with the NCTM's Principles and Standards for School Mathematics. A multi-dimensional instructional observational tool, the Mathematics Scan, was used to measure mathematics instructional quality in nine dimensions. Eight pre-service teachers participated in the study. This chapter also describes their improved instructional practices in all dimensions.

In chapter ten "The PBL-TECH Project: Web-Based Tools and Resources to Support Problem-Based Learning in Pre-Service Teacher Education," Thomas Brush, Krista Glazewski, Anne Ottenbreit-Leftwich, John Saye, Zhizhen Zhang and Sungwon Shin discuss PBL-TECH, a project that provides a framework of problem-based-learning with the support of technology tools for collaborative learning. This chapter also identifies a set of Web 2.0 tools and resources to support the modeling and development of technology-enhanced problem-based instruction for K-12, and suggests that it is necessary for teacher educators and preservice teachers to increase their abilities to model and use the PBL-TECH strategies.

Petrea Redmond from Australia and Jennifer Lock from Canada authored "TPACK: Exploring a Secondary Pre-service Teachers' Context." This article documents a preliminary exploration of pre-service teachers' competency related to the TPACK concept. A self-rate survey was conducted with 55 secondary, preservice teachers at a regional university in Australia. The findings suggest that the preservice teachers are developing the necessary confidence in working with the technology, and designing innovative teaching and learning experiences with the TPACK framework.

Nancy Sardone and Barbara Cordasco authored chapter twelve "Pen Casting in a Teacher Education Program." They explored the use of pen casting for teacher candidates to prepare lessons in a variety of content areas. In their study, 16 teacher candidates created lessons with pen cast recording for their student teaching internship. Reactions from these teacher candidates, K-12 students and parents were collected and coded into themes of usefulness, attitude, and best uses of pen casts as an instructional method. This chapter offers another example of technology integration in preservice education.

In "Aspects of an Emerging Digital Ethnicity," Nan Adams and Thomas DeVaney describe their work on the development and validation of The Digital Ethnicity Scale (DES). The development process was conducted with more than 2000 respondents. The initial item set was retested and refined, resulting in a two-section final version of the DES, which contains a three-factor solution with 12 items for the first section, and a four-factor solution with 16 items for the second section. The chapter is included in this section as it provides reference to assessment work in the process of technology integration design in preservice education.

IMPACT STUDIES

In this section, three quantitative studies are included that examine the effects of certain variables on learning-related outcomes such as achievement, engagement, attitudes or behaviors. In these three studies, t-tests, ANOVA, and multiple regression were employed.

A study by Lauren Happel, Sanghoon Park and Ron McBride entitled "The Effects of Student Response Systems (SRSs) on Eighth Grade Pre-Algebra Students' Achievement and Engagement" begins the fourteenth chapter. This study examines the effects of using a student response system (SRS) with eighth grade, prealgebra students' achievement and engagement. Participants were 32 students from two intact pre-algebra classes with 16 students in each class. Posttests and engagement surveys were administered after a four week pre-algebra lesson, and data were analyzed using independent samples t-tests. The results indicate that students in the SRS group have significantly higher achievement and engagement than the students who did not use SRS in the classroom.

Chapter fifteen "Do Gender and ADHD Affect Media Multitasking Attitudes and Behaviors?" describes a study by Lin Lin, David Bonner and Kim Nimon. This study investigates gender and attention deficit/hyperactivity disorder (ADHD) as factors in adolescents' media multitasking attitudes, self-efficacy, and activity levels. Participants were 120 adolescents, half of whom had ADHD. Data were collected from three survey instruments. Two-way ANOVA analyses were used to evaluate the effects. Results revealed a significant interaction of gender with condition on media multitasking self-efficacy, attitude, and activity levels.

In chapter sixteen "Examining Factors Affecting Beginning Teachers' Transfer of Learning of ICT-Enhanced Learning Activities in Their Teaching Practice," Douglas Agyei and Joke Voogt report a study that examined the extent to which beginning teachers' transfer of learning of ICT- ABL to their teaching practice could be influenced by learner characteristics, characteristics of the professional development program, and school environment characteristics. Participants were 100 beginning teachers. Data were collected through an Email questionnaire. Multiple regression analysis was performed.

K-12 APPLICATION AND PROFESSIONAL DEVELOPMENT

In the first four sections, chapters are focused on studies with preservice teachers' practice. This last section of the book features K-12 related studies on inservice teachers' technology applications, school administrative support to teachers, and professional development in K-12 schools. Four chapters are presented.

Authored by John Cowan and Mayra Daniel, chapter seventeen "How People, Tools and Rules Enhance or Inhibit Technology Use in the K-12 Classroom: A Design-Based Activity Systems Analysis" presents a study that explores K-12 teachers' viewpoints of factors that support or inhibit the integration of digital media into a course for K-12 English Language Learners. The study used a design-based approach. Data were collected from 21 inservice teachers, including a short instructional video they created and narrative responses they wrote in the course. Data analysis yielded a summary of participants' reflections on the elements of rules, tools, people and division of labor. School functioning levels, from low to high, were determined by the capacity of a school to support teacher technology use, and the administrative rules that govern technology use.

In chapter eighteen "The Challenges and Supports of Teaching Geometry in a 1:1 Classroom," Anthony Dove describes a study that examined the challenges and supports that influenced teachers' instructional practices and technology integration while participating in a long-term professional development program. The program focused on teaching Geometry with The Geometer's Sketchpad (GSP). Participants were four geometry teachers. Multiple qualitative methods were used to gather data, including observations, interviews, emails, and lesson artifacts such as worksheets, GSP files, and websites. Cross-case analysis suggested that teachers faced challenges of time to complete activities and cover the curriculum, learn the affordances and constraints of GSP, and manage student discourse. Professional development was found to support teachers' needs to overcome the challenges.

In chapter nineteen, Mark Simpson and Sheila Bolduc-Simpson introduce "Teachers Teaching Teachers Technology: An Innovative PK-12 Professional Development Program" as an action research project studying the design, development, implementation and assessment of a professional development program for the training of PK-12 educators to use Web 2.0 technologies for the teaching of writing in their content areas. Participants were 22 educators in five counties in southwest Florida. Data were collected using pre-series, formative, summative and post-series tools, and on-site class visits. Findings indicated that use of the series was effective but that involvement by stakeholder school districts was necessary. Components of an effective professional development program model were suggested.

In the final chapter "Using Technology to Promote Mentoring and Reflection between Beginning and Experienced Math Teachers," Denise Johnson, Farrah M. Jackson and Nancy Ruppert introduce a two-year project, Fostering Effective Teaching Through Support (FETTS), which was designed to virtually connect beginning math teachers with experienced math teachers. Participants were experienced and beginning teachers from three North Carolina counties. Various technologies were tested and used to virtually connect mentees and mentors from various locations across the state. Data was collected by analyzing responses in online modules, blogs, surveys, and in professional growth feedback cycles. Results revealed that some technologies promoted reflection and mentoring interaction by providing convenience and programmatic integration while others challenged participants with technical specifications and a lack of ease of use.

Finally, we would like to take this opportunity to express our congratulations and our appreciation to the book review board, the eight book editors, and the authors of all the manuscripts contributed to this book. We believe that this outstanding collection of papers will be a welcome addition to the literature in the field of information technology in teacher education.

May 1, 2013

Senior Book Editors
Leping Liu
David C. Gibson
Cleborne D. Maddux

SITE BOOK REVIEWERS 2013

Peter Albion, University of Southern Queensland, Australia
Cindy Anderson, Roosevelt University, United States
Leanna Archambault, Arizona State University, United States
Youngkyun Baek, Boise State University, United States
Savilla Banister, Bowling Green State University, United States
Beth Bos, Texas State University, United States
Glen Bull, University of Virginia, United States
Livia D'Andrea, University of Nevada, Reno, United States
Aaron Doering, University of Minnesota, United States
Candace Figg, Brock University, United States
Penny Garcia, University of Wisconsin-Oshkosh, United States
Mark Hofer, College of William and Mary, United States
Natalie Johnson, Arkansas State University, United States
Kathryn Kennedy, International Association for K-12 Online Learning
Kioh Kim, University of Louisiana-Monroe, United States
Lin Lin, University of North Texas, United States
Chrystalla Mouza, University of Delaware, United States
Priscilla Norton, George Mason University, United States
Marilyn Ochoa, University of Florida, United States
Mark Rodriguez, Sacramento State University, United States
Merryellen Schulz, College of Saint Mary, United States
Scott Slough, Texas A & M University, United States
Debra Sprague, George Mason University, United States
James Telese, University of Texas, Brownsville
Tandra Tyler-Wood, University of North Texas, United States
Roberta Weber, Florida Atlantic University, United States
Jana Willis, University of Houston-Clear Lake, United States
Thomas Winkler, Institute for Multimedia and Interactive Systems, Germany
Harrison Yang, State University of New York-Oswego, United States
Melda Yildiz, Kean Univ

Revisioning Teacher Preparation for Mobility: Dual Perspectives

Peter R. Albion
University of Southern Queensland, Australia
Peter.Albion@usq.edu.au

Romina Jamieson-Proctor
University of Southern Queensland, Australia
Romina.Jamieson-Proctor@usq.edu.au

Wendy Fasso
CQUniversity, Australia
w.fasso@cqu.edu.au

Petrea Redmond
University of Southern Queensland, Australia
Petrea.Redmond@usq.edu.au

Abstract: Widespread availability of smartphones and similar devices with connection to the Internet is influencing the evolution of higher education across disciplines. For teacher educators there is an additional consideration of how to prepare teachers to use such devices in their own practice once they graduate. This paper will address some related issues and report results from a study conducted in two Australian universities. The evidence confirms that obtaining the best results from adoption of mobile technologies in teacher education will require adjustments to course design and to the behaviors of both pre-service teachers and teacher educators.

Background

Educational technology advances affect teacher education differently than other university disciplines. All disciplines share a focus on how educational technology can enhance learning and teaching within the discipline at university but teacher education has an additional challenge to consider how the introduction of new technologies affects how graduates will approach learning and teaching in their own professional practice. In addition to adopting new technologies to enhance the learning of pre-service teachers, teacher educators need to adapt their programs to prepare graduates for using the new technologies in their own future practice. In this paper we address these dual perspectives with respect specifically to the emergence of mobile technologies in education.

Smartphones

The smartphone, that is a mobile phone with Internet access and functions common to personal computers (ACMA, 2011), is rapidly becoming a staple of everyday life in modern societies. Of the 89% of Australian adults owning a mobile phone in April 2011, 37% had a smartphone (ACMA, 2011) but just a year later that proportion had risen to 52% (Ipsos, 2012). Where the ACMA report found that users accessing the Internet with their mobile phone had increased by 63% from 2.4 million to 3.9 million between June 2010 and June 2011, Ipsos found that 58% of smartphone owners used their phone to go online every day and 74% did not leave home without it.

According to Norris and Soloway (2011), we are entering an age of *mobilism,* in which access to mobile personal computing devices will be commonplace. They distinguish between *mobile* devices, those small enough to be *always* carried, and *portable* devices such as laptops, netbooks and tablets, which can be carried but are too large to be placed in a pocket or bag and are less likely to be always available. Mobility is the key to ubiquitous access to services, information, and educational opportunities, either stored on the device or available through its connection to the Internet. Norris and Soloway (2011) predicted that by 2015 every K-12 student in the USA will be using their own mobile device. Other observers agree that mobile devices and associated software will be adopted by K-12 schools in the near term (Johnson, Adams, & Cummins, 2012b). Given the rapid uptake of smartphones in Australia and the history of 1:1 computing in Australian schools (Albion, 1999) we expect that Australian schools will experience similar trends. The *Teaching Teachers for the Future* project (Romeo, Lloyd, & Downes, 2012) did much to build the Information and Communication Technology (ICT) in education capacity of graduating teachers. However, not all participating institutions included work related to mobility. Hence, there is still much work needed to assist graduating and continuing teachers to work effectively with mobile devices in their classrooms.

Flexible learning

In 2006, 70% of full-time Australian undergraduates were working almost 15 hours per week on average, 15% were working more than 20 hours, and almost 5% were working full-time (James, Bexley, Devlin, & Marginson, 2007). Undergraduate students also include mature students with family commitments. In 2009, 24% were 25 years or older and 15% were older than 30 (DEEWR, 2010). The proportion varies across disciplines but in 2006, 45% of teacher education students were 25 years or older and 10% were 40 years or older (DEST, 2006). Commitments to family and work may limit the availability of students to attend classes on campus. Hence many Australian university students are selecting distance or online study for all or part of their degrees. Implicit in those decisions is their desire for flexibility to study at times and places of their choosing, which is not possible with scheduled classes on campus or even with distance or online study that is dependent upon delivery of bulky printed materials or media that must be accessed using a computer, whether via network or using locally stored content.

Universities challenged to match the needs and expectations for flexible study are using Learning Management Systems to facilitate online access to resources and activities for learning and teaching. Nationally, from 2001 to 2010 multimodal enrolments (partially on campus and partially off campus) rose from 4% to 8% (DEEWR, 2011). At one of the universities in this study, the proportion of web-based enrolments increased by more than 400% from 2006 to 2010 (USQ, 2012) and in 2012 up to 70% of students in the 4-year Bachelor of Education program were studying some subjects online. At the same time, students enrolled on campus are likely to access materials and activities from online sources made available to all students irrespective of mode of study. These changes in enrolment patterns reflect the priority being given by students to flexible study options. Smartphones and related devices will be increasingly important elements of future flexible study options. Hence it is important to understand the potential and the implications of mobile technologies for learning and teaching.

Literature review

Researchers have suggested that mobile devices enable, or even require, new pedagogies. Norris and Soloway (2011) described a move from a teacher-centric "I teach" pedagogy to a "We learn" pedagogy in which the teacher learns with the students. This movement from pedagogies of scarcity, through which difficult to access information was transmitted from teacher to learner, toward pedagogies of abundance (Weller, 2011) is a necessary accommodation to a world affected more by information overload than scarcity. Networked mobile devices that permit instant access to rapidly changing information from around the globe have rendered human memory of information less necessary and sometimes potentially dangerous because it is out of date.

Generalizability of early mobile learning (m-learning) research was limited by the differing capabilities of devices (Trifonova, 2003). Studies using PDAs, cellphones, and other devices offered insights into m-learning (Cobcroft, Towers, Smith, & Burns, 2006) but the introduction of the iPhone in 2007 delivered a mobile device combining capabilities such as PDA, cellphone, web browser, music player, and camera. Other smartphones followed and capabilities continue to expand, opening possibilities expected to be soon adopted in higher education and K-12 (Johnson, Adams, & Cummins, 2012a; 2012b). A recent review (Pollara & Kee Broussard, 2011) noted the variety of devices featured in m-learning research but confirmed the increasing pervasiveness of the mobile phone. Most older learners own mobile phones and the 10 to 16 age group is a key target for telecommunication companies (Franklin, 2011). Norris and Soloway (2011) reported benefits for learning with smartphones that they attributed to increased time on task because of the high likelihood that the device would be available at any time.

Increasingly versatile smartphones can be used in diverse learning contexts, varying by both time and place, to support learning activities that make use of convenient access to information. Pedagogies developed to enable a teacher to deliver information in a fixed location (classroom) will need to be replaced by pedagogies of abundance (Weller, 2011) that are capable of being implemented with flexibility in time and space to accommodate the needs of learners with a variety of commitments beyond study and a variety of mobile devices available.

This need for transformed pedagogies has been recognized and research efforts have been committed to exploring pedagogies using mobile technologies with outcomes offering both practical suggestions and principles for ongoing design (Herrington, Mantei, Olney, Ferry, & Herrington, 2009). The 11 key principles emerging from that study included real world relevance of learning activities; using mobile tools in non-traditional and mobile contexts; encouraging personalized, spontaneous and exploratory uses; and "prod*using*" by using mobile learning to produce and consume knowledge. Work by other researchers arrived at a more compact description using three constructs: *authenticity*, *collaboration*, and *personalization* (Kearney, Schuck, Burden, & Aubusson, 2012). Although there is not yet a definitive theory of mobile learning there are signs of convergence around key ideas.

Teacher educators need to consider mobile learning from two perspectives, namely, how mobile learning can enhance teacher preparation and how best to prepare graduating teachers for mobile learning in their K-12 classrooms. This paper will be guided by two questions related to those perspectives:
1. What lessons for implementation of mobile learning in universities can be drawn from the experience of pre-service teachers with a mobile device, specifically the iPod Touch?
2. What lessons for preparing teachers to work with mobile devices can be drawn from their experience with a mobile device, specifically the iPod Touch?

Method

This project, from which this paper reports results obtained from teacher education students, was conducted within teacher education and nursing education programs at two Queensland universities during two consecutive teaching semesters in 2011 and 2012. The main aim of the project was to investigate the affordances and constraints associated with mobile devices for enhancing distance and online student learning opportunities. The iPod Touch was selected for use because it offers very similar capabilities to a popular smartphone (iPhone), lacking only the telephony and 3G data capabilities, but was significantly less expensive and avoided the logistical complications of initiating and managing a large number of short-term registrations on the mobile telephone network.

Each university had 40 iPod Touch devices (20 each for education and nursing) for distribution on a 'first come' basis to students responding to invitations issued at the beginning of each semester in selected subjects. At the end of each semester the iPods were returned for reuse. Each student who accepted the invitation completed a research consent form and an acceptable usage agreement form. The iPods, and iTunes gift cards ($30) to support the purchase of relevant software, were distributed to the volunteers by regular mail.

This paper presents data from undergraduate students taking ICT and pedagogy courses within the teacher preparation programs at their respective universities. The ICT and pedagogy courses explore the use of ICT for teaching and learning in school classrooms in order to prepare students for integration of ICT during professional experience placements and may include students from Early Childhood, Primary, Secondary, and Special Education specializations. Although the host courses at the two universities performed similar functions within their respective programs, there were some differences in the specifics of course operation between the universities and between the first and second semester of project operation in each case.

University 1: The selected course included all schooling sectors. Assessment tasks required collaborative exploration of digital tools and facilitation of a digital learning event to inform peers about a new tool. It also required students to demonstrate how they met relevant professional and employer standards for ICT use. Students developed an e-portfolio to present evidence and reflections of ICT integration during professional experience.

During the first semester of the project a member of the research team facilitated the host course. In addition to 19 students who responded to the invitation and accepted an iPod Touch to use for the semester, there were two additional students who participated using their own iPhones. Three students withdrew during semester, citing workload pressure. The course was offered online, using a Learning Management System (LMS), which was based on Moodle, to store documents, recorded lectures, tutorial activities, additional readings and online discussions. Synchronous weekly tutorials in Wimba were offered to the whole class. No materials were modified for specific use on the iPods but a separate area in the LMS provided information about using the iPods and discussion forums for both learning and social purposes. Students shared how they used their iPods on their three-week professional experience placement as well as during the Christmas break which fell in the middle of the semester. They also used a wiki to share ideas related to learning and working with a mobile device. The iPod research area was available to all course participants but only project participants interacted in that space.

Arrangements for the second semester of the trial were similar to the first except that a new member of the Faculty who was not associated with the project was the facilitator of the host course. The same member of the research team was responsible for issuing invitations and liaising with the 18 students who accepted the invitation to participate in the second semester. The general direction of the course remained as it was in the previous semester but the structure and operation were somewhat modified by the new facilitator. As in the first semester, course materials and activities were not modified to accommodate the iPods.

University 2: The selected course explored how ICT provides a platform for teaching and learning, creativity and innovation. The same member of the research team facilitated the host course in both semesters of the project. The course was designated as an e-learning course in which students accessed study materials presented as text, images, audio or video through a Moodle LMS. In addition to the regular materials prepared for access using a standard computer, the facilitator arranged for mobile learning materials, formatted for a small screen, to be available as an option. Materials ordinarily delivered using Flash-based applications were either transcribed or converted to be compatible with iOS devices. Tutorials related to the iPod Touch were created and an online synchronous session, using Elluminate, was scheduled to introduce the devices and recommended apps.

Timing for the mail-out to distribute the devices to participants in the first semester of the project was problematic. To allow time for students to settle into an intense set of courses, recruitment began with an online class meeting in the first week but the first mail-out was delayed until the end of the second week and it was Week 4 before the list of 19 participants was finalized. Participants were advised at the outset about the data collection processes but were not pressed to complete them immediately. Rather they were encouraged to take time to become familiar with the device. Five participants withdrew during the semester, citing workload pressure. Early in the semester it became apparent from student discussions and reflections that the iPod Touch was considered to be an "aside" to the course. Tutorials were adjusted to more explicitly treat the iPod as a device with potential to support learning and planned activities were modified to include mobile options. The process of making the iPod Touch relevant for learning in the course was important for creating opportunities for discussion about its affordances and that resulted in more students expressing interest in participation in the project.

In the second semester of the project 24 participants were recruited from the beginning of the semester. The devices were mailed in the second week. Rather than instructions being delivered in an initial meeting as in the first round, they were provided by email, which ensured that participants had a record for reference. The course was adapted to better integrate the use of the iPod Touch into the design and learning materials. For example, where digital images were explored, the use of the iPod to generate and share images was encouraged.

Data collection

An instrument was developed using published scales (Albion, Jamieson-Proctor, & Finger, 2010) and additional scales specific to the project. The substance of all items remained the same for pre-test and post-test but some items were adjusted to reflect prospective responses in the pre-test and responses based on experience in the post-test. The items addressed interest in, and attitude toward, using ICT for learning, expected (actual in the post-test) ease of use of the iPod Touch for learning, expected (actual in the post-test) usefulness of the iPod Touch for learning, frequency of use of ICT (iPod Touch in the post-test) for study activities, and desirability of a mobile device for study. Each scale, other than 'frequency of use', used a 5-point Likert scale from strongly disagree (1) to strongly agree (5). The frequency of use measure used a 6-point scale (1=Not Used; 2=Once/twice a semester; 3=Once/twice a month; 4=Once/twice a week; 5=Once a day; 6=Several times a day). Questionnaires were administered online using LimeSurvey® (www.limesurvey.org) in the first and last weeks of each semester. Data were transferred to SPSS 19 for analysis. Scores were calculated and reported as average ratings. Table 1 lists the scales with sample items from the pre-test version and Cronbach's alpha reliability calculated for both pre-test and post-test. In all cases alpha values were high, indicating excellent internal reliability. Although the focus of this paper is on data collected from pre-service teachers, the reliability values were calculated using all available data including that collected from nursing education students. Reflections by students and facilitators, focus group interviews with participants, and records of online discussions were used to collect qualitative data. These data were analyzed thematically.

Scale	Sample items from pre-test version	# items	Cronbach's alpha Pre-test (N = 94)	Post-test (N = 49)
Attitude to ICT for learning	I currently use ICT for study extensively I have the technology skills I need to use ICT in my study	13	.91	.95
iPod Touch ease of use for learning	Learning to operate the iPod Touch will be easy for me The iPod Touch will make communicating with my peers easier	6	.91	.92
iPod Touch usefulness for learning	Using the iPod Touch in my course will enable me to accomplish tasks more quickly Using the iPod Touch will improve my course results	6	.91	.97
ICT [iPod in post] frequency of use for study	I use ICT to access course study materials through the university website I use ICT to communicate with my instructor/s	30	.92	.97
Desirability of mobile devices for study	… it will help me get better results … it will improve my career or employment prospects in the long term	13	.92	.98

Table 1: Characteristics of scales used in the questionnaires

Results

All participants were invited to complete the online questionnaires at the beginning and end of their semester. With 80 iPods available in each of two semesters across nursing and education courses, there were 160 potential responses across the project. Table 1 displays 94 completed responses for the pre-test and 49 for the post-test. Online distribution (no face-to-face class meetings) may have limited the response rate. Respondents were requested to enter a code in the questionnaires to enable anonymous matching of pre-test and post-test responses. For this analysis the data were further reduced to just education students for whom matched pairs of responses to the pre-test and post-test could be extracted. Those totaled 28, 17 for one university and 11 for the other.

Independent samples t-tests compared pre-test and post-test means for participants from the two universities on each of the semesters. There were no significant differences between the universities for responses collected during the first semester of the trial. For the second semester University 2 returned significantly greater means for usefulness (3.76 cf. 3.25) of the iPod Touch for learning measured on the pre-test ($t = 2.185$, df = 28, $p = .044$, $d = .83$) and for desirability (3.75 cf. 2.48) of mobile devices for learning measured on the post-test ($t = 2.636$, $df = 15$, $p = .021$, $d = 1.36$). In both cases equal variances were not assumed. Effect sizes are calculated as Cohen's d.

Scale	University	N	Pre-test Mean	SD	Post-test Mean	SD	t	df	p	d
Attitude to ICT	University 1	17	4.34	.55	4.48	.50	-2.54	16	.022	-.27
	University 2	11	4.40	.61	4.18	1.10	.536	10	.604	.25
Ease of use	University 1	17	3.47	.53	3.16	.77	1.88	16	.079	.47
	University 2	11	3.59	.74	3.11	1.10	1.19	10	.263	.51
Usefulness	University 1	17	3.24	.71	2.38	1.12	3.23	16	.005	.92
	University 2	11	3.48	.62	2.80	.81	1.99	10	.075	.94
Frequency of use	University 1	17	3.73	.74	1.70	.56	10.07	16	.000	3.09
	University 2	11	3.88	.69	2.78	1.21	3.21	10	.009	1.12
Desirability of mobile device for study	University 1	17	3.74	.54	2.60	1.16	3.99	16	.001	1.26
	University 2	11	3.84	.55	3.70	.77	1.63	10	.135	.21

Table 2: Combined pre-test and post-test mean ratings and significant differences on scales

Table 2 reports pre-test and post-test means and standard deviations together with significance values for paired samples *t*-tests conducted for each university using combined data from both semesters. Table 3 displays equivalent data for individual semesters where paired samples *t*-tests detected significant differences between pre-test and post-test means. The numbers of responses for the individual semesters were small and the relevant t-test statistics should be interpreted with caution.

Semester	University	Scale	N	Pre-test Mean	SD	Post-test Mean	SD	t	df	p	d
1st semester	University 1	Usefulness	10	3.30	.78	2.45	1.19	2.66	9	.026	.84
		Frequency of use	10	3.65	.48	1.82	.56	7.92	9	.000	3.51
		Desirability	10	3.82	.55	2.70	1.21	2.76	9	.022	1.19
2nd semester	University 1	Attitude	7	4.30	.58	4.56	.50	-4.77	6	.003	-.48
		Frequency of use	7	3.86	1.04	1.53	.55	6.56	6	.001	2.80
		Desirability	7	3.63	.54	2.47	1.16	2.80	6	.031	1.28
	University 2	Usefulness	6	3.44	.36	3.03	.70	2.61	5	.048	.74

Table 3: Semester pre-test and post-test mean ratings and significant differences on scales

Preliminary analysis of qualitative data has revealed broad trends relevant to the questions addressed in this paper.

University 1: Data from the first semester at University 1 were analyzed thematically and considered from the perspective of activity theory (Albion, Jamieson-Proctor, Redmond, Larkin, & Maxwell, 2012). Key themes that emerged were access, convenience, and mobility but these three and other concepts were often linked in a single statement. For example, a student reported using the iPod to "listen to lectures while I walked my dogs." Most participants did not report changes to communication but changes to interaction with course materials were more commonly reported. References to access in responses to an open-ended question about the most useful aspects of the iPod Touch were mainly about accessing recorded lectures or other course materials. Similar themes emerged in the second semester of use. Students commented on access to study materials, including audio recordings, and ability to respond to email and forums in different locations away from their computer. Some also mentioned using educational applications with K-12 students during professional experience.

Students in both semesters commented on size as a limitation. Example comments included "size of the screen was far too small to spend any real amount of time using the device" and "screen size of the device was small and at times it made it hard to read study material". However, there was also recognition that "tablet or iPad would be better, but they are often too big." The reliance on WiFi for Internet connection was also experienced as a limitation. Students commented that "without an Internet connection access to course materials can be limited to what has been synced to the device prior to leaving Internet access" and "only being able to use the internet where

WiFi was available was a disadvantage." There were also issues reported with formatting of the university website and some course materials were not well adapted for mobile devices.

University 2: University 2 response to open-ended items revealed similar themes. Students noted the "ability to access the internet and work offline with materials for courses", easy access to "podcasts and videocasts", that the iPod "saved me carting my laptop ... more work done as I would just whip it out and do an assignment when I was waiting." A key difference at University 2 was the adjustment of the course in the second semester to more actively integrate the iPod Touch so that class activities made more frequent, specific reference to the iPod.

Although the second group of participants generated little data through questionnaires and other focused methods, examination of their assessment work revealed marked differences compared to participants in the first semester. In the first trial, 3 of 19 participants mentioned the iPod, identifying video functions as valuable, and one wrote about the need for teachers to "be mindful of the outcomes they are trying to achieve ... and not just use [the iPod] for the sake of including a technological tool." One noted the functionality of the iPod as "web browser, media player, apps, camera and much more" and used it in teaching plans for capturing video for upload to YouTube. In the second trial, 13 of 24 students reflected on the iPod Touch or mobile phones in their first assessment. Their comments related to apps for specific learning such as phonics, vocabulary and numeracy; utility uses such as the iPod as a remote mouse permitting teacher mobility in the classroom; access to remote files using Dropbox; content creation by allowing "children to film, cut and paste, record sounds, add sounds to other applications"; sharing and collaborating because "these tools allow children to be able to take an image ... and send it all the way across the world while holding it in your hand." One student noted that all expectations for student use of ICT could be met using the iPod Touch. Students also demonstrated awareness of the need to guide children about appropriate use such as "asking permissions from others before taking photo, video or audio recording of them" and "giving accreditation to other peoples' work or words". In the second assessment several students integrated iPods into lesson plans with a variety of activities including recording data using photographs, audio and video; and conducting surveys using services such as polldaddy.com. Compared to the first semester, students moved from offering rare suggestions about using the iPod Touch to integrated explanations of how the device enhanced pedagogy.

Discussion

Of 70 pre-service teachers who accepted the offer to work with an iPod Touch, 64 completed the pre-test and 39 the post-test questionnaires, with 28 pre-post pairs able to be matched. Although the response rate was low (40%) the analysis identified some trends in the data at each university, some consistent and some contrasting. At both universities, students reported positive attitudes toward the use of ICT for learning and that was maintained, or in one case increased, across the semester. The host courses at both universities addressed ICT for learning, which probably contributed to the students' positive attitudes. There were no significant changes in the ease of use scale, suggesting that the iPod Touch did not present any usability challenge to students at either university.

Measures of usefulness and desirability of a mobile device for learning decreased from pre-test to post-test, in some cases significantly. The qualitative data from both universities included comments about small screen size and limitations of WiFi connectivity that may partially explain why the reality of using the iPod Touch did not match initial expectations. In some cases reported difficulties in accessing the LMS and other materials not explicitly formatted for mobile devices will have contributed to reduced perceptions of usefulness and desirability. The frequency of use scale recorded the largest decrease, implying that the iPod Touch did not support the range of activities for which participants used ICT. The 30 item pre-post scale covered a variety of uses of ICT, some of which would not be possible using the iPod Touch. Analysis at the item level may reveal more meaningful patterns.

Based on their comments many students from both universities saw the iPod Touch as an interesting novelty rather than central to their learning. That impression will have been reinforced by any difficulties encountered in using it with course materials and activities, especially for those unfamiliar with its operation and least able to solve problems they encountered. This interpretation is consistent with the facilitators' observations. It seems likely that some of the issues lie with the LMS (Moodle) being poorly configured for mobile access and some materials, such as PDF files, being inappropriate for the small screen because text does not reflow and requires scrolling when magnified to a readable size. Alternative formats, such as HTML and ePub, may be more suitable.

What was learned about implementing mobile learning at universities? Although some online learning materials and activities were easily accessible using the iPod Touch others would require conversion. Some of the issues raised in student responses about screen size and other device characteristics may have reflected this mismatch while others may have arisen from unrealistic expectations. Implementing mobile learning will require varying degrees of redesign of course materials and activities to suit handheld devices. In the short term, until familiarity with device capabilities can be assumed, it will also require user education for both facilitators and students and some management of expectations. There is a tendency to consider the potential of mobile devices for delivering content to learners but, as was evident in some data from University 2, there is also potential for the devices to be used to capture and create content that can be shared with other participants in a course. A shift of that kind may be more confronting because it challenges the traditional transmissive pedagogies of scarcity to recognize the possibilities of pedagogies of abundance based on information being readily available to all.

What was learned about preparing teachers to work with mobile devices? Experience with mobile devices is an important foundation for thinking about how such devices might be used for learning and teaching. Students in all groups expressed appreciation of the opportunity to explore the potential of the device. However, the greatest impact was apparent in the second semester at University 2 where the course was modified to explicitly deal with the iPod Touch and its potential. The impetus from explicit discussions encouraged students to explore a wider range of possibilities and the opportunity to include the products of those efforts in assessment pieces meant that the time allocated to working on those pieces was available for exploration of the iPod Touch and its affordances. If graduating teachers are to be prepared for working with mobile devices in their classes then it will be necessary to ensure that they have access to devices together with time and reason to explore the potential. Building assessment activities around the use of mobile devices appears to be one effective approach to achieving that outcome.

Acknowledgement

This *Distance Education Hub (DEHub)* project was funded by the Australian Government Department of Education, Employment and Workplace Relations (DEEWR).

References

ACMA (2011). *Australian Communications and Media Authority Communications Report 2010-11*. Retrieved from http://www.acma.gov.au/webwr/_assets/main/lib410148/communications_report_2010-11.pdf.

Albion, P., Jamieson-Proctor, R., Redmond, P., Larkin, K., & Maxwell, A. (2012). Going Mobile: Each Small Change Requires Another. In M. Brown (Ed.), *Future Changes, Sustainable Futures. Proceedings of ascilite 2012*. Wellington, NZ.

Albion, P. R. (1999). Laptop Orthodoxy: Is Portable Computing the Answer for Education? *Australian Educational Computing, 14*(1), 5-9. Retrieved from http://www.acce.edu.au/journal/journals/vol2014_2001.pdf.

Albion, P. R., Jamieson-Proctor, R., & Finger, G. (2010). Auditing the TPACK Confidence of Australian Pre-Service Teachers: The TPACK Confidence Survey (TCS). In C. Maddux, D. Gibson & B. Dodge (Eds.), *Research Highlights in Technology and Teacher Education 2010* (pp. 303-312). Chesapeake, VA: Society for Information Technology in Teacher Education.

Cobcroft, R., Towers, S., Smith, J., & Burns, A. (2006). *Literature Review into Mobile Learning in the University Context*. Brisbane: Queensland University of Technology Creative Industries Faculty.

DEEWR (2010). *Students: Selected Higher Education Statistics*. Retrieved from http://www.deewr.gov.au/HigherEducation/Publications/HEStatistics/Publications/Pages/2009FullYear.aspx

DEEWR (2011). *uCube - Higher Education Statistics*. Retrieved from http://www.highereducationstatistics.deewr.gov.au/

DEST (2006). *Survey of Final Year Teacher Education Students*. Retrieved from http://www.dest.gov.au/sectors/school_education/publications_resources/profiles/documents/FinalYrTeachStudentsSurveyReport_pdf.htm.

Franklin, T. J. (2011). The Mobile School: Digital Communities Created by Mobile Learners. In G. Wan & D. M. Gut (Eds.), *Bringing Schools into the 21st Century* (pp. 187-203). New York: Springer.

Herrington, J., Mantei, J., Olney, I., Ferry, B., & Herrington, A. (Eds.). (2009). *New Technologies, New Pedagogies: Mobile Learning in Higher Education*. Wollongong: University of Wollongong.

Ipsos (2012). *Our Mobile Planet: Australia - Understanding the Mobile Consumer.* Retrieved from http://services.google.com/fh/files/blogs/our_mobile_planet_australia_en.pdf

James, R., Bexley, E., Devlin, M., & Marginson, S. (2007). Australian University Student Finances 2006: Final Report of a National Survey of Students in Public Universities. Retrieved from http://www.universitiesaustralia.edu.au/documents/publications/policy/survey/AUSF-Final-Report-2006.pdf

Johnson, L., Adams, S., & Cummins, M. (2012a). *The NMC Horizon Report: 2012 Higher Education Edition.* Austin, TX: The New Media Consortium.

Johnson, L., Adams, S., & Cummins, M. (2012b). *The NMC Horizon Report: 2012 K-12 Edition.* Austin, TX: The New Media Consortium.

Kearney, M., Schuck, S., Burden, K., & Aubusson, P. (2012). Viewing Mobile Learning from a Pedagogical Perspective. *Research in Learning Technology, 20.*

Norris, C. A., & Soloway, E. (2011). Learning and Schooling in the Age of Mobilism. *Educational Technology, 51*(6), 3-12.

Pollara, P., & Kee Broussard, K. (2011). Student Perceptions of Mobile Learning: A Review of Current Research. In M. Koehler & P. Mishra (Eds.), *Society for Information Technology & Teacher Education International Conference 2011* (pp. 1643-1650). Nashville, Tennessee, USA: AACE.

Romeo, G., Lloyd, M., & Downes, T. (2012). Teaching Teachers for the Future (TTF): Building the ICT in Education Capacity of the Next Generation of Teachers in Australia. *Australasian Journal of Educational Technology, 28*(6), 949-964.

Trifonova, A. (2003). *Mobile Learning - Review of the Literature* (Technical Report No. DIT-03-009). Trento: University of Trento.

USQ. (2012). *University of Southern Queensland 2011 Annual Report.* Toowoomba: University of Southern Queensland.

Weller, M. (2011). A Pedagogy of Abundance. *Spanish Journal of Pedagogy,* 249, 223-236.

The Role of Handheld Computing in Facilitating Teacher Resilience through Problem Solving

Irina Falls
School of Education
University of North Carolina at Pembroke
United States
irina.falls@uncp.edu

Rita Hagevik
Science Education
University of North Carolina at Pembroke
United States
rita.hagevik@uncp.edu

Abstract: Becoming an effective teacher that thrives not only survives involves much more than finishing a licensing higher education program. This study explored problem-solving strategies that student teachers used during their internship semester to cope with professional challenges and to develop resilience. The research questions in this study included: What strategies support the development of resilience? How are teachers approaching the professional dilemmas encountered? How can handheld devices facilitate reflective problem-solving? Six student teachers from early childhood education, special education, and science education used mobile computing devices for a variety of professional and personal purposes and reflected upon and documented uses. Data was analyzed using a case study approach. Major themes included risk factors such as low self-confidence, and protective factors such as strong motivation to teach, and critical reflection skills. Mobile technology devices proved to be easy to use and very helpful in the problem solving process.

Introduction

Increasing novice teacher effectiveness and retention especially in problematic teaching districts has been a topic of concern and study for many years. While many studies have focused on the multiple challenges that teachers face in both rural (Zost, 2010) and urban areas (Tait, 2008; Margolis, 2008; Huisman, Singer, & Catapano, 2010; Castro, Kelly, & Shih, 2010), researchers recently have shifted their interest towards the concept of "teacher resilience" by investigating the specific factors that enable certain teachers to remain and be successful in their profession (Gu & Day, 2007, Beltman, Mansfield, & Price, 2011).

While resilience appears to be an essential factor in teacher retention (Yonezawa, Jones, & Singer, 2011), defining it and conceptualizing the mechanisms through which some teachers cope with adversity and become effective, satisfied professionals, is a complex endeavor and therefore there is not an agreed upon definition to date in the literature (Beltman et al., 2011).

While some authors argue that resilience is a mixture of personal and environmental attributes, most agree that it can be shaped at least in part. Bernshausen and Cunningham (Zost, 2010) identified several characteristics of resilient teachers which included: skillful in their teaching area, a feeling of acceptance by the school and the community, the ability to adjust and prevail over challenges, a higher level of determination and a strong desire not to fail, and a positive outlook about themselves, their school, and life in general.

Currently, resilience is perceived by the majority of authors not so much as an innate quality of the individual to "bounce back", but rather as the result of a complex and dynamic process in which a series of factors interact (Day & Gu, 2007; Howard & Johnson, 2004; Castro et al., 2009). Thus, by responding to difficult situations with a resilient "nature", an individual learns how to shape their own learning and how to improve problem-solving skills. Studies of the intricate interplay between risk and protective factors conclude that resilience can be learned and will ultimately produce teachers who "stay in the profession [and] do not just survive, but thrive as confident and healthy professionals." (Beltman et al., 2011, p. 196)

In their review of the teacher resilience studies since 2000, Beltman et al. (2011) found evidence of two types of factors whose interplay might lead to resilience: risk/challenging factors and protective factors. Individual risk factors include low self-confidence, difficulty asking for help, conflict between personal beliefs and school practices while contextual risk factors might be related to family, school/classroom characteristics, or other professional work contexts.

Protective factors (supports) in teacher retention have been extensively studied, although like the risk factors, they were not always explicitly related to the concept of "resilience". Among the individual protective factors perception of self-efficacy (Tschannen-Moran & Hoy, 2007), capacity to problem solve (Yost 2006), personal strengths and characteristics such as strong motivation to teach (Gu & Day, 2007), and critical reflection (Bobek, 2002; Gu & Day, 2007) are cited as being essential. Some authors stress the importance of students' ongoing reflection for analyzing and solving dilemmas and for getting a better perspective of the teaching and learning context and the role of oneself in it (Kuechle, Holzhauer, Lin, Brulle, & Morrison, 2010).

In the context of the above data, it seems that the process of building teacher resilience is the missing link between the knowledge and skills acquired during the teacher preparation programs and their application in the classroom for becoming effective and fulfilled professionals. Exploring how novice teachers approach and solve the personal and professional dilemmas as they happen by documenting the events and strategies immediately is important for capturing some nuances and even emotional reactions that could be lost in later reports. Mobile technology devices seem to be the tool of choice for such notations.

In teacher education, there is evidence suggesting that student teacher performance and self-efficacy can be improved using technology (Kopcha, & Alger (2011). More recently, ubiquitous handheld computing offers countless potential uses in field investigations (Soloway, Grant, Tinker, Roschelle, Mills, Resnick, et al., 1999; Franklin, Sexton, Lu, & Ma, 2007; Bennett & Cunningham, 2009). Mobile technology has changed not only the way teachers work with information and assessment in schools, but also the way they interact with their environments and situations. Ubiquitous computing has been proven to facilitate increased communication and knowledge access as well as being useful for planning, organizing, and restructuring students' activities (Franklin et al., 2007). While most studies to date have concentrated on how teachers use mobile devices to improve instruction and learning, some authors have seen the potential of using mobile devices to address problems encountered during field experience and internship. Peng, Su, Chou, and Tsai (2009) and Seppälä & Alamäki (2003) focused on the advantages of using mobile devices to facilitate the discussion of teaching issues between the preservice teachers and their university supervisors. Bennett and Cunningham (2009) used handhelds tools to support formative assessment in the elementary classroom to engage students in an active constructivist model of learning while Chen (2011) confirmed the benefits of teachers using the Mobile Assessment Participation System (MAPS) in self and peer- assessments by students in the classroom. However, to date there are no studies explicitly using mobile devices to capture without delay the challenges and processes the preservice teachers encounter during their student teaching period or to investigate how these mobile devices can mitigate challenging factors and increase protective ones.

Method

Research Questions

The study's main purpose was to explore the various professional dilemmas encountered by preservice teachers during their internship semester and to discover how they manage the transaction between the protective and risk factors as described in the teacher resilience literature.

1. What are the main professional dilemmas identified by the student teachers?
2. In what ways can mobile technology mitigate risk factors and increase protective factors for student teachers?
3. How can mobile devices change the way student teachers solve problems or professional dilemmas in the classroom?
4. How can handheld computing support student teachers in developing as reflective practitioners that are resilient?

Participants

A total of 6 undergraduate students in their semester of student teaching were recruited from a public university in the Southeast United States. The preservice teachers were pursuing a teaching license in their internship semester (student teaching) of their plan of study, and enrolled in the following teacher education programs: 3 in Special Education, 1 in Early Childhood Education, and 2 in Science Education. They were enrolled to fulfill their internship in the spring semester 2012 and have not taught as lead teachers before this internship. The participants are all females, of ages between 26 and 42 years of age and included the following races: White (Caucasian)-3, African American-2, and Native American-1.

Procedure

The handheld computing devices used were iPads2 and were distributed to students at no charge for the duration of the semester (16 weeks). None of the study participants owned or had used a portable device before except smartphones. The participants attended a two-hour training session that included the following:

Training in problem solving techniques. The participants were informed about the procedures to follow in documenting and reflecting events and practices, as well as in the use of the handheld mobile devices and their applications. Procedures for getting support in coping with challenging events were also put into place by establishing communication pathways with the university supervisor, mentors, and colleagues.

Establishing the methods, timing, and rules for noting and keeping records of the challenging events and reflections. The participants were asked to record and upload their problems/dilemmas once a week. They were also scheduled to communicate with the university supervisor periodically.

Basic training in using the mobile devices and the applications required for the project. The participants were instructed to use the mobile devices (iPads) for several purposes including the following:
  a. Searching for possible solutions to the encountered problems/dilemmas
  b. Implementing the chosen solution such as individualizing instruction for a child, organize activities for a group of children, behavior management.
  c. Using the various productivity applications to manage scheduling, tasks, and time planning.

Seven major categories of challenging situations were offered to the preservice teachers for organizing their problem solving/dilemmas using the reflective problem-solving strategy and the hand-held devices: (1) the first day of teaching, (2) working as a team with the cooperating teacher, (3) classroom behavior management, (4) sensitivity to the needs of children with difficult home circumstances, (5) observations by the university supervisor, (6) inclusion practices, and (7) breaking through with a difficult student (Kuechle et al., 2010). However, the participants were encouraged to add any other challenging situations to these general categories.

The student teachers were instructed to use an application - "I can do it – Motivation!" (Bonfire Development Advisors, Inc., 2012) - that was already installed on their iPad. This app streamlines the basic problem solving steps and walks users through three easy steps to identify their blocking thoughts and feelings, and to rephrase them to be more actionable. The content of the problem solving notes were then emailed to the researchers.

There were several apps downloaded on the iPads that the participants were instructed to use; they included notes, draw diagrams, and visually organizing thoughts. In addition, the students were free to use the mobile devices as needed for both professional and personal needs.

Because of their mobility, handheld devices were supposed to facilitate note-taking in various contexts while ideas are still fresh and therefore help solve problems and remember facts. Involving preservice teachers in the learning of problem solving steps and resilience building processes using handhelds devices certainly lent to an active, constructivist learning experience.

Data collection
1. Weekly reflections that the student teachers were required to submit as part of their internship seminar.
2. Problem solving notes of professional dilemmas or problem situations occurred in a specific format using the iPad application "I can do it – Motivation!" (Bonfire Development Advisors, Inc., 2012).
3. Exit interviews were semi-structured interviews to gather information about both the most important experiences and personal characteristics that may evidence resilience, as well as use of mobile devices to solve problems. The interview prompts included the following topics: background information about the participants and the internship school, preparation for teaching, sources of support available, problem solving skills, perceived teaching effectiveness, and use of the mobile devices.

Data analysis
The weekly reflections, problem solving process documents submitted by the participants, and the final semi-structured interviews were qualitatively analyzed as a whole through content analysis. Two categories of information were identified:
1. Types of risks/challenges and protective factors documented by the student teachers
2. The role of mobile technology devices in facilitating the problem solving process and in mitigating the risk factors.

Using the structure of risk factors and protective factors described by Beltman et al. (2011), the data was assigned to various categories and subcategories. For example, risk factors could be individual (negative beliefs, low self-confidence) or contextual (related to the particular school or classroom or to professional workload and difficulty). The individual protective factors included personal attributes, self-efficacy, coping skills, teaching skills, professional reflection and self-care while the contextual protective factors addressed professional and personal support. Although the data collected was analyzed rather deductively (i.e., according to Beltman's existing coding system), the subcategories remained flexible and amenable to the additions of new ones if necessary. Two researchers reviewed every document for content analysis with an inter-rater reliability of 86%.

Results

Resilience factors

The main Risk/challenge factors expressed by the participants have been grouped into five main categories. The most frequently expressed challenge was related to classroom management and coping with disruptive students. This category belongs to the contextual risk factors, in this case the context being the classroom. The student teachers did not feel prepared to cope with students who had disruptive or defiant behaviors and wished they had more training. One student teacher writes *"*MD came into the class with the attitude of wanting to work, but when I gave her the assignment she just closed up on me. When asking her to write she would not respond to anything I asked her. I need to get help with this situation. I panicked. What do I do? What did I do wrong?" while another noted "[…] had a student today who was disrupting the class by giggling, making noise, and attempting to coerce his peers into joining in to his negative behavior. I needed to stop the disruptive behavior so we could move on with the lesson but had no idea how to do that without stopping the other students from learning. I wish I have learned more classroom management skills because you don't really know how much you can do until you are actually in the classroom." Two students mentioned that not being present at the beginning of the semester when the clinical teacher established the classroom rules was a disadvantage in maintaining an orderly environment. The students' problem solving process showed that they searched for suggestions and solutions to behavior problems in common sense and their peer student teachers rather than their clinical teacher, university supervisor or professional literature.

The next risk factor often mentioned was the teacher workload, in addition to actual classroom teaching. This category belongs to the contextual risk factors, in this case the context being the professional work. This category was mentioned especially often by the special education students. The student teachers were surprised and felt overwhelmed by the amount of paperwork involved and by the nonteaching activities that the special education teachers in particular were asked to perform: "There is so much more to teaching than the classroom…. I really need to be aware of the home environment of children because so many come from either poverty or special circumstances"; "There is a lot of planning involved in teaching- overwhelming […] especially when you do not know exactly how to do it."; "I watch my clinical teacher work every day on paper work for new and existing students and it is amazing to see how she handles the stress". The reflections showed that this concern was less evident towards the end of the semester, when supposedly they acquired strategies to manage their schedule and workload.

Concern about emotional involvement with their students and work stress (Personal factors – emotional management) was another frequent topic of worry for the interns. The majority were worried about not being able to separate personal from work related involvement. One student teacher said about a student coming from a family who neglected her where she was not groomed and had the same clothes for a whole week "I'm concerned that my heart strings will want to take over when I am a teacher and how do I balance my emotions with all of my students?" One student teacher specifically expressed her wish to be able to control their emotions "Will I be able to control my emotions or will I break down and cry?" The student teachers became quite involved with the school performance of some students and even contacted their families. One student related "I had a student who would come to the class every morning high, you could not smell or anything but his eyes were bloodshot and he wanted to sleep the whole time. He was also a senior. He was like "I don't care" and I continued telling him "you really can do it" and then one day he came to me and said "What can I do to make up all this work?" And finally he started doing his work, his parents were not cooperative. [So you contacted his parents?] Yes, I told them he really needs to do this, but they said oh well, we really hope he graduates from high school, and the clinical teacher said "don't worry about it", he is not going to do it, but he started trying, he would be on time now. He finally started to try harder and his grades went up. I will go to the school to see if he continued improving and graduate." One participant even expressed concern about being so "emotionally drained and stressed" that she might not be able to effectively parent her own child at home. "This week I feel like I am over my head, with school and with my family. I think I can be a great teacher, but what do I do about being a parent for my own child?"

Time management and organization was often mentioned as a significant challenge due to the multitude of tasks the teachers are expected to accomplish. Several of the problems participants needed to solve were fatigue and stress. One student teacher writes "I need to go through this morning sessions because I feel so tired." During the exit interview another student teacher said "I feel like I have walked into a world were multi-tasking is a must. I made the discovery that teachers have a lot of things placed on them, some at very short notice. Would have liked to know in advance how a day of work would look like, organization of events, planning."

Finally, relationships with their colleagues was a concern for special education teachers who worried that regular education teachers did not communicate enough with them regarding inclusion of children with special needs and coordinating the learning goals included in the Individual Education Plan. "I am concerned about my role as a Special Education teacher and working with the General Education teachers" said one student teacher referring to a session in which they worked on a child's upcoming meeting with the parents. Relationship with colleagues was also a concern for two of the other student teachers in relation with assessment of students and planning meetings for the whole school.

The main Risk/challenge factors found in the collected data could also be grouped into five general categories. Flexibility was the quality that the student teachers mentioned most often as necessary for coping with various situations in the classroom. "What would help me be more successful in teaching is trying to be a more 'go with the flow person', to be more flexible, make adjustment, sometimes in the middle of a lesson. I used to be more of a planner and stick with the plans but teaching would challenge that." To have problem solving skills means to find solutions to situations in which the answer is not immediately apparent. It takes the ability to explore various options and to be willing to accept and apply unusual resolutions. As a result, flexibility is part of problem solving as a protective factor in the resilience process.

The second most often mentioned protective factor identified in teachers' reflections was having a sense of competence, pride, and confidence in their work and their abilities to be effective. Although most student teachers did not feel very confident in their teaching or behavior management, they agreed that an effective teacher needs to know she is competent and leads the children on the learning path. Through the reflections during the internship, the students discovered and commented on their personal and professional growth and the process of building self-confidence and self-efficacy as they became more experienced. As the student reflections progressed later into the semester, they were showing more confidence in their ability to teach and to handle unexpected situations such as behavioral manifestations. The common theme at the beginning was that they felt just like visitors in the classroom, whereas gradually they began to recognize they can have a role and the students listen to and respected them as participants in the educational process. "I have more responsibility in the classroom which is accompanied with more independence" said one student teacher while another remarked "I know the routines and what needs to be done in the mornings, during class, and after school and I am able to get stuff done without anyone asking me to do it". This process was not easy and during many weeks they often doubted themselves, questioning and arguing back and forth their choice to become a teacher.

Helping students succeed and having high expectations of them was mentioned by four of the six student teachers as being an important ingredient of teacher success. One participant said that having high expectations of your students comes from self-confidence in ones abilities. "I love children, I want to teach them and watch them grow; I have confidence in my ability to plan lessons" said one participant when asked what will make them an effective teacher. Another participant mentioned that in order to survive in this profession you need "to believe that all children can succeed and keep telling them they can do better."

Intrinsic motivation for teaching in the form of declared commitment to the profession and desire to make a difference in the lives of children was implied by all interns through various remarks during their reflections and interviews. One participant said "I wanted to be a teacher ever since I was in preschool. Both my parents are teachers and I often ask them for ideas. I know that I can do this even though it is not going to be easy all the time." Another student teacher stated "[...] questioning why teachers are not paid more or more recognized for the work they do! It truly is a profession that is demanding but very rewarding and sometimes pay is not the main reason you do it."

The last main category of protective factors was related to the availability of mentorship during the first years of teaching years. This was mentioned by three of the six interns who expressed the needed to consult with an experienced teacher in addition to the clinical teacher and the university supervisor. This necessity can be explained by the fact that a mentor would be someone neutral who is not in a position of evaluating their performance, his or her only role being to strictly provide suggestions and feedback. The mentor therefore is perceived as a nonjudgmental person to whom the interns could talk more openly.

Use of mobile technology

During the exit interviews the interns revealed their use of the iPads during the student teaching period. All but one student stated that they used their iPads daily for various purposes. These uses were grouped in the following broad categories: professional use, personal use, and use for problem solving. The problem for which the iPads were used could be related to work (professional) or to personal life but it stand as a separate category because a problem solving process was involved. For this category the solution was not clear from the beginning as was the case with the other uses.

Use of iPads for professional purposes

All students used the iPad to help them in planning their lessons, either by using it to write lesson plans on the go or by looking for applications or videos to use in their teaching. Another universally common use of the iPad was to reward the students by letting them use it for educational purposes. Still other students used the iPads to individualize instruction. For example, one intern would give the iPad to a student who needed help with reading and would let him play reading games while his classmates were involved in higher level reading activities. In the younger grades the iPads were used for playing educational games in small groups - "Animal Words", "Tic-Tac-Toe", "Puzzles", "Crayola LCC"- while in the science classes they were used to investigate various subjects through the science apps. Another professional use was for jotting down notes while in the classroom. *"The iPad is so easy to grab and so easy to access. You jot down things that you would forget otherwise"*. Interns also used the iPads for networking with their colleagues and for sharing or asking for teaching tips.

Use of iPads for personal purposes

The interns admitted that it was easy to use the iPad for keeping a personal calendar, to-do lists, or for playing mindless games to relax after a long day at school. Although it might seem that this use has nothing to do with resilience, one of the personal protective factors that play an important role in building resilience is taking care of oneself (Beltman et al., 2011). Social networking, playing games, surfing the web, are considered important activities for relaxation and mental health and the student teachers were using the available devices to fulfill these needs.

Use of iPads for problem solving

Although there is sufficient evidence in the data collected in this study that the student teachers used the iPad to solve many problems encountered in their internship semester, the participants did not keep a record of their challenges/professional dilemmas in a structured format as suggested initially. They seemed overwhelmed by the workload of the internship and followed the recommended problem solving steps only partially. Despite the fact that the participants were documenting some of the problems encountered, listed several barriers and "blocking thoughts", and provided possible courses of action, the final step of choosing a solution and implementing it was not acknowledged in the data. The writing up of encountered problems was an additional task that was not required by the internship and therefore was perceived as optional. In future studies the problem solving steps should be included in the required reflections in order to be able to have a periodic and documented record of the challenges they face and the solutions they consider in solving them. Some of the problems the mobile devices were used in are described below.

Individualization of instruction was used often by all participants. For example, the iPad was used as "reward for students who finished tasks to use looking at science apps", "downloaded several educational games that D.S. could do", "really helpful to use with the English Language Learners[…] had pictures of the words learned in our weekly topic".

Another frequent use of iPads was to cope with emotionally difficult situations. One student was embarrassed to dress up as character in the "Wizard of Oz" story – as all teachers decided - because he thought his authority in the classroom would be diminished and he would feel ridiculous and unable to perform his role as lead teacher. Another study participant described how she as extremely nervous the first day of teaching and used the problem solving steps to identify her emotions and come up with a plan.

Behavior management of difficult children in the classroom was logged as a problem by four out of the six participants. One of the students shared with the other participants ClassDojo (Class Twist, Inc., 2012), an application that is a classroom tool helping teachers improve behavior in their classrooms quickly and easily. It also captures and generates data on behavior that teachers can share with parents and administrators. Although this was a solution found through their professional learning group instead of the traditional problem solving steps, it seemed to work very well in all the classrooms and supported the case of the benefits of using mobile devices for resilience building.

Both science education interns reported looking up answers to student questions (give it to the student who asked). The same students also described instances in which they researched content and strategies for lesson plans. Four out of six students reported that they used the mobile technology devices to make lessons more interesting and capture the attention of difficult children in class (e.g., "[…] app like a Whiteboard and you can record yourself talking and you can draw on the whiteboard at the same time then you can connect it to the projector and present it in class.").

Another way in which the iPads were used for problem solving was to take notes for later write up of puzzling situations or for incorporating certain student behaviors in lesson planning ("Jot down notes for myself, for example when I was outside.")

Finally, the mobile device was used to demonstrate the clinical teachers how technology can be used and hoping they would be willing to use mobile technology more frequently in the classroom ("used the iPad sometimes to teach my clinical teacher about the various uses [role reversal]"). One particular student reported that she would have liked to use her iPad during formative assessment but her clinical teacher was not in favor because she was not used to it and insisted that the student teacher conducts the assessments the "way it was always done."

Discussion

The purpose of this article was to explore whether the kinds of professional dilemmas student teachers encounter in the classroom and the processes used to cope with them can be better understood as well as mitigated through the use of mobile devices. The focus was on the problem solving process as a main contributor to the development of resilient teachers that do not only survive but strive in adverse environments. By providing the student teachers with mobile devices (iPads) a variety of possible strategies to cope with challenges and develop resilience were uncovered. The results indicate that mobile technology devices not only facilitate many tasks and activities in the day of a teacher, but also add countless possibilities to professionally and personally supporting the teacher and to solving problems.

The student teachers identified several problems but three of them seemed pervasive: managing teacher workload in addition to classroom teaching, coping with emotional involvement at the workplace, and time management and organization. Classroom management seem to be a concern for most teachers independent of the region where they teach or the years of experience and this finding should be an indication that teacher education programs might not be doing enough to prepare their graduates for this challenge.

On the other hand, finding that all participants have found difficult to separate their emotional involvement with the children in their classrooms and were concerned about maintaining an emotional balance between the work place involvement and their own family life was unexpected. Although teachers' emotional involvement is mentioned by some authors (Vanoverbeke & Cavanaugh, 2001; Oplatka, 2004), it is evident that there is nothing in the teacher education programs to prepare them for this effect. Since a sense of wellbeing and emotional control seems to be an intrinsic part of the resilience process, the teacher candidates need to be warned about it and provided with adequate strategies to cope with it.

Finally, the time management and organization challenge seemed to be mentioned by all participants while two of them explicitly mentioned that it would have been extremely helpful if, before beginning their internship they would have knowledge about what a typical day of a classroom teacher looks like and what is the sequence of events. During their higher education program teacher candidates have many field experience requirements but they are not asked to spend an entire day in a classroom.

Many of the problems described may not have been as accurately described and the attached emotions correctly identified without the help of mobile technology devices.

Mobile devices proved very effective at mitigating risk factors and increasing protective factors for student teachers in several ways. As anticipated, the mobile devices served both as easily accessible tools to record notes anytime and anywhere as well as instruments capable to deliver the needed solution. As recording instrument, the "I can do it – Motivation!" (Bonfire Development Advisors, Inc., 2012) proved to be and adequate, if not ideal, tool to document dilemmas and to guide the teachers through the problem solving steps including acknowledging and identifying their emotional reactions to the situation. However, a more appropriate application is needed for solving professional dilemmas since these need more time to explore and research various options before settling on implementing one of them. The iPads were also used by all participants to write notes and short messages related to classroom events that needed to be remembered such as ideas for future lesson plans or observations about a particular child.

The mobile devices also provided easy solutions to several professional challenges such as individualizing instruction, educational gaming in small groups of children with similar abilities, quick answers to students difficult questions by letting them search the web and then share the result, and task and time management. An unanticipated use of the mobile devices and their applications was for social networking and playing games as relaxation activities although Beltman et al. (2011) have found that self-care is an important characteristic of a resilient teacher.

The results of this study indicated that mobile technology devices can be a powerful tool for both documenting and facilitating resilience building in beginning teachers. Applications for education and personal productivity purposes exist in such a vast number that every teacher can find at least one containing a solution to particular problems. However, the most efficient way to find out about the best applications is to be part of a professional learning community focused on mobile technology in the classroom. It is widely known that teachers are increasingly embracing the mobile devices for instructional purposes and student assessment but it is less known how this technology is transforming their personal and professional life.

Finally, handhelds have proven to be extremely useful for increasing the ease with which the student teachers were able to take notes about events and behaviors that they later reflected on and made decisions about. Teacher reflection has been identified as one of the most powerful ((Bobek, 2002; Gu & Day, 2007; Kuechle et al., 2010) protective factors in building resilience. By using mobile devices the teachers can now take short notes anywhere and anytime about things they want to come back to and reflect on.

Conclusion

Teacher resilience seems to be an operational term that defines teachers who not only survive in a difficult profession and high needs school environments, but teachers who are also effective and enjoy their work. As demands on teachers continue to increase, teacher education programs are faced with the daunting task of preparing their candidates not only with knowledge and skills but also with the ability to successfully cope with the professional challenges of the job. While limited in several ways, the results of this study suggest that mobile devices were successful in providing easy access to documenting challenges and in improving the problem solving strategy and repertoire of solutions for student teachers. In addition, the results indicate that when given the opportunity, student teachers will use technology to take care of their personal needs as well as their professional ones. Such evidence serves to inform teacher education programs about the missing components that should be added to their curriculum in order to increase resilience in their teacher candidates.

References

Beltman, S., Mansfield, C., & Price, A. (2011). Thriving not just surviving: A review of research on teacher resilience. *Educational Research Review, 6*(3), 185-207. doi:10.1016/j.edurev.2011.09.001

Bennett, K., & Cunningham, A. C. (2009). Teaching Formative Assessment Strategies to Preservice Teachers: Exploring the Use of Handheld Computing to Facilitate the Action Research Process. *Journal Of Computing In Teacher Education, 25*(3), 99-105.

Bobek, B. L. (2002). Teacher resilience: A key to career longevity. *Clearing House, 75*(4), 202. Retrieved from http://0-search.ebscohost.com.uncclc.coast.uncwil.edu:80/login.aspx?direct=true&db=ehh&AN=6519729&site=ehost-live

Bonfire Development Advisors. (2012). i Can Do It - Motivation! Version 3.0.0 [Mobile application software]. Retrieved from http://itunes.apple.com/

Castro, A. J., Kelly, J., & Shih, M. (2010). Resilience strategies for new teachers in high-needs areas. *Teaching & Teacher Education, 26*(3), 622-629. doi:10.1016/j.tate.2009.09.010

Class Twist, Inc. (2012) ClassDojo, Version1.2.0 [Mobile application software]. Retrieved from http://itunes.apple.com/

Day, C., & Gu, Q. (2007). Variations in the conditions for teachers' professional learning and development: Sustaining commitment and effectiveness over a career. Oxford Review of Education, 33(4), 423–443.

Franklin, T., Sexton, C., Young, L., & Hongyan, M. (2007). PDAs in Teacher Education: A Case Study Examining Mobile Technology Integration. *Journal Of Technology & Teacher Education, 15*(1), 39-57.

Gu, Q., & Day, C. (2007). Teachers resilience: A necessary condition for effectiveness. *Teaching & Teacher Education, 23*(8), 1302-1316. doi:10.1016/j.tate.2006.06.006

Howard, S., & Johnson, B. (2004). Resilient teachers: Resisting stress and burnout. Social Psychology of Education, 7(4), 399–420.

Huisman, S., Singer, N. R., & Catapano, S. (2010). Resilience to success: Supporting novice urban teachers. *Teacher Development, 14*(4), 483-499. doi:10.1080/13664530.2010.533490

Kopcha, T. J., & Alger, C. (2011). The impact of technology-enhanced student teacher supervision on student teacher knowledge, performance, and self-efficacy during the field experience. *Journal of Educational Computing Research, 45*(1), 49-73. Retrieved from http://0-search.ebscohost.com.uncclc.coast.uncwil.edu:80/login.aspx?direct=true&db=ehh&AN=66481752&site=ehost-live

Kuechle, J., Holzhauer, M., Lin, R., Brulle, A., & Morrison, S. (2010). Teaching Ms. Kerbin: A Unique Approach to Student Teacher Reflections and Their Use with Preservice Candidates. *Action in Teacher Education, 32*(3), 25-39.

Margolis, J. (2008). What will keep today's teachers teaching? Looking for a hook as a new career cycle emerges. Teachers College Record, 110(1), 160–194.

Oplatka, I. (2004). Women Teachers' Emotional Commitment and Involvement': A Universal Professional Feature and Educational Policy. *Education & Society, 22*(2), 23-43.

Peng, H., Su, Y., Chou, C., & Tsai, C. (2009). Ubiquitous knowledge construction: Mobile learning re-defined and a conceptual framework. *Innovations in Education & Teaching International, 46*(2), 171-183. doi: 10.1080/14703290902843828

Schmitz, G.S. & Schwarzer, R. (2000). Selbstwirksamkeitserwartung von Lehrern: Längsschnittbefunde mit einem neuen Instrument [Perceived self-efficacy of teachers: Longitudinal findings with a new instrument]. Zeitschrift für Pädagogische Psychologie, 14 (1), 12-25.

Seppälä, P. P., & Alamäki, H. H. (2003). Mobile learning in teacher training. *Journal Of Computer Assisted Learning, 19*(3), 330. doi:10.1046/j.0266-4909.2003.00034.x

Soloway, E., Grant, W., Tinker, R., Roschelle, J., Mills, M., Resnick, M., et al. (1999). Science in the palm of their hands. Communications of the ACM, 42, 21–26.

Tait, M. (2008). Resilience as a contributor to novice teacher success, commitment, and retention. Teacher Education Quarterly, 35(4), 57–75.

Tschannen-Moran, M., & Hoy, A. (2007). The differential antecedents of self-efficacy beliefs of novice and experienced teachers. *Teaching & Teacher Education, 23*(6), 944-956. doi:10.1016/j.tate.2006.05.003

Tschannen-Moran, M., Hoy, A. W., & Hoy, W. K. (1998). Teacher efficacy: Its meaning and measure. *Review of Educational Research, 68*(2), 202-248.

Vanoverbeke, C., & Cavanaugh, J. (2001). How Do Teachers Avoid Emotional Involvement with Students?. *English Journal, 91*(2), 31.

Wagnild, G.M., & Young, H.M. (1993). Development and psychometric evaluation of the Resilience Scale. *Journal of Nursing Measurement, 1,* 165-178.

Yonezawa, S., Jones, M., & Singer, N. (2011). Teacher Resilience in Urban Schools: The Importance of Technical Knowledge, Professional Community, and Leadership Opportunities. *Urban Education, 46*(5), 913-931. doi:10.1177/

Yost, D. S. (2006). Reflection and self-efficacy: Enhancing the retention of qualified teachers from a teacher education perspective. Teacher Education Quarterly, 33(4), 59–76.

Zost, G. (2010). An Examination of Resilience in Rural Special Educators. *Rural Educator, 31*(2), 10-14.

Knowledge and Practices Relating to Netbook Use: The Voices of Primary School Children in St. Vincent and the Grenadines

Coreen J. Leacock
School of Education
The University of the West Indies
Cave Hill Campus, Barbados
coreen.leacock@cavehill.uwi.edu

S. Joel Warrican
St. Vincent & the Grenadines Community College
St. Vincent & the Grenadines
jwarrican@gmail.com

Andrea Veira
St. Vincent Girls' High School
St. Vincent & the Grenadines
akveira@gmail.com

Abstract: This study explores the knowledge and practices with regards to the use of the Netbooks among students in primary schools in St. Vincent and the Grenadines. Sixty-three students from six schools were interviewed: 31 from Gr3 (14 girls, 17 boys) and 32 from Gr5 (17 girls, 15 boys). Three broad categories of issues were identified: knowledge relating to the technology; use of the machines; and misuse of this resource. Evidence suggests that the students had some technical knowledge related to use for specific purposes and technical tricks for outfoxing systems; that they used the netbooks for a variety of activities both at home and at school, though they face restrictions at school; that some students were exposed to inappropriate content on the Internet, often at the instigation of older individuals. A main conclusion is that there is a need to educate the students for safe and beneficial use of the netbooks.

Introduction

As is the case in most countries, computer technology has made its way into educational institutions at all levels in St. Vincent and the Grenadines (SVG). In its bid to ensure that its citizens develop twenty-first century skills, in 2010, the Government of this multi-island state in the Caribbean embarked on an initiative that involves gradually putting computer technology in the form of netbooks into the hands of all students in the country, under a One-Netbook-Per-Child scheme. Thus, students in primary, secondary and tertiary institutions in the country are expected to benefit from this initiative. As previously reported (Leacock & Warrican, 2012), it was deemed necessary in part to address the disparity between the "haves" and the "have-nots" in relation to out-of-school access to technology; the expectation being that the benefits of having such access to electronic technology would not only be evident in the students' current academic life, but could reach beyond into their future endeavours. The SVG Ministry of Education (2011) projected that with increased skills and confidence with technology, the citizens of SVG would be better able to generate new employment opportunities for themselves and to virtually offer their products and services to others.

The Netbook Initiative is part of a larger educational reform in SVG, which is being monitored for evaluation purposes, as commissioned by the Government of SVG. Monitoring activities include the collection of baseline data about the practices of teachers and students relating to electronic technology with a view to identifying areas for which teachers and students may require training to meet the IT standards for use (Leacock & Warrican, 2012). It should be noted that there was very little training for teachers and none for students before the netbooks were distributed. Lessons learned from this initiative can shed light on the experiences of schools, teachers and students in SVG as they adapt their practices to incorporate this powerful technology. It is hoped that these lessons can be instructive to other Caribbean countries with multiple landmasses and similar terrain as well as other countries considering technological innovation.

In their 2012 paper, Leacock and Warrican presented the beliefs and practices of teachers in SVG in relation to the use of electronic technology in their classrooms at the start of the laptop initiative. In this paper however, the focus is on students, specifically those at the primary level. Its purpose is to explore students' knowledge and practices with regards to the use of the Netbooks allocated to them by the education officials. Answers were sought to the following broad questions: What knowledge do primary school students have about technology? For what purposes do the students use their netbooks?

Children's Use of Technology: Concerns and Contradictions

There is a tendency when educational innovations are introduced to give little attention to the voices of the children who are affected. Especially where technology is involved, it is often assumed that children will be eager to use the technology and that, being "digital natives", they will somehow manifest the knowledge and skills needed to make optimum use of it (Bennett, Maton & Kervin, 2008). There is the general belief that these so-called digital natives are all comfortable using the technology and are more knowledgeable than their "digital immigrant" teachers (Prensky, 2001). However, being born in this digital age is no guarantee that twenty-first century children are competent and at ease with technology (Li & Ranieri, 2010) and hence should be fed a steady diet of it; that they know how to use it for optimum benefits or how to use it safely. These issues have been the subject of discussion and some advice has been given. For example, in highlighting guidelines for using technology with young children, Parikh (2012) includes the admonition to limit children's use of technology and media, presumably for health reasons; while others write of the possible dangers that children can face as they make use of the Internet, including being taken advantage of by commercial websites that request personal information in excess of what is required for personal identification (Kim & Yi, 2010) and running the risk of intentional or inadvertent exposure to inappropriate content such as pornography (Treyvaud, 2008; Hope, 2010). These warnings and dangers are not unfounded and should alert the adults who supervise young children to pay attention to technology related activities.

In the opinion of some (e.g. Hope, 2010), the potential for danger has led schools to overreact and place unreasonable restrictions on children's use of technology such as the Internet. Indeed, Selwyn (2010) reported that children in a study conducted in the UK reported a clear divide between their use of ITC at home and at school, with use in school being limited by rules and regulations governing areas such as the delivery of curriculum content and filtering of Internet content. He found that home use of the Internet included a wide range of activities while school use centred around seeking information, and that school computers were primarily used for writing up work and making presentations. It is therefore not surprising that Selwyn and Husen (2010) reported that despite the fact that technology is hailed by education officials as having educational benefits, secondary school students placed less value on ITC use for educational purposes than they did on technology use in other areas of their lives. Finally, Baytak, Tarman and Ayas (2011) point out that studies that explore home and school use of computers tend to be focused on students in the upper grades, and that studies that concentrate on the primary grades are also important. Indeed, younger children are increasingly exposed to technology in both settings (Lacina, 2007/2008; Espinosa, 2006).

These concerns and apparent contradictions provide a basis for raising questions about the views, beliefs, competencies and practices of children in schools in SVG. These students have been given access to netbook computers that they can use at home and at school, along with wireless Internet access at their schools.

The Research

In order to explore the topic of primary school children's use of the netbooks at home and at school, a qualitative interview study was conducted.

Participants

Six schools, 5 government-run and 1 private, were selected from five of the ten educational districts across the country. For the government-run schools, one school was selected from each of the five geographical regions in SVG. A sample of students was purposively selected from among the Grade 3 (7-8 years old) and Grade 5 (9-10 years old) students. The principal was asked to identify five students from each of these grades to be interviewed. General guidelines for selection included that the students should be articulate and should have been allocated a netbook. The principals were also asked to include at least one student who has demonstrated unusual skill with the technology. This was to allow for the exploration of the sources of students' knowledge. Sixty-three students were interviewed in all: 31 from Grade 3 (14 girls, 17 boys) and 32 from Grade 5 (17 girls, 15 boys).

Procedure

Students were interviewed by a trained research assistant either individually or in groups, depending on what was possible at the school. The interviews were conducted in a room away from the students' regular classrooms to provide an environment that would allow the students to speak freely. The students' responses were initially recorded in writing by the interviewer, but were later compiled in a spreadsheet, organized by question and examined for emerging themes.

Interview Planning

Prior to the interviews, an interview schedule was produced. This schedule contained questions arranged under the sub-heads knowledge of computers; use of computers at home and at school; feelings and beliefs about the netbooks; and challenges and triumphs. The instrument was vetted by officials of the Ministry of Education and school principals and was piloted prior to implementation.

Findings

The themes that emerged from the students interviewed were compiled under three overarching headings: (1) Knowledge; (2) Uses; (3) Misuse and Misconceptions. Each of these is explored below.

Knowledge

The first question invited the students to talk about what they know about computers. Perhaps the first thing that jumped out is the fact that almost all of the students made some reference to playing games, and typically, they spoke of computers in terms of what they do with the machines. The response of Jan, a Grade 3 girl illustrates a typical response:

> There are netbooks that you can play games on, like spelling, through the Internet. They have batteries that sometimes die, there is a screen, a keyboard and a mouse. (Jan, Gr 3)

Additionally, as illustrated in Jan's response, students could identify parts of the machines that they had. Students reported knowing how to perform certain actions with the netbooks: downloading and installing software; changing configurations on the machines; dealing with crashes and working around restrictions like applying or changing passwords. Note the following discussion that ensued among a group of Grade 5 students when one of them remarked on the fact that sometimes things go wrong.

> **Interviewer**: Are you able to fix things that go wrong on the netbooks?
>
> **Corey**: The Facebook *Aww Snap* error comes up and when the Facebook chat not working, I fix them. I change the Internet proxy settings to access sites so that they work.

> **Jaden**: I delete all games and reinstall them. I then try YouTube (*a restricted site*) and it works. Press *ctrl del* to restart when it sticks, and *Fn* and *F11* for the sticking of the cursor. I know cheat codes for games from online...

This exchange indicates that not only did the students have technical knowledge to circumvent glitches with the netbooks, they also had the meta-language to discuss their actions. Further technical knowledge emerged when the discussion turned to encounters particularly with restricted sites, such as some email and social networking sites.

> **Interviewer**: How do you get around lack of access to restricted or banned sites?
>
> **Lyra**: I use Hotmail and Twitter and delete everything from my history. I download everything and then go to Internet settings and bookmarks to clear them.
>
> **Jeva**: I access Facebook by clicking on 'Learn more', which gives you the box to type in the site Facebook.
>
> **Corey**: I delete everything by using *ctrl del*.
>
> **Jaden**: I delete history, refresh it, create space and use Internet (*Freeing up memory to facilitate Internet use*). I also access YouTube this way through mp3skullplayer.com.
>
> **Corey**: Y8 (*a gaming site*). After forbidden access, I go to history and delete everything.

Again, this illustrates how students obtain and use technical knowledge to get around challenges they face, though in some cases the students' responses were somewhat naïve, not always demonstrating comprehensive understanding. Another point of interest as mentioned earlier is the students' knowledge of the meta-language associated with the technology. In several instances, students made references to "downloading" (e.g. Firefox and music); "searching on Google"; experiencing "crashes"; and using "apps"; "flash drives" and "browsers". They tended to use this language with ease, even if their interpretation of the result of their actions associated with the language was not always accurate.

Another emerging feature relates to the sources of the students' knowledge. It is noteworthy that when the students mentioned the source of their knowledge about computers and how to do things with the netbooks, for the most part, there were no references to school or teachers. Typically, students seemed to be acquiring their knowledge from relatives and friends: "*My cousin who is 13 years old helped me*" (Keith, Gr 3); "*If the netbook is freezing, my sister tells me how to unfreeze it... My sister taught me to use video, chat and exchange pictures*" (Shanna, Gr 5); and Becca, Gr 5, reported that her brothers taught her about games and simulations. In some cases, these sources of information were younger. Apart from learning from other children, there is evidence that many of the students learned through exploration on their own. For example, Mark, a Grade 5 boy reported:

> I felt very happy to get the netbook because I knew it would be interesting. I had a laptop with Windows 7. I prefer laptops to see videos because the netbook has *Aww Snap* errors when you turn it on. So I try things to fix it. When I turn it on, I press *ctrl d c* or *ctrl qd* then all the function keys including *Esc*.

As was reported by other students, Mark tried things until something worked. It was also common for the students to report sharing their discoveries with their classmates and other students. Thus, a knowledge network appears to be emerging among the students.

Based on evidence then, it appears that the students interviewed had some knowledge of computers, though it often related to use for specific purposes and technical tricks for outfoxing systems. Considering that the sources of their information appear to be, for the most part, slightly older children or personal investigation, suggests that these students were not afraid to explore the technology or to ask questions when they needed help. Of note though is that sources selected tended to be their peers or themselves. They were also not timid about sharing their acquired knowledge with others.

Uses of the Netbooks

The second broad area that emerged from the interview data relates to the use of the netbooks. Students reported that they used their netbooks in diverse places: school, home, their parents' workplaces, relatives' homes, public library and Internet cafes; indeed, anyplace where they have access to an open wireless network. It was also apparent that the students used the netbooks anytime they found themselves with free time. The students reported a variety of purposes for which they use their netbooks. These include playing games, watching videos, listening to music, social networking and doing school work.

Games

The students, both girls and boys, spoke primarily of using their netbooks to play games, and here some gender-related issues emerged. For example, boys tended to report playing "action" games: "*I can access games like car racing, Gun Mayhem, Mass Mayhem and fighting games.*" (Jamal, Gr 5); "*I play Need for Speed, Most Wanted, G-Switch and Pistol*" (Jared, Gr 3). Girls tended to choose a wider variety of games: "*I play Cooking, Barbies, Dress Up, money addition...*" (Avril, Gr 3); "*I play games on G-Switch and Y8*" (Tara, Gr 3). Both girls and boys reported playing educational games: "*I play games like Dress up, maths and language arts games*" (Sally, Gr 5); "*I play more educational games like BrainPOP, PBS Kids and Spelling City in class*" (Milan, Gr 5). It is noteworthy that the students reported playing educational games both in and out of the school setting.

Videos and Music

Watching videos and listening to music were also common activities reported by the students. The most popular was watching music videos on YouTube (a banned site), though some students reported listening to music that they or someone else downloaded via the internet. Some of them also reported watching cartoons on their netbooks: "*I do home-work, play music from YouTube using Firefox*" (Ziva, Gr 5); "*I like to play music in Devices* [a folder that registers input from external sources]. *My cousin downloads music then gives me on a flash drive to play*" (Roland, Gr 3); "*I watch Big Buck Bunny movie and Kittens which were already on the netbook*" (Sharon, Gr 3). Of note is that a general complaint was that YouTube froze or crashed regularly and they had to find ways of rectifying this annoyance. Speaking of freezing machines, Jaden, Gr 5, said "*It only happens with some songs on YouTube*". Students reported watching videos and listening to music both at home and at school, although in some cases, students reported having to do so clandestinely while at school.

Social Networking

Another popular activity reported by the primary school students interviewed relates to social networking. Students reported using Skype, Facebook, and Twitter to get in touch with friends and family: "*I can practically access anything, even Skype*" (Evan, Gr 5); "*I talk to friends ...and family on Facebook*" (Aldon, Gr 5); "*I use Hotmail and Twitter and delete everything from my history*" (Lyra, Gr 5). More often than not, however, the students were not engaging in these activities on their own; other family members were involved. Students reported that mothers, fathers, aunts, uncles, siblings and cousins also used their netbooks for social networking: "*My sister uses it to access her Facebook account and I access stuff from her account*" (Jamal, Gr 5). Apparently though, not all students could engage in this activity freely, even at home. Ava, a Grade 3 student reported "*My big sister uses it at* [secondary school]. *She goes on Facebook but I can't... Mummy checks to see what I'm doing and punishes me when I'm on Facebook*". This reluctance of parents to allow these young children to use social networking sites may be related to the belief that social networking sites are considered to be unsafe and that these children can easily be duped by unscrupulous individuals.

Educational Uses

Though it was not the first activity they mentioned, many of the students reported using their netbooks for educational purposes. In the school setting, this included searching for information, playing educational games to reinforce concepts covered in class and to a lesser extent, producing works. For example, Kyle, a Grade 3 student reported "*We look up stuff like the environment and pollution, rainforests, snakes and other animals. I even looked up food chains on my own. I research things*". Students reported doing this activity at the request of the teachers, but also on their own initiative: "*I use my netbook to do research when the teacher tells us to, like on turtles and mammals. We also looked up the digestive system before the teacher taught us*" (Tamara, Gr 3). Of note is the language used by Ashanna, a Grade 3 student: "*Without the teacher's permission I research things like leatherback turtles, crop roots and soil. Other times when the teacher gives permission it is to look up things like the natural resources of SVG*". This seems to suggest that some teachers exercise strong control over students' use of the netbooks in school. Students reported using their machines in school to do art, music, write letters, and practice typing. Furthermore, some of the students believed that their performance in school work had improved with their use of their netbooks for educational purposes: "*My marks have improved for language and social studies. I think*

I'm better at problem solving now too" (Naomi, Gr 5); "*I get help for Math by searching for it on Google and my marks improved from 40s to 50s as I was weak at Math*" (Zahra, Gr 5). Students reported using their netbooks at home to complete homework assignments and to practice activities done at school.

In this section, the main purposes for which students reported using the netbooks were explored. What became evident as they spoke is that not only do they use the machines, but others in their households also use them. It is also evident that though the computers are being used in the classroom, the scope of this use is limited. This is probably because the schools have no clear plans for the integration of this technology in the classroom, and teachers are playing it safe, frowning on and discouraging activities that are not directly related to the current academic pursuits of their charges. Thus, while their teachers remain restrained, these digital natives are not shy about using their machines for a variety of purposes.

Misuse of Technology

One concern that surfaces when children are afforded access to the Internet is the potential of this resource for adverse effects. For example, there is the worry that these impressionable ones may be exposed to inappropriate content on the web. The issue of inappropriate sites emerged during the interviews. The students were asked if they ever used the netbooks for any purpose for which they may get into trouble at home or school. Rather than speaking of accessing banned sites or of meddling with the configurations of the machines, several of the students raised the issue of accessing pornographic sites.

> "*I was caught on* [an adult site] *by Jaden and Corey and I got in trouble in the music room for it*" (Aldon, Gr 5).

> "*I accessed* [inappropriate content] *through a friend's netbook on* [adult site]. *I went to Village X, left netbook to use bathroom and came back to see it on* [the adult site] *with bad stuff that someone did*" (John, Gr 3).

> "*I checked for* [adult sites] *online after seeing my cousin do it on his computer. I got in trouble in school for checking* [inappropriate content], *my computer was taken away for a month. I accessed* [an adult site]" (Roland, Gr 3).

In addition to these comments, all of the Grade 3 students at one school (3 girls and 2 boys) admitted visiting at least three inappropriate sites. What emerged as they spoke of their activities is that generally, introduction to such content came through older people: older siblings, aunts, uncles and friends. Also disturbing is the fact that these students reported using the school's wireless access point to gain entry to these sites, despite the fact that the administrators of the Internet service indicate that such sites are blocked.

Another form of misuse was seen in the student's treatment of the netbooks. For example, several of them expressed dislike for these machines, preferring the machines that they owned prior to the initiative.

> "*The netbooks don't allow certain things like Youtube.com. On Google in school a lot of sites are also blocked so I prefer my own computer...*" (Bethany, Gr 5).

Perhaps because they are accustomed to faster machines with fewer restrictions, some students experienced some frustration when using the netbooks. This may account for the misuse or abuse of some of the machines. For example, some students reported repeatedly removing batteries in their efforts to reset the machines. At least one student admitted behaving destructively towards the machine:

> "*I get upset when* [inappropriate content] *comes up ...I cuss the laptop when I can't beat Neverball. I take out the battery and pelt* [throw] *it* [a]*way. The laptop gets on dotish* [behaves foolishly]; *Internet not working; ants are on the laptop. My cousins pound keys*" (Neil, Gr 3).

This diatribe was delivered with some disgust at the machines. The reference to ants indicates that perhaps Neil's computer was not kept clean. This speculation found some support in the fact that the interviewer reported that often when the students brought their netbooks to the interview, they were dirty, covered with food as if the students were eating while using the machines. This suggests that, despite being happy to have this technology available to them, some of the students apparently did not know how to take care of them.

Conclusion

The students in this study demonstrated an affinity for the technology, in keeping with Prensky's (2001) concept of the digital native. Unlike their teachers who seemed reluctant to use the technology (Leacock & Warrican, 2012), these students were not timid about exploring this resource. Although it was the first time some of them even touched a computer, they readily embraced the technology and learned and used the meta-language with some ease. Perhaps because of this displayed affinity, these students were not given formal instructions that would clarify the concepts related to the language that they are using.

Also noteworthy is the fact that the students use their netbooks both at home and at school, although school use is somewhat restricted. This may be attributable to several possible factors. First, since the teachers are uncertain about the technology, they appear to be very conservative in the use that they encourage among the students. Second, because there is no definitive technology integration plan at the schools, teachers may decide to err on the side of caution and restrict use to academic purposes only. Third, since the wireless network used by the schools has restricted access to many of the sites that the students want to use (e.g. email and social networking sites), students' use of the netbooks at school is somewhat curtailed, leading some of them to find ways to circumvent the restrictions. This state of affairs is similar to what Selwyn (2010) found in primary schools in the UK: the students found their school use of the technology very different from their home use. To them school use was restrictive and boring. It is perhaps for this reason that some students in SVG used their netbook clandestinely in schools.

Finally, Hope (2010) wrote of overreaction of schools to the possible dangers of unrestricted access to the Internet. However, in the case of the students in this study, access to certain sites was restricted but students either found ways to circumvent these restrictions or sadly, were seduced to explore such content after being exposed to it by older people. This suggests that restrictions alone may not be adequate. This study suggests that curiosity can entice these digital natives to inappropriate content on the web, and consequently, an education programme designed to promote safe and appropriate use of web resources may be necessary. Indeed, a programme of safe use is also relevant for the use and care of the hardware. If as Parikh (2012) points out, overuse of technology can be detrimental to young children, then safety in terms of quantity of use may also have to be drawn to the attention of not only the students, but also their parents and their teachers.

It is indeed laudable that the authorities in SVG are seeking to ensure that the citizens of this small state have the opportunity to develop the technological skills that are part of what are being called twenty-first century skills. However, the findings of this study suggest that there is a need for a programme of training not only for the students, but also for their teachers and parents. There is also a need for a system of monitoring young children's use of the technology both at home and at school. Thus, the lesson learned here is that accurate knowledge and good habits should be encouraged through appropriate programmes that accompany computer integration initiatives in schools.

References

Baytak, A., Tarman, B., & Ayas, C. (2011). Experiencing technology integration in education: Children's perspectives. *International Electronic Journal of Elementary Education, 3* (2), 139 – 151.

Bennett, S., Maton, K., & Kervin, L. (2008). The 'digital natives' debate: A critical review of the evidence. *British Journal of Educational Technology, 39*, 775 – 786. doi: 10.1111/j.1467-8535.2007.00793.x

Espinosa, L. M., Laffey, J. M., Whittaker, T., & Sheng, Y. (2006). Technology in the home and the achievement of young children: Findings from the early childhood longitudinal study. *Early Education & Development, 17* (3), 421 – 441.

Hope, A. (2010). Seduction of risk and school cyberspace. *Australasian Journal of Educational Technology, 26* (5), 690 – 703.

Kim, S. & Yi, S. (2010). Is privacy at risk when commercial websites target primary school children? A case study in Korea. *Children & Society, 24*, 449 – 460.

Lacina, J. (2007/2008). Computers and young children. *Childhood Education, 84* (2), 113 – 116.

Leacock, C.J. & Warrican, S.J. (2012). Laptops and Learning: Beliefs and Practices of Teachers in St Vincent and the Grenadines. In P. Resta (Ed.), *Proceedings of Society for Information Technology & Teacher Education International Conference 2012* (pp. 1933-1938). Chesapeake, VA: AACE. Retrieved from http://www.editlib.org/p/39872.

Li, Y. & Ranieri, M. (2010). Are 'digital natives' really digitally competent?—A study on Chinese teenagers. *British Journal of Educational Technology, 41*, 1029 – 1042. doi: 10.1111/j.1467-8535.2009.01053.x

Ministry of Education (2011). *Improvement of education through the use of information and communications technology: ICT in education policy.* Kingstown, SVG: Author.

Parikh, M. (2012). Technology and young children: New tools and strategies for teachers and learners. *Young Children, 67* (3), 10 – 11.

Prensky, M. (2001). Digital Natives, Digital Immigrants Part 1. *On the Horizon, 9* (5), 1 – 6. Online at http://dx.doi.org/10.1108/10748120110424816.

Selwyn, N. & Husen, O. (2010). The educational benefits of technological competence: An investigation of students' perceptions. *Evaluation and Research in Education, 23* (2), 137 – 141.

Selwyn, N. (2010). Primary schools and ICT – What can we teach our pupils? *Literacy Today, 62*, 28 – 29. Retrieved from Education Research Complete (EBSCO), Oct 12, 2012.

Treyvaud, R. (2008). Journey to the new world: Young people and cyberspace. *Screen Education, 49*, 94 – 99.

"Is There Anybody Out There": Twitter as a Support Environment for First Year Teachers' Online Induction Workshop

Yehuda Peled
Western Galilee and Ohalo Colleges, Israel
ypeled@macam.ac.il

Efrat Pieterse
Open University of Israel, and Western Galilee College, Israel
efratpi@openu.ac.il

Abstract: This research examines the benefits of Twitter as a support tool to enhance social interaction among participants in an online induction workshop; to aid the workshops' moderator in monitoring the group and enhance and support the early-service teachers' growth and resilience. The 2344 tweets that were posted during the induction workshop enabled the workshops' moderator constant monitoring of the participants' progress, lows and highs. They reveal a process of socialization among the participants which leads to personal and professional support, thus enhancing the new teachers' professional growth.

Introduction

First Year Teachers

The transition from pre-service teacher to being wholly responsible for one's own classroom is, in many cases, overwhelming (Utsumi & Kizu, 2006). Novice teachers struggle with the challenges of their new jobs. They describe daily difficulties with the students in their classrooms (Johnson & The Project on the Next Generation of Teachers, 2004). They describe not knowing what to teach or how to teach it (Kauffman et al., 2002). At the same time, they are trying to acclimate to the norms and modes of professional interaction in their new workplace (Kardos, Johnson, Peske, Kauffman & Liu, 2001). It is important to pay attention to new teachers and their struggles, since teachers' early experiences determine their sense of success with their students (Johnson & Birkeland, 2003), their long-term performance in the classroom (Gold, 1996), and their decisions as to whether or not to remain in teaching (Gold, 1996).

Induction, Mentoring and Support

For the most part, new teachers experience their early career challenges in professional isolation (Kardos & Johnson, 2007). Thus, at the time when they are most in need and most vulnerable, they are often left to 'sink or swim'. Formal mentoring, which pairs new teachers with veteran colleagues, is currently the main strategy used to address new teachers' isolation, frustration, and failure (Kardos & Johnson, 2010). Mentoring requires "real-time" interactions, and although 21st Century technologies may be used to support mentoring (see Maxwell, Harrington, & Smith, 2010), the personal relationship between the mentor and mentee and timely interventions are pivotal to the mentoring process (Ganser, 1996).

One-to-one mentor assignments, in themselves, cannot meet the myriad needs of new teachers (Kardos & Johnson, 2010), thus an induction program is required to complete the process and give the novice teachers additional support. The theory behind induction programs holds that teaching is complex work, that pre-employment teacher preparation is rarely sufficient to provide all the knowledge and skill necessary to successful teaching, and that a significant portion of this knowledge can only be acquired on the job. This view holds that through induction programs, schools can provide an environment where novices can learn how to teach, survive, and succeed as teachers. Induction programs are thus often conceived as a "bridge" from student-of-teaching to teacher-of-students (Ingersoll & Strong, 2011).

Although the overall goal of these teacher development programs is to improve the performance and retention of beginning teachers, induction theorists have identified multiple objectives and emphases such programs may hold (e.g. Feiman-Nemser, 2001; Ganser, 2002). Teacher induction can refer to a variety of different types of activities for new teachers—orientation sessions, faculty collaborative periods, meetings with supervisors, developmental workshops, extra classroom assistance, reduced workloads, and, especially, mentoring (Ingersoll & Strong, 2011).

Teachers' Resilience

Teacher resilience is a relatively recent area of investigation. While the stresses that face teachers in their daily lives have been well documented (e.g. Goddard & Foster, 2001; Tait, 2008), the term 'resilience' was initially used to explain the capacity of individuals to adapt and thrive despite experiencing adversity (Masten, Best & Garmezy, 1990). As an emerging field of research, and in part due to the complex nature of resilience, teacher resilience has been conceptualized in the literature in a range of ways (Le Cornu, 2009). Beltman, Mansfield, and Price, (2011) found 24 papers that explicitly discussed resilience, and whose conceptualizations and definitions incorporated common ideas. In summary, teacher resilience is a dynamic process or outcome that is the result of interaction over time between a person and the environment (e.g. Day, 2008; Tait, 2008).

Microblogging

Microblogging is an online publishing blogging tool, which allows a small amount of text-based content to be displayed on the user's page (Java, Song, Finin, & Tseng, 2007). Twitter is a Microblogging environment. By allowing for no more than 140 characters in a post called a "tweet", it enables users to publish brief text updates in real-time as well as asynchronous communication (Luo & Franklin, 2012).

Although microblogging primarily serves as a communication tool, its unique affordances in education have been investigated in recent years (see Bishop, 2012; Luo & Gao, 2012; Luo & Franklin, 2012) and more specifically in teacher education (see O'Hare, Quartermaine & Cooke, 2011). Some research has been published on support for teachers in their first year at school (see Beltman, Mansfield & Price, 2011) and a number of reviews on the topic of induction have been published over the past two decades (for a recent anthology, see Wang, Odell, & Clift, 2010). The following article will discuss the role of microblogging – specifically Twitter, as an environment, which strengthens a first year teachers' resilience through an on-line induction workshop. In this paper, we will discuss the ways an online mentoring environment (Twitter) for first year teachers', when used as part of an inclusive program, strengthens various aspects influencing teaches' resilience.

Content

Internship in teaching has been operating in the Israeli education system since 2000. The internees, usually in their fourth and last year, integrate into the education system. During that period, they benefit from two support frameworks; (1) a mentor from the school under the responsibility of the school's principal and inspector and (2) a weekly internship workshop, at one of the colleges of education. The workshop is moderated by a faculty from the hosting institute (Ministry of Education, 2004). The workshops' moderator's responsibility is complex; expediting this kind of workshop demands a wide range of capabilities such as the establishment of small learning groups in an intimate atmosphere, professional teaching and class management experience and a wide ranging professional knowledge in the moderator's specific content area. Participating in the internship workshop is one of the conditions for an internee receiving a teaching certificate (Ministry of Education, 2009).

The objectives of the internship workshop is to support the internee in personal, theoretical and practical aspects and thus help him or her conceptualize the events encountered at school and convert them into an asset for professional development (Levi-Fridman, Rychenberg & Sagie, 2006). From the professional development aspect, the workshop aims to improve the trainees' reflective thinking skills as well as their teaching and class management skills (Harrison & Yaffe, 2008). From the social-emotional aspect, the workshop aims to create a support framework for the teachers in their first year of teaching. This weekly peer meeting of people who are all facing the same challenges, opens an opportunity to share. The participants themselves raise the issues they want to discuss, usually reflecting events they encountered during the week at school. In the workshop internees share their thoughts, feelings, frustrations, and their range of experiences and how they chose to deal with them (Sagie & Regev, 2002).

In the last few years, some of the internship workshops have become online workshops, with the result that the early-service teachers do not physically meet their peers and or the workshops' moderator. As the workshops' objectives are to share, support, and learn from each other under the expert guidance of the workshops' moderator, an online workshop is a challenge. Unlike discussion groups, forums or any other form of online environment where people participate and contribute to the group voluntarily, in the internship workshop, participation is mandatory and is part of the early service teachers' obligations for receiving a teaching certificate. In a face-to-face workshop meeting weekly over the course of a year, the moderator ensures that each participant is active and contributes to the workshop and the group. The moderator gets to know them, learns of their working environments, their needs, weaknesses and strengths, and is able to direct and adapt the workshop to meet the needs of all the participants. One of the researcher-authors, who have been moderating internship workshops since 2002, was asked last year to moderate an on-line workshop. This raised number of questions such as; how will he keep in touch with the participants in a way that will enable him "to see their eyes", to listen to their small complaints, their successes, how they overcame a specific situation, and how will he be able to encourage their mutual peer support on a daily basis. In order to insert a component into the online workshop, which allowed the participants to share, the induction workshop's moderator decided to use Twitter. The ongoing assignment for the entire year was to tweet four times a day. The tweet can be on any subject or issue, whether in school or home. The objective of such intensive and frequent tweeting was to create an ongoing flow of information, which the participants will be privy to through the use of a specific hashtag, a format which associates a user created tag with an event or a context using a prefix symbol, # (Chang, 2010).

In light of the above description, the following research questions were formalized: (1) how are the visibility and presence of the participant represented online through Twitter and (2) to what extent can tweeting act as a substitute for, or meet the same objectives as, face to face social interaction?

Methodology

Seventeen early-service teachers participating in an internship online workshop were asked to tweet four times a day using a hashtag designated for that purpose. The tweets were collected every week for twenty eight weeks and were analyzed with ATLAS.ti software. In order to develop a grounded theory, a content comparative method (Glaser and Strauss, 1967) was used. The initial analysis enabled the identification of nine major categories which were grouped from sub-categories. The categories were validated and refined until an 85% matching was achieved by three analyzers (see figure 1). The participants filled a 20-item attitudes survey regarding the Twitter activity and a focus group interview was conducted at the end of the year.

Participants

The group consisted of eleven female and six male early service teachers aged 23-33 years old. The participants in the induction course were from a variety of teaching fields and age groups; 83% of the participants had no previous experience in Twitter, 75% had previously participated in online courses. Only 25% of the group had participated in an intensive social media activity such as forums, blogs, Facebook etc.

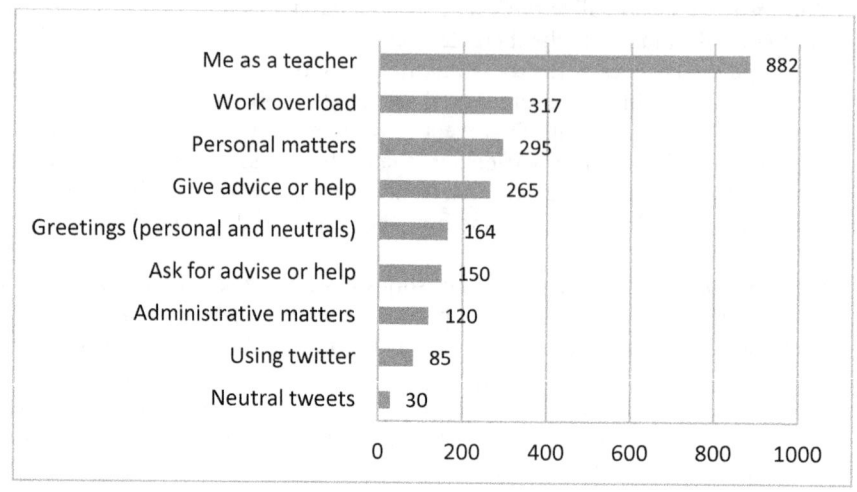

Figure 1: Distribution of Tweets by Categories

Findings

Only two participants stopped tweeting altogether, one after 3 months the other after 4 months. 2344 tweets were posted during the induction course, an average of 150 tweets per participant. Maximum and minimum number of tweets was 391 and 31 respectively. Although tweeting was intensive and continuous, most of the participants did not add their peers as followers, which may explain a very low rate of re-tweets and posts which have been marked as favorites. Content analysis of the tweets revealed three major themes in which the participants were engaged: Some of the Tweets hence quoted are longer than 140 characters due to translation into English from Hebrew.

Visibility and Presence

We asked in what way the tweets represent the participants' daily routine. A major part of the tweets (1213) dealt with the participants' daily life at work and home. Some of them were neutral, describing the upcoming activity: *"teaching 4 hours today. 2 are behind me. 2 to go."* or activity within school *"school staff meeting today. Think-tank – how to deal with students' disciplinary issues"* other tweets related to home and personal issues *"It was a very long and rewarding day. Tomorrow's lessons to prepare then to bed. Laundry and dishes can wait and stink. I have no time for them ☺"*. Others report on difficulties and missing class *"woke up with a virus. Stayed home. Feeling much better"*.

To What Extent Can the Workshop's Moderator Identify Difficulties and Problems

Being connected to Twitter through mobile devices and the daily tweets enabled the workshops' moderator to be attentive to any change in mood or to identify a call for help from any of the participants, thus enabling a real time intervention by the moderator or the participants. For example, the following tweets were a cause for alarm, which evoked an immediate telephone call from the moderator to the tweeter *"I'm so desperate" "I don't know what to do tomorrow at school. I hate the thought of going there tomorrow" "I don't want to teach any more" "There's *nobody to talk to in this school...".* There were also tweets concerning personal issues, which are not related to school *"I crashed my car. Luckily no one got hurt. I hope to be at school on Monday"* This is evidence that the Twitter method did fulfill some of the support-sensing role that happens in a face-to-face setting when one can see and feel the mood of the group.

What Are The Main Issues of Concern to Early-Service Teachers?

Looking into the sub-categories of "Me as a teacher" shows tweets representing the following topics: (1) professional insights (170 tweets), for instance, *"a first year teacher is a worker on the assembly line. It will take some time to move up to QC [quality control]"*; (2) reflection as teachers (128 tweets), for instance *"in regard to my teaching yesterday, today was much better and tomorrow's will be even better"*; and (3) feelings towards their teaching as a profession (106 tweets), for instance *"another day of wondering about my future as a teacher"* This is evidence that first year teachers contemplate on their future as teachers, their attitude changes according to their daily encounter with various challenges.

Spill The Beans - Sharing of Difficulties and Success

The microblogging environment was a place to pour out the heart and 'Let off steam'. 218 tweets (not counting responses) revolved around the issue of work overload, time shortage, fatigue and concerns about the opinion of the school inspector who visits them in class. These tweets caused the most reaction and discussion among the participants. For instance, *"Today was the worst day this year. I've survived to tell. Tomorrow a new day"* or *"a teacher needs to be qualified in another area so when he has enough he can leave"* which received the following comment *"There is a burnout in every profession, but the burnout in teaching is faster. Looking for an additional profession at this early stage does not say good things about the teacher"* and another comment *"a teacher who's looking for another profession shouldn't have chosen to be a teacher in the first place. A teacher should be a teacher whole heartedly".*

Some of the tweets, especially towards the end of the year related to their understanding of the importance of the tweeting for their professional development: *"Thank you for the workshop, for the tips and for sharing"*, they also commented on the advantage of twitter: *"The Discussions are great, they shed light on what is going on with other teachers"* Some of the responses in the open end question: *"The ability to recognize additional experiences experienced by students who are in a similar position to mine and thus to compare my situation to their own situation. I could through tweets find myself positive reinforcement"* and *"The day to day communication with the workshops' participants enables the sharing of feelings and occurrences in real-time"* and *"the most important thing is that the Twitter made me feel as part of a group. I always found new things brought up by the other members of the group. Whenever I did not log in [to Twitter], I felt as if I'm skipping class and missing important stuff".*

Most of the tweets were not addressed to a specific person. Only 577 tweets were addressed to the workshop's moderator or specifically to one of the participants. Contrary to that, 75% of the participants mentioned in the survey that the daily presence in Twitter encouraged the sharing of information and knowledge among the workshop's participants. 78% confirmed that the activity enhanced communications between the participants and the workshops' moderator. Another important aspect was the moderator's response speed to questions, queries or calls for help.

Discussion and Conclusion

Twitter is a microblogging social media tool with posting characteristics which are shared by a Blog and a Talkback, thus the posts are personal and usually do not expect a comment. Unlike most social media tools, it is difficult to follow a chain of posts and comments in Twitter. This phenomena raises the question as to if this is tantamount to "talking to the wall" – or, in other words, posting one's thoughts and feelings without being acknowledged? Although there were some reservations expressed by the participants to tweeting on a regular basis as they are *"extremely busy with our daily chores at school"*, after the initial period of acclimatization to tweeting the majority of the participants shared their feelings and thoughts with the group. From the moderator's point of view, it allowed him to monitor their daily mood changes and follow issues which, at the time, were the center of their existence.

Apart from two participants who followed the rest of the group, using nodeXL to map the connection between the participants confirmed that none of the participants followed any of their peers but, there was an interaction between the participants – asking for advice and help, response to advice and help requests and greetings (see figure 1). Apparently, they were using the hashtag to monitor what is being said, as, in a small group such as this one, following a hashtag is sufficient to stay informed of any new tweet. This is evidence that they might not have created affiliation with their peers as expected. In a follow up research which is currently running the researches emphasized the importance of social network habits, in order to enhance a support group.

As Twitter was used in an online induction workshop where the participants have not previously met, it served as a social interface creating an atmosphere of sharing. The turning point in that regard came when one of the participants, when informed of a forthcoming new baby, resulted in a continuance stream of posts personal in nature apart from the customary Mazal-Tov (good luck in Hebrew). The frequency of these increased as the participants got to know each other (virtually).

During the course of the study, there was a gradual increase in posts. The posts, which were asking for professional advice, and the response from group members, showed willingness on the part of group members to provide help and offer advice. This can be a factor in increasing confidence both for the asker and the answerer. This, in its turn, leads to an increase in the participants' resilience which, as Castro, Kelly & Shih (2009) point out, is based on an increase in teachers' confidence and coping strategies which are an important factor in overcoming challenging situations or recurring setbacks. Malloy & Allen, (2007) determined that a resilient teacher is one who is able to recover from and overcome difficulties quickly and efficiently. Such teachers also show greater perseverance and thrive in the teaching environment. This can be seen from an increase in the ways that the early-service teachers dealt with increasingly difficult situations whilst supporting each other. This to benefited both sides and encouraged the development of a reciprocal, mutually supportive relationship between the early-service teachers, and, at the same time, helping create professional and peer relationships, which are an important factor in the process of increasing teachers' resilience (Sammons et al, 2007).

As to research question # 1 (how are the visibility and presence of the participant represented online through Twitter) and # 2 (to what extent can tweeting act as a substitute for, or meet the same objectives as, face to face social interaction?) We can, conclude that compelling the online workshop participants to be present in an online social environment did not create an atmosphere of sharing and support among them as happens in a face to face (F2F) workshop. On the other hand, the workshops' moderator was able to keep track of the moods and attitude of each of the participants on a daily basis, remembering that a group participating in a F2F workshop meets once a week, the Tweeting has a huge advantage over F2F workshop in regard to the ability of the moderator to react in real time to any change in the participants mood or need as it arises.

Although the network analysis does not show a development of a social interaction among the participants, the questionnaire, indicates that the activity in the Twitter encouraged the sharing of information, contributed to better communication and support from the moderator and among the workshops' participants.

Thus, we can see a community of practice evolving as the school year progresses. The opportunity and the ability to pause for a moment, to reflect upon one's experience and offer advice or support demonstrates the change that early-service teachers go through due to their activity in Twitter.

References

Beltman, S., Mansfield, C., & Price, A. (2011) Thriving not just surviving: A review of research on teacher resilience. Educational Research Review, 6(3), 185-207.

Bishop, M. (2012). Virtual Teacher Talk: Blogging With and By Pre-Service Teachers. A Dissertation submitted to the Education Faculty of Lindenwood University. Accessed September 10, 2012 at: http://gradworks.umi.com/3426991.pdf.

Castro, A. J., Kelly, J., & Shih, M. (2009). Resilience strategies for new teachers in highneeds areas. Teaching and Teacher Education. 26(3), 622-629.

Chang, H. C. (2010). A new perspective on Twitter hashtag use: Diffusion of innovation theory Proceedings of the American Society for Information Science and Technology, 47(1), 1-4. Retrieved from http://onlinelibrary.wiley.com/doi/10.1002/meet.14504701295/full.

Day, C. (2008). Committed for life? Variations in teachers' work, lives and effectiveness. Journal of Educational Change, 9(3), 243-260.

Ganser, T. (1996). Preparing mentors of beginning teachers: An overview for staff developers. Journal of Staff Development, 17(4), 8-11.

Glaser, BG., & Strauss, AL. (1967). The Discovery of Grounded Theory: Strategies for Qualitative Research. New York: Aldine De Gruyter.

Goddard J., & Foster R. (2001). The Experiences of neophyte teachers: A critical constructivist assessment. Teaching and Teacher Education 17, 349-365.

Gold, Y. (1996). Beginning teacher support: Attrition, mentoring, and induction. In J. Sikula, T. J. Buttery, & E.

Harrison, J., & Yaffe, E. (2008). in Swennen, A., & Klink, M. (Eds.) Teacher Educators and Reflective Practice Becoming a Teacher Educator, Springer Netherlands, 145-161.

Ingersoll R.M., & Strong, M. (2011). The Impact of Induction and Mentoring Programs for Beginning Teachers: A Critical Review of the Research. Review of Educational Research, 81(2), 201-233.

Java, A., Song, X., Finin, T., & Tseng, B. (2007). Why We Twitter: Understanding Microblogging. Joint 9th WEBKDD and 1st SNA-KDD Workshop, August 12, *2007*. Retrieved September 10, 2012 from: http://aisl.umbc.edu/resources/369.pdf.

Johnson, S. M., & Birkeland, S. E. (2003). Pursuing a ''sense of success'': New teachers explain their career decisions. American Educational Research Journal, 40(3), 581–617.

Johnson, S. M., & The Project on the Next Generation of Teachers. (2004). Finders and keepers: Helping new teachers survive and thrive in our schools. San Francisco: Jossey-Bass.

Kardos, S. M., Johnson, S. M., Peske, H. G., Kauffman, D., & Liu, E. (2001). Counting on colleagues: New teachers encounter the professional cultures of their schools. Educational Administration Quarterly, 37(2), 250–290.

Kardos, S.M., & Johnson, S.M. (2010). New teachers' experiences of mentoring: the good, the bad, and the inequity. Journal of Educational Change, 11(1), 23-44.

Kauffman, D., Johnson, S. M., Kardos, S. M., Liu, E., & Peske, H. G. (2002). ''Lost at sea'': New teachers' experiences with curriculum and assessment. Teachers College Record, 104(2), 273–300.

Le Cornu, R. (2009). Building resilience in pre-service teachers. Teaching and Teacher Education, 25(5), 717-723.

Levi-Fridman, I, Rychenberg, R., & Sagie, R. (2006). The evaluation segment of the teachers internship program in Israel. Tel-Aviv, Mofet Institute (Hebrew).

Luo, T., & Franklin, T. (2012). "You got to be follow-worthy or I will unfollow you!" Students' Voices on Twitter integration into classroom settings. In P. Resta (Ed.), Proceedings of Society for Information Technology & Teacher Education International Conference 2012 (pp. 3685-3688). Chesapeake, VA: AACE. Retrieved from http://www.editlib.org/p/40173.

Luo, T., & Gao, F. (2012). Designing microblogging-based class activities. In P. Resta (Ed.), Proceedings of Society for Information Technology & Teacher Education International Conference 2012 (pp. 2939-2944). Chesapeake, VA: AACE. Retrieved from http://www.editlib.org/p/40037.

Malloy, W.W., & Allen, T. (2007). Teacher retention in a teacher resiliency-building rural school. Rural Educator, 28(2), 19-27.

Masten, A., Best, K., & Garmezy, N. (1990). Resilience and development: Contributions from the study of children who overcome adversity. Development and Psychopathology, 2, 425-444.

Maxwell, T. W., Harrington, I., & Smith, H. J. (2010). Supporting primary and secondary beginning teachers online: Key findings of the education alumni support project. Australian Journal of Teacher Education, 35(1), 42-58.

Ministry of Education – Israel – management directive 1B. (2009).

Ministry of Education – Israel – management directive 9B. (2004).

O'Hare, S., Quartermaine, L., & Cooke, A. (2011). Issues involved in supporting pre-service teachers' learning in an online environment Teaching and Learning Forum 2011. Accessed September 10, 2012. https://lsn.curtin.edu.au/tlf/tlf2011/refereed/ohare.html.

Sagie, R., & Regev, H. (2002). The first years teacher's challenges. Dapim, 34, 10-45 (Hebrew).

Sammons, P., Day, C., Kington, A., Gu, Q., Stobart, G., & Smees, R. (2007). Exploring variations in teachers' work, lives and their effects on pupils: Key findings and implications from a longitudinal mixed-method study. British Educational Research Journal, 33(5), 681-701.

Tait, M. (2008). Resilience as a contributor to novice teacher success, commitment, and retention. Teacher Education Quarterly, 35(4), 57-75.

Utsumi, L., & Kizu, J. (2006). Mentoring alternative certification teachers: Perceptions from the field. National Association for Alternative Certification Online Journal 1(1), 48-67.

Wang, J., Odell, S., & Clift, R. (Eds.). (2010). Past, present, and future research on teacher induction: An anthology for researchers, policy makers, and practitioners. Lanham, MD: Rowman & Littlefield and Association of Teacher Educators.

Assessment Practices that Support
Deeper Learning in Online Learning Communities

David Gibson
Alexander Halavais
Nils Peterson
USA

Philipp Schmidt
South Africa

Chloe Varelidi
France

Mozilla Badges Informal Workgroup
david.gibson@curveshift.com

Abstract: This article is a research-based position paper that describes a framework of eight assessment practices that support deeper learning in online learning communities using digital badges. The narrative defines deeper learning and outlines a case for elevating formative, performance-based assessments over summative assessments of deeper learning skills. Self- and peer-assessment is viewed as a key requirement of deeper learning that simultaneously supports the scalability of deeper learning assessment practices in open online learning environments.

Introduction

The proliferation of social media and tools (e.g. Pinterest, Facebook, Dropbox) and the rise of new media literacy practices (e.g. social voting, folksonomies, similarity matching) make it easier than ever to imagine giving and receiving feedback from peers, including strangers who share only your current interest, whether that is in finding a new product, or learning about how something works. If we can learn what we need to from anyone at anytime, do we still need experts to pass judgment on us in order to have valid assessment? In the online map tool Waze, the community of all other drivers near you sends observations, alerts, and news, while the underlying map locates exactly where you are and an automated voice tells you where to turn next. Are high-quality, reliable assessments of road conditions taking place in this kind of environment? At the same time as social media is changing and gamifying the experience of self-directed tool use, a new open learning environment movement in formal education is promoting massive access to online open courses (MOOCs). How can an expert give useful information and feedback to thousands of people? Can such a learning environment support deeper learning of higher order skills? Can digital badges be used in these contexts to support deeper learning?

An examination of the literature on deeper learning and open learning environments suggests a set of eight assessment practices discussed below that support deeper learning outcomes. By "assessment practices" we mean a set of processes and protocols that provide helpful feedback to people to begin or advance their learning and to help guide their deeper learning contributions to the community. The term "deeper learning" has been defined by the Hewlett Foundation (2010) as learning that addresses five groups of abilities:

- Mastering core academic content,
- Critical thinking and problem solving,
- Working collaboratively,
- Communicating effectively, and
- Learning how to learn independently.

Historically, deeper learning has been accomplished in both formal and informal "communities of practice" (Lave & Wenger, 1991). These settings often include feedback from an expert mentor as well as peers at various stages of learning. In the judo dojo for example, everyone is responsible for helping their peers learn, and the "sempai," those who have "gone before" and have more skill, are particularly obligated to instruct the "kohai," those with less experience (Bright, 2005; McDonald & Hallinan, 2005). This sort of self and group-assessment has also been traditionally fostered in doctoral and advanced professional programs in institutions of higher learning (Davenish et al, 2009; Weidman & Stein, 2003). However, the traditional communities that developed before the Internet, social media, and online voting schema, have a relatively high cost and are difficult to scale, limited by the number and size of the learning contexts and the availability of expert mentors. Now, in addition to the digital infrastructure that has supported a rapid expansion in diverse communities of practice, global shifts toward a knowledge economy have created an acute need for deeper learning by larger and larger numbers of people. It is therefore a good time to reflect on how to create online community practices that support intensive, community-driven assessment interactions (e.g. guiding expertise, validating achievement) that can scale organically to serve new social demands.

Online, collaborative environments with open and free access provide a relatively new way for anyone, anytime, to learn new things, remotely meet people, and potentially achieve understanding in a supportive community. The unique affordances of the new online approaches allow learners to:

- Find distributed communities in narrow topical niches that may not exist locally;
- Engage in and influence communities asynchronously and at their own pace;
- "Learn by lurking" and easily find their way into open communities as observers;
- Engage models, simulations, and other forms of assessment that may be automated;
- Manage personal reputation within a community (often as an outcome of assessment); and
- Inexpensively publish portfolios of work to an audience of peers or a broader public.
- Accumulate the community wealth of resources, specialized language, answered questions, practices and know-how over time in taxonomic, searchable and shareable forms.

Informal assessment practices in these online communities often emerge to meet a variety of needs (e.g. polling for opinions, finding new resources, building trust networks) and take advantage of unique digital affordances through mechanisms such as badges, asynchronous communications, and peer-based recommender systems. Our purpose here is to look across the commonalities among these practices and offer a framework for the future development of assessment practices.

A set of eight practices discussed below support deeper learning outcomes. New software, instruments, and protocols that support these practices can help formalize the processes of assessment far beyond a casual sharing of comments. In the practices that follow, we assume that the online learning community remains open and elective. Members can casually drop in and out at will over time, but by virtue of these practices, the casual associations among peers can provide formal learning outcomes, for both individuals and the learning community.

1. Expertise & Knowledge of the Learning Community

Central to the idea of a "community of practice" is the ability of any member of a community to learn from experts through observations and increasing participation in the community. This knowledge-in-action is precisely the sort of essential deeper learning that is missing in many formal learning environments. While there is a range of interest-driven communities, communities of practice in particular (CoP) are those in which knowledge in a particular domain is nurtured and in which members contribute to building a common store of solutions, practices, and "ways of seeing" (Hung, 1999). These practices develop and are maintained over time, through the actions of their participants. In particular, networks of social interaction lead to the informal sharing of tacit knowledge. Lave and Wenger refer to the process of learning beginning with "legitimate peripheral participation"; that is, the engagement by new members of the community in early tasks and positioning to observe the work of more expert practitioners. The practices learned can often be at odds with the formal training and documentation systems and the formal organization chart (Orr, 1996).

There are, however, ways of making the process of learning more transparent, assessing that process, and improving the development of a community of practice. Essential to the effective CoP is the combination of learning-while-doing and reflections and discussion of that practiced action (Buysee, Sparkman, & Wesley, 2003). That reflection can take many forms, from basic examination of technical skill, to ethical explorations of the social effects of professional practice (Hatten & Smith, 1995).

While Lave and Wenger focused mainly on physical sites of interaction, significant work has shown that interactions online can support such communities, including those related to online learning environments (Gray, 2004). But groups that are mediated online tend not to be the tightly-knit communities the original CoP theorists investigated. Brown and Duguid in The Social Life of Information (2000), modified the CoP model to account for those in which the participants were bound only by weak ties and a shared system of exchanging messages and documents, often across organizational boundaries. Such inter-organizational weak links can be particularly important in encouraging innovation and organizational learning (Blackler, 1995).

2. Internal and External Validation of Knowledge/Skill

In addition to the argument from legitimate peripheral participation, peer-assessment of expertise is itself an essential ingredient of developing expertise. To emphasize the point, although there are a range of skills, knowledge, and practices that might be said to make up expertise, "evaluative skill is the basic cognitive ability that characterizes all these areas" (Weiss & Shanteau, 2003). The process of acquiring evaluative skills requires practice in evaluating and communicating. This need not be unidirectional; peer assessment is often of benefit to both parties in learning more about their topic of interest. Effective peer assessment not only provides the subject of the assessment with a better idea of her skill level, and illuminates a path toward improvement; it also improves the assessor's skill at discerning good work. Likewise, asking and answering questions can improve the abilities of both the questioner and respondent (Barak & Rafaeli, 2004). In addition, assessments, when well designed for the peer environment, not only improve outcomes, but can encourage continued participation and involvement (Boud, Cohen, & Sampson, 1999; Keppell et al., 2006). In other words, good assessment practices encourage participants to learn the skill of assessment, perhaps the essential skill for a learning society (Boud, 2000).

What determines if the community makes things (e.g. knowledge, assessment decisions) of high quality? Duguid (2006) discusses the arguments of quality assurance in open projects such as Wikipedia. The two most cited rationales are 1) enough eyes on a problem leads to improvements and 2) the good stuff will spread and outlast the bad stuff. However, co-production of cultural knowledge is not linear and higher numbers of eyes and more time do not by themselves guarantee quality. Systems that validate quality must acknowledge the boundaries of peer communities at both the bottom (e.g. the criteria for effective quality) and the top (e.g. the decision-making processes that use the criteria to admit new knowledge and practices). For example in open source software communities of practice, the bottom is comprised of the physical chips that ultimately must "run" if the software is to be effective and the top is comprised of the hierarchical control structures that decide whether or not to accept new code into the code base. Similar structures are needed in other communities of practice, which leads to the idea of tokens and reputation.

New tokens of achievement such as badges (see https://wiki.mozilla.org/Badges) can function as both extrinsic and intrinsic motivations that work in concert (Covington & Müeller, 2001). Of key importance is making sure that extrinsic motivations are not punitive, and encourage risk-taking that leads to greater self-realization and self-directed learning. In other words, a token such as a certificate, degree or badge can be a pointer or reference to a process by which a learner engages in and receives validation from a community that practices authentic assessment. The metadata attached to a digital badge can also guide students who are seeking direction, while also providing transparency and motivation for moving from the periphery of a community to its core. Ideally, such a token can celebrate not just the accomplishment of co-discovered goals, but the engagement of the community in assessing and guiding the progress of the learner.

3. Transparent, Authentic Artifacts of Practice

The new assessment mechanisms and processes being outlined here - peer feedback concerning authentic artifacts shared in an open community of practice leading to badges of achievement - provide better internal and external validation of deeper learning than paper-and-pencil bubble tests and short answer quizzes. This is so for two reasons: 1. digital media learning allows a richer array of performance, and 2. computers are involved, which offers an expanded degree of computational power and flexibility beyond traditional "grading" by a teacher. Technology-enabled mechanisms include peer assessment, automated documentation and feedback, and interactive tutoring, which can complement the social construction of signs and symbols of the meaning and value of complex knowledge and skills in a community. The targets of assessment - the intended results of a learning experience - need to be measured in more than one way in order to provide a reliable indication of acquired knowledge and skills.

Assessing what someone knows and can do involves "a model of how students represent knowledge and develop competence in the subject domain, tasks or situations that allow one to observe students' performance, and an interpretation method for drawing inferences from the performance evidence thus obtained" (Pellegrino, Chudowsky, & Glaser, 2001, 36). These are referred to as the student, task and evidence model in the conceptual assessment framework of evidence-centered design (Mislevy, Almond & Steinberg, 2003), where "the student model specifies the variables in terms of which we wish to characterize students. Task models are schemas for ways to get data that provide evidence about them. Evidence models contain two components, which are links in the chain of reasoning from students' work to their knowledge and skill: The evaluation component of the evidence model contains procedures for extracting the salient features of students' performances in task situations (i.e., observable variables), and the measurement component contains machinery for updating beliefs about student-model variables in light of this information" (p.8).

The student model is more than a characterization of a single student, it also contains what we know about how all students acquire and use knowledge. In this sense, it reveals the contours of the learning community's understanding of knowledge. The task model is a situation in which those skills are called upon and required. As such, it is an authentic context in which the community's knowledge and skills are employed. The evidence model is the inference procedure used to make a judgment. A transformational goal of education is to help people acquire the ability to make judgements (Mezirow, 1997), which entails transparency of the processes and examples of community practices (Dirkx, 1998; Taylor, 2008). If these aspects are present, then participants will have incentives to participate in both the construction of knowledge and reflecting on their contributions and those of others.

4. Assessment as a Core Skill

Like democracy, peer-to-peer assessment works best with everybody educated on the issues and involved in the decisions. Thus, the community assessment framework needs to bring people along in the skills needed to provide helpful, timely feedback that improves performance. Three essential skill areas are involved, which mirror the three components of evidence-centered design (Mislevy, Steinberg and Almond, 1999): 1. knowing what tasks, artifacts, practices belong with the community; 2. knowing what good performance looks like; and 3. being able to link the differences between an actual and ideal task, artifact, or practice performances and advice or information that helps a community member improve.

How are these skills promoted as a core skill? By promoting community norms for feedback, sharing worked examples of performances, using open scoring tools such as informative rubrics, and employing simple rules that relate scores to meaningful feedback that improves performance. Examples of communities that build assessment as a core skill include musicians, who teach each other how to listen, adapt and respond; doctors, who learn to diagnose illnesses; real estate brokers, who learn to estimate land and house values; and scientists, who learn skills of skepticism and critique concerning experiments and results.

5. Incentives for Participation

Assessment structures and practices in open learning environments invite participation and have flexibility "designed in" that respects individual choices. The process and experience of belonging in the community is designed to be an enjoyable and enlightening experience that fosters learning, personal growth, belonging, and giving and receiving feedback. Badges, stars and grades for example, help promote desired behaviors and practices by recognizing and rewarding people for learning, participating, helping others, and offering critical advice. Incentives for participation can include other rewards, such as reputation in a community of scientists measured by citations and reviews; recognition and promotion into leadership within a community based on demonstrated value as a committee member; and increased salary based on certifications acquired during professional practice.

Four types of recognition can be developed for each of the major aspects supporting how people learn: for example, badges might be awarded for 1) knowledge gained, 2) personal profile development, 3) community role development, and 4) providing helpful advice and feedback to others. The incentive and recognition system might include "leveling" so that people understand early progress, completion of benchmark processes and products, and can see a developmental path for expanded reputation within the community.

6. Rich problems in real-world settings

Open learning environments tend to focus on complex problems, because a wide diversity of people are drawn to the community for an exchange of practical ideas to help them solve their real-world problems. As the problems are shared and solutions considered, naturally occurring partnerships form among members of such communities; the members engage in dialog to find common ground and mutual benefits by working together. It is fluid and dynamic rather than a purely mechanistic process of differences leading to creative solutions. The build-up of expertise in the community leads to new forms of validity sanctioned by the community. Davidson (2011, p. 352) calls this "collaboration by difference."

As we've outlined here, working with others to solve complex real-world problems entails increased use of deeper learning capacities as well as a need for broad, multiple measures to validate learning and achievement. This occurs because solutions and decisions involved in real-world settings need to a) meet several criteria of success, b) involve and prioritize more than one viable outcome, c) be evaluated with negotiable values for individuals and the community, and have other characteristics that make them potentially as complex as the problems they address. Therefore, open learning environments have to be watchful for the introduction of overly simplistic or mechanistic problems, solutions and assessments, which can detract from deeper learning and distract the community from rich dialog and a flexible exchange of ideas.

7. Diversity of Autonomous Learners

Online learning is envisioned that provides maximum autonomy for the learner as well as scaffolding that allows individuals to take their own paths through the materials. A key to encouraging self-directed learning is help people base their decisions upon an understanding of their own strengths, interests and aspirations as recognized and appreciated in the community. For some time, researchers have recognized that the autonomous learner seeks to plan learning processes and engage in self-assessment to reach individualized goals (Moore, 1973).

The assessment system must therefore accomplish a number of things in order to meet the needs of an autonomous learner. It must be highly transparent: the kinds of knowledge needed in order to demonstrate mastery must be clear and openly described. It is not enough to merely indicate a level of expertise, as learners may arrive at one particular point in the curriculum via one of many different paths. A learner must know what the assessment aims to demonstrate, and what assessments (if any) should be accomplished before tackling any given task.

The assessment system should also provide multiple ways of assessing the same knowledge, and acknowledge that a given skill or element of knowledge may be tested in multiple ways, each with its own perspectives on feedback. Some assessments may draw more heavily on peers' ability to analyze and discuss the work of the learner, while other assessments may be accomplished alone.

To assure that the assessments meet the diverse needs of the learning community the learning community can be directly involved in the construction and evaluation of the assessment instruments. As Stefani (1998) suggests, involving students directly in the creation of assessment tasks, and carefully monitoring differences between the ways experts, peers, and learners themselves evaluate work can provide insight into assessments that are accurate and provide effective feedback to students. If the assessment instrument, the learner's work and the assessment results are each public, learners can learn by observing other the community's assessment activities; an example of "legitimate peripheral participation."

8. Mechanisms for the System's Evolution

A successful community of practice must be responsive to changes in its contexts (knowledge, technology, social setting) and change its practices and assessments of those practices to reflect the changing context. A group needs a mechanism that enables it to come together and decide that whatever assessment framework they have established to measure aptitude in an area of knowledge (e.g., JavaScript expertise) either is not working, or has stopped working because the profession or larger community has adopted new practices. Vital to this process is collecting a broad portfolio of evidence in order to be able to inform the ways in which the assessment framework is maintained and changed.

Conclusion

Communities that produce deeper learning outcomes can be developed online, based on open, public and peer to peer interactions, enhanced by the addition of appropriate assessment affordances, including a focus on formative feedback, community recognition signaled by symbols such as badges, and outcomes validated by the collections of evidence that support them.

Deeper learning can be fostered in scalable, effective open learning environments if there are support structures - the tools, processes, and symbols valued by the community - that enable community-building, the sharing of its unique knowledge, the advancement of the interests of its individual members, and the appropriate design of assessment activities. To measure deeper learning outcomes, assessment must be a public process, unlike a high-stakes test. Public peer-to-peer assessment has several important consequences for the learner and for the community of learners:

- Learners can understand the knowledge and experience of the learning community by understanding what is assessed and how it is assessed.
- External people as well as the community's own members can verify and place value on the community's processes, products and results. A public assessment process that includes the work, the assessment instrument, and the assessment results facilitates credibility of the accomplishment outside of the community.
- Community values become transparent and open for discussion and continuous improvement of authentic practices.
- Community members can learn from the assessments provided to others, comparing the work and the feedback received to better gauge the meanings of the community's assessment practices. Learners can socialize to the norms of the community as well as develop new levels of knowledge and skills by giving and/or receiving peer assessments.
- Badges and other tokens of and incentives for accomplishment can be understood within the community in terms of the kinds of performances that they denote.
- The real-world problems and approaches of the community supply a rich field of practice and development for the learner.
- Individualized development pathways are acknowledged, supported and valued.
- By exposing the aggregate results of the assessment activities the community can examine the success of its assessment practice in order to improve its practice and processes.

Founded in the science of how people learn, the literature views deeper learning as emerging from the dynamic interplay between people with specialized knowledge, working together to solve problems, in a community that is formed by shared interests and practices, and providing constructive feedback to continuously improve performance. An assessment framework of practices that incorporates the eight principles will lead to more effective learning in open environments, and implementation of systems that address these principles will lead to better learning experiences for all.

Acknowledgements

The authors would like to thank Erin Knight and Carla Cassilli for their in-depth comments, interactions and discussions that have helped shape this work. Many other people, too numerous to mention, made valuable comments on the online drafts; their insights also improved our thinking. Gibson takes responsibility for this shortened version of the work and apologizes to the co-authors for any omissions.

References

Barak, M., & Rafaeli, S. (2004). On-line question-posing and peer-assessment as a means for web-based knowledge sharing in learning. International Journal of Human-Computer Studies, 61(1), 84-103.

Blackler, F. (1995). Knowledge, knowledge work and organizations: An overview and interpretation. Organization Studies, 16(6), 16–36.

Boud, D. (2000). Sustainable assessment: Rethinking assessment for the learning society. Studies in Continuing Education, 22(2), 151–167.

Boud, D., Cohen, R., & Sampson, J. (1999). Peer learning and assessment. Assessment and Evaluation in Higher Education, 24(4), 413–436.

Bright, M. I. (2005). Can Japanese mentoring enhance understanding of Western mentoring? Employee Relations, 27(4), 325-339.

Brown, J. S., & Deguid, P. (2000). The social life of information. Cambridge, MA: Harvard Business School Press.

Covington, M. V., & Müeller, K. J. (2001). Intrinsic versus extrinsic motivation: An approach/avoidance reformulation. Educational Psychology Review, 13(2), 157–176.

Davidson, C. N. (2011). Now you see it: How the brain science of attention will transform the way we live, work, and learn. New York: Viking.

Gray, B. (2004). Informal learning in an online community of practice. Journal of Distance Education, 19(1), 20–35.

Hewlett Foundation (2010). Education program: Strategic plan. The William and Flora Hewlett Foundation. Retrieved from http://www.hewlett.org/uploads/documents/Education_Strategic_Plan_2010.pdf

Hung, D. (1999). Activity, apprenticeship, and epistemological appropriation: Implications from the writings of Michael Polanyi. Educational Psychologist, 34(4), 193–205.

Keppell, M., Au, E., Ma, A., & Chan, C. (2006). Peer learning and learning-oriented assessment in technology-enhansed environments. Assessment & Evaluation in Higher Education, 31(4), 453-464.

Lave, J., & Wenger, E. (1991). Situated learning: Legitimate peripheral participation. Cambridge, UK: Cambridge University Press.

McDonald, B., & Hallinan, C. (2005). Seishin habitus: spiritual capital and Japanese rowing. International Review for the Sociology of Sport, 40(2), 187-200.

Mezirow, J. (1997). Transformative Learning: Theory to Practice. New Directions for Adult and Continuing Education, 1997(74), 5-12. doi:10.1002/ace.7401

Mislevy, R., Steinberg, L., & Almond, R. (1999). Evidence-Centered Assessment Design. Educational Testing Service. Retrieved from http://www.education.umd.edu/EDMS/mislevy/papers/ECD_overview.html

Mislevy, R., Steinberg, L., & Almond, R. (2003). On the structure of educational assessments. Measurement: Interdisciplinary Research and Perspectives, 1, 3–67.

Moore, M. G. (1973). Toward a theory of independent learning and teaching. Journal of Higher Education, 44(12), 661–679.

Orr, J. (1996). Talking about machines: An ethnography of a modern job. Ithica, NY: Cornell University Press.

Pellegrino, J., N. Chudowsky, and R. Glaser, eds. (2001). Knowing what students know: The science and design of educational assessment. Committee on the Foundations of Assessment, Board on Testing and Assessment, Center for Education, National Research Council. Washington, DC: National Academy Press.

Stefani, L. A. J. (1998). Assessment in partnership with learners. Assessment & Evaluation in Higher Education, 23(4), 339–350.

Weidman, J. C., & Stein, E. L. (2003). Socialization of doctoral students to academic norms. Research in Higher Education, 44(6), 641-656.

Weiss, D. J, & Shanteau, J. (2003). Empirical assessment of expertise. Human Factors, 45(1), 104–116.

Designing for Critical Thinking and Learning: Online Communication Platforms in Teacher Education

Tina L. Heafner
Teresa M. Petty
Michelle Plaisance
Abiola Farinde
University of North Carolina at Charlotte, USA
theafner@uncc.edu, tmpetty@uncc.edu, mplaisan@uncc.edu, afarinde@uncc.edu

Abstract: Windows into Teaching and Learning (WiTL), a study at a large urban research university in the United States, provided teacher candidates enrolled in online summer courses access to meaningful, quality virtual clinical experiences during those months when clinical settings were unavailable. Additionally, WiTL was engineered to explore differences in communication and engagement in synchronous versus asynchronous learning environments. WiTL had surprising corollary outcomes, such as, the presence of conditions that enhanced student engagement and promoted the use of critical discourse to make meaning of clinical experiences. Evaluating the level of discourse and questioning using a cognitive framework, Revised Bloom's Taxonomy, we conclude that synchronous learning provided higher levels of engagement and questioning through immediacy and less authoritative structures not present in asynchronous text.

Introduction

Windows into Teaching and Learning (WiTL), an innovative online teacher education initiative, created a technology-mediated learning environment that integrated diverse virtual clinical experiences coupled with synchronous and asynchronous dialogue. In this manuscript, we situate teacher candidate learning in two WiTL online methods courses within a discourse and questioning framework, Revised Bloom's Taxonomy (RBT) (Anderson, Loren & Krathwohl 2001), in order to identify and describe differences in approaches that promoted high levels of engagement, learning, and dialogue. Our primary goal was to create an online learning environment that supported analytical and judicious thinking, one where candidates were able to critically and socially construct meaning as they viewed relevant teaching by experts in the field. The research outcomes described in this article focus on a comparative examination of interactions within online learning contexts. We utilized the RBT to classify cognitive development, permitting the categorization of higher order thinking within synchronous and asynchronous educational environments. Determining when and under what conditions higher-level thinking and questioning occurred was a primary interest. We believed that for optimal learning to be observed, candidates' discourse needed to occupy the upper levels of the RBT. At these upper levels, students possess a high level of metacognitive awareness (Szabo & Schwartz 2011; Valcke, Wever, Zhu, & Deed 2009) and engage in critical thinking and deliberative discourse (Murchú & Muirhead 2005), both desired project outcomes.

Review of Relevant Literature

Good education preparation programs know effective teacher qualities and attributes of learning environments; however, current programs fall short in providing prospective teachers access to meaningful opportunities to deeply examine teaching episodes that closely align with university coursework (Darling-Hammond 2010). In response, innovative ways to approach teacher preparation are sought. Utilized as a tool to enhance learning and improve educational experiences, technology serves as a pathway for connecting teacher candidates with schools (Szabo & Schwartz 2011). Evidence of the expanding use of technology is visible in the expansion of online courses, with over 4.6 million students enrolled in at least one course online annually (Allen & Seaman 2010). With growth, questions concerning quality and design in association with higher levels of learning, especially in teacher education, emerge.

Researchers describing interaction patterns of preservice teachers enrolled in both synchronous and asynchronous online environments, found that, while synchronous communication was more frequent, asynchronous interaction between participants was more in-depth and serious (Bonk, Hanson, Grabner-Hagan, Lazar, & Mirabelli 1998). Similarly, while there are positive attributes to using synchronous communication environments, such as the ability to establish a social presence within the classroom community, asynchronous opportunities produce deeper, more meaningful discussions (Im & Lee 2003). Beyond the obvious benefits of asynchronous communication, such as flexibility and convenience (Branon & Essex 2001), traditional thinking has positioned this platform as being more conducive to the higher-level reflection and questioning thought to be desirable in teacher education programs. In contrast, using Dewey's definition of critical thinking to rate teacher reflectiveness and a content analysis of online discussions, Levin, He, and Robbins (2006) found that candidates were more reflective and reached higher levels of critical thinking in synchronous discussion. In addition, candidates' pre-post surveys showed preferences for synchronous communication, citing as one reason their appreciation of "being challenged to think intensely and learn from peers in a short time frame" (p. 448). Ng'ambi (2006) also examined the use of synchronous texting to create collaborative questioning as students shared in the critical reading of an assigned text. Students reported that they found the real-time, collective and ongoing experience increased reflective and higher order thinking. Other researchers (Krentler & Willis-Flurry 2005; Offir, Lev & Bezalel 2008; Schellens & Valcke 2006) connect engagement in online discussions with learning outcomes and suggest that engagement is linked to critical thinking skills of the participants (Mauriano 2006). Recognizing that requirements to participate in online discussions do not always produce the level of interaction or quality desired (Buraphadeja & Dawson 2008; Dennen 2005; McLoughlin & Mynard 2009), structuring of tasks, writing prompts, and feedback to promote, encourage, and model intellectual engagement become important considerations. Otherwise, online discussions fall short of achieving desired critical discourse and higher-order thinking (Jarosewich et al 2010). In sum, both asynchronous and synchronous learning have been documented as reflective and thought-provoking; however, experiences and outcomes vary, suggesting a need for research examining levels of thinking in both learning environment structures.

Within higher education, multiple online learning environments are utilized to further instruction by providing more time and opportunities for engagement and reflection (Ertmer, Sadaf, & Ertmer 2011). The effectiveness of online learning communities is rooted in students' cognitive interaction, specifically whether teacher candidates are engaging in higher-order thinking. In order to measure students' cognitive growth, this study uses RBT of cognitive objectives (Anderson & Krathwohl 2001) as a content analysis tool to determine whether asynchronous or synchronous discussion forums produced different levels of thinking among teacher candidates. The content and structure of RBT allows it to serve as an evaluation tool used to classify cognitive development. It not only permits analysis of learning outcomes, but also the cognitive process, which occurs throughout a learning experience (Valcke, Wever, Zhu, & Deed, 2009).

Method

Data were collected from a convenience sample of thirty teacher candidates enrolled in two online content area methods courses. Researchers utilized two cooperating schools in two geographically distinct districts as a result of university faculty connections to community partnerships and ongoing work. From these schools a purposive sample of twelve middle and secondary teaching professionals was selected based on educational background, content expertise, teaching experience, commitment to serve as mentor teachers, and administrative evaluation as accomplished. Prior to the commencement of the methods course, the teacher mentors worked with the researchers to select exemplary content-pedagogy lessons to be videotaped and archived in the months prior to the beginning of the methods courses. Course instructors utilized a laptop, wireless headset, and Webcam to facilitate the recording of asynchronous sessions. During these sessions, the instructors "narrated" the lessons through written comments, captured on screen using Microsoft Word. After the lessons, instructors added additional audio narration using Camtasia Screen Recording Software (http://www.techsmith.com/camtasia.html) to provide a context for each lesson and to include learning cues for targeted instructional strategies and successful teacher behaviors.

Each methods course began with the shared viewing of six synchronous sessions that were delivered via Wimba (http://www.wimba.com), allowing class members to observe the mentors' teaching real-time for one academic block. During the observation sessions, course instructors were present in the clinical setting using a desktop computer with Internet connection, webcam and wireless headset, and texting interface to post comments. The methods instructor provided a narrated context for each classroom and lesson at the beginning of the observation. Candidates were given access to text chat to communicate with one another throughout the observation. Immediately following each of these synchronous lessons, the teacher mentor hosted a live debriefing via Wimba, during which candidates were encouraged to explore the pedagogical methods they had just observed through questioning and dialogue. Later in the course, following the shared synchronous experience, candidates were assigned the task of viewing aforementioned archived asynchronous sessions. In contrast to the live debriefing, candidates were asked to engage in an online threaded discussion with the teacher mentors utilizing a password-protected forum that had been established in NiceNet (www.nicenet.org). The threaded discussions occurred over two weeks and provided the candidates an opportunity to capitalize on the teacher mentors' expertise. The project yielded multiple data sources; however, the data central to this study are the synchronous text chat logs, asynchronous threaded discussion, and transcribed synchronous debriefings. We defined our guiding research question as: What are the differences in levels of engagement, learning, and dialogue in synchronous and asynchronous online learning environments?

Data Analysis

Using content analysis (Charmaz, 2006; Krippendorf, 1980), specifically, a conceptual analysis of critical thinking, we sought to quantify and tally levels of questions and comments in learning contexts associated with the asynchronous and synchronous observation experiences through a systematic and iterative coding process. We examined data looking for implicit and explicit occurrences of the language codes of RBT (see Figure 1). While explicit terms were easily identified, coding for implicit terms relied on individual and collective interpretations. Due to potential for subjectivity, five levels of analyses and a structured coding process were used to cross-validate data interpretations.

	Cognitive Process Dimension					
	Remember (Describing, naming, defining)	**Understand** (Interpreting, classifying, explaining)	**Apply** (Implementing, demonstrating, illustrating)	**Analyze** (Exploring, contrasting, differentiating)	**Evaluate** (Justifying, appraising, arguing)	**Create** (Generating, constructing, designing)
Factual (Discipline specific, terminology, details)						
Conceptual (Classifications, principles, generalizations)						
Procedural (skills, techniques, methods)						
Meta-Cognitive (Reflective, strategic, contextual)						

(Knowledge Dimension)

Figure 1: Data Analysis Coding Chart for RBT

First, we independently evaluated data sources using a RBT framework. Each researcher individually sorted participant text chats and NiceNet comments into the six RBT categories. Independently we used a descriptive organization chart that included RBT verbs and question stems. Second, we met in dyads to confirm and question individual coding. Definitional comparisons of categories were made using examples from the data. When agreement was not consistent, we discussed differences until consensus was achieved. Third, we convened to discuss categorized and sorted data. Each dyad presented collective findings. When agreement was not present between dyads, we undertook rationalized category sorts for each example. Additionally, we contextually examined data within complete discussion threads and text chats to further explore coding fit. Fourth, we individually re-evaluated data as coded to confirm category fit. When participant statements were questioned, these were highlighted and discussed in dyads. Once in agreement, frequencies were tabulated for each RBT category. Fifth, dyads met as a whole group to verify coding changes and gain final consensus. We discussed interpretations of data based on frequencies. Patterns were identified by data source and examples of differences were selected that best represented frequency and coding patterns.

Results

In examining transcripts of the post-project focus groups with the candidate participants, a strong preference for synchronous communication opportunities emerged. Of the 30 candidates, 21 commented favorably on these types of interactions. For example, one candidate stated,
> So it wasn't necessarily even so much the questions for the teachers afterwards as it was peers of mine and the things they were observing; questions that we had that we answered back and forth- it made the whole experience much richer... [The synchronous text chat] made me observe or see things I might not have otherwise.

This feeling of sharing in the experience arose often in the data, along with the idea that access to peers via synchronous texting kept students more engaged in the clinical experience. As one candidate articulates, "[in traditional clinical experiences] you're sort of passively observing where I felt that this one was more actively observing because we had peer discussions going on during the class."

Perhaps more important are the patterns of communication that emerged during comparative analyses of opportunities to communicate about the teaching they observed. Table 1 illustrates the frequency of output per category in the RBT. Based on the previously described analyses, we arrived at two important insights. First, synchronous communication opportunities yielded significantly larger proportions of output that were reflective of higher order thinking. A relationship between levels of engagement and the immediacy and interactive structure of video-observation was noted. Second, the presence and interjection of a perceived authority figure, either in the form of the course instructor or the mentor teacher, lowered the level of questioning and critical thinking. The unconstrained dialogue offered through constructivist synchronous text chat was linked to higher-level discourse.

Bloom's Level	Asynchronous	Synchronous	Synchronous
	During observation	*During observation*	*Post lesson- debrief*
Remembering	236	68	96
Understanding	69	125	42
Applying	41	21	12
Analyzing	27	85	1
Evaluating	71	144	12
Creating	30	28	5
Total	474	471	168
Total HOTS*	128	257	18
Percentage HOTS*	**27%**	**55%**	**11%**

*Higher Order Thinking Skills (HOTS)

Table 1: Frequency of Candidate Output, Synchronous v. Asynchronous

Immediacy and Engagement in Synchronous Environments

Using RBT to analyze synchronous and asynchronous discussions, data findings show that synchronous learning environments yielded higher levels of critical thinking. During synchronous communication, a greater number of candidates' questions and comments were categorized in the top three tiers: *analyzing*, *evaluating*, and *creating*. This high-level input focused primarily on content knowledge, pedagogical practices, and classroom instruction. In contrast, asynchronous communication produced fewer examples of higher-order thinking. Often, these questions and comments remained in the middle or lower tiers, addressing classroom management and organization. As illustrated in Table 1, student synchronous communications generated a tallied score of 85, 144, and 28, respectfully for *analyzing, evaluating,* and *creating*. In comparison, in asynchronous communication settings students' summative scores were significantly lower (27, 71, and 30, respectfully) for the same tiers.

In this collaborative, immediate-response communication environment, students' questions and comments possessed depth and greater levels of critical thinking. Examples of this occurrence range among the top three tiers of RBT. Although not exhaustive, the selected questions and comments reveal the strength of synchronous communication in promoting higher order thinking. Evidence of c*reating*, which occupies the top tier of RBT could be found in the following students' questions and comments:
- I was thinking that it might be good for a different teacher to do the remediation rather than the student's regular teacher. The different teacher may just present something a little differently that sets off the light bulbs for the students, just a thought.
- I think the goal for me should be how to create kind of a scavenger hunt type of unit so they can not only be interested but start learning the reasoning behind it.

Students generated an even greater number of *evaluation* questions. Higher levels of thinking are apparent in the questions and comments below:
- You know that she is a good, experienced teacher because of the level of talking among the students...they all seem to be talking about the task at hand and not anything else...they all seem to be really into the activity which is great.
- It is good that he is giving more than one way to get to an answer.
- Mixing genders may have spurred more in-group discussion. It appears that most groups are like-minded in responses.

Below is a representative sample of students' questions and comments that comprised the third tier of RBT-*analyzing*.
- I wonder if the use of the calculators hinders this ability to maintain skill level for basic math.
- She is starting out with simple facts about population and government. Setting the groundwork for deeper work about the culture.

The presence of higher order thinking questions in synchronous communication is also strengthened by the decrease of these questions in asynchronous communications. Conversely, asynchronous questions and comments, more commonly present in the middle and lower tiers of RBT (applying, understanding, and remembering) were often fact-based, general, managerial questions. Questions address topics of time management, teachers' preferences, classroom procedures, seating arrangements, discipline, homework, class size, classroom organization, and etc. Examples include:
- What strategies do you use to encourage your students to their homework?
- How long do you typically spend with middle school students teaching them the rules and procedures for your class?
- What is your classroom management plan?
- If students are normally not required to raise their hands, is this because of the class size or because of their age/maturity level?

Constructivist Questioning in the Absence of Authority

An additional theme emerged during analyses of candidate interaction throughout the synchronous observations. On many occasions student interaction began in the lower tiers of RBT; however, over the course of several exchanges the level of questioning increased. Candidates appeared to find affirmation in their peers' comments and used them as scaffolding to more elevated thinking. These trends were supported by candidates' comments in the post project focus groups where students were asked to share their preference for the synchronous or asynchronous experiences. As an example, one candidate explained:
I did like the fact that we were all watching the same thing and could make comments about it and talk about our same viewing with different perspectives. So I thought it was really beneficial not just to have other people seeing what I was seeing, but be able to teach me things I didn't pick up on.

This and many similar comments suggest that questioning was constructivist in nature, with candidates collectively shaping their understanding based on a shared experience and unencumbered discourse. As evidence, the following synchronous exchange occurred via text chat as one group of students observed a math lesson toward the end of the school year:

> **Candidate #1** said: Sorry, I know you already stated this...but when is their EOC for this course? (*remembering*)
> **Course Instructor** said: They took it on Monday.
> **Candidate #2** said: Do you know how much longer they are in school for? (*remembering*)
> **Candidate #1** said: Once a class takes their EOG or EOC...and they pass...do they start doing math that is for next year? (*understanding*)
> **Candidate #3** said: great question
> **Candidate #2** said: He did say earlier that whatever they were doing was getting them ready for next year.
> **Candidate #1** said: Thanks!
> **Candidate #4** said: I had a teacher that I observed not long ago that said to me that it is always good if you have the time to teach more than just let them be there quiet. (*applying*)
> **Candidate #3** said: It does seem like a waste of everyone's time to be in school and not learn anything.
> **Candidate #1** said: Class full of bright students allows this to happen. I can't imagine trying to motivate lower level students to continue learning after the EOC. (*applying*)
> **Candidate #4** said: Good point, Beth.
> **Candidate #3** said: Maybe some cooperative learning activities and more game-type learning would motivate them a little more. (*creating*)
> **Candidate #1** said: I agree!
> **Candidate #3** said: Make the students think they're playing instead of learning. (*creating*)

In addition to this trend of student-generated surges of questioning, we noted a pattern throughout both the synchronous and asynchronous communication opportunities. We found that the presence of authority, either in the form of a course instructor or a mentor teacher, consistently impacted the types and levels of questions that were posed. First, when instructors allowed for unrestrained dialogue with little to no intervention, the level of questioning increased. Conversely, as instructors became more engaged, student questioning levels consistently dropped to the lower tiers. Candidate feedback and analyses of the synchronous communication logs indicate that the reason for this shift was that instructors introduced new foci and redirected dialogue to different topics. While one candidate noted, "it was nice to see the different instructors giving questions and making me think about what I was watching as I was watching it," in retrospect, this redirection, though well-intentioned, may have been unfortunate in that candidates often returned to the lower tiers of RBT following each instructor intervention.

There were; however, fewer interruptions in the synchronous text chat. Data reported in Table 1 support this finding, where higher order dialogue accounted for 55% of synchronous text chat interactions when the mentor teacher was not present, as compared to only 11% when mentor teachers or course instructors participated in the communication. Additionally, questions posed directly to mentor teachers or in the presence of the instructor focused mainly on "safe" topics, like classroom management and logistical concerns. This shift also helps to explain the enormous difference in higher-order exchanges in the synchronous environment (where authority was often uninvolved) versus asynchronous environments (where questions were posed directly to someone with perceived authority). The following questions posed during an asynchronous chat with one mentor teacher support this finding:

> **Candidate #1**: Hi, I was wondering how you go about establishing guidelines for group activities so that your students stay on task while they are completing them? (*understanding*)
> **Candidate #2**: Good morning. I have a couple of questions that coincide. What challenges do you face when your student come in at the beginning of the year and how do you I guess overcome those challenges as far as academic wise, getting them to where they need to be? (*understanding*)
> **Candidate #4**: Good afternoon. Thank you for answering our questions today. My question is how long you been teacher? And how was your first semester at the school you decided to work? (*remembering*)
> **Candidate #5**: Thank you so much for answering our questions. I have a question about the curriculum you had mentioned about you implementing a new curriculum for the students this year. I wanted to find out how much input you have in making that type of decision on what you are able to present in your classroom? (*understanding*)

Furthermore, the hierarchical structure of the asynchronous text chat created a one-way transference of knowledge between the novice and expert. While peers may have joined the question thread, the asynchronous discussion structure did not provide candidates an unconstrained forum for interaction and critical discourse in the absence of authority. The high frequency of *remembering* questions (n=236) comprised over 55% of the asynchronous posts. Comparatively, less than 27% of the asynchronous questions exhibited higher-order thinking, whereas, 55% of synchronous posts showed evidence of higher levels of questioning. The authority-directed learning structure prevalent in the asynchronous discussion forum inhibited critical discourse. In the absence of any authority figure in synchronous text chats, candidates ventured into areas that they had previously avoided. Because the higher levels of RBT require candidates to critically evaluate what they are observing, and even to challenge it, they appear unwilling to do so in the presence of someone with more tenure, we suspect for fear of offending mentor teachers or appearing inexperienced. As an example, a candidate noted in the post-project interview:

> I think also with the online observations…we could almost see the negative things in the classroom. I don't know if I am saying that correctly, but as far as for me, I am a little embarrassed to point out things to the teacher face to face that I might notice, that are like "okay, what is this?...but online you feel a little bit comfortable because you are not actually face to face with the teacher. I guess that's one pro of the online (clinical experiences).

Implications and Recommendations

From the results, we conclude that the immediacy and democratic structure of synchronous text chat promoted higher levels of cognition. The format of the synchronous text chat created unconstrained learning environments not present in the authoritative-oriented asynchronous text chat. We suggest that remote observations, coupled with unimpeded constructivist synchronous dialogue provided the opportunity for more critical discourse, affording candidates the unique opportunity to venture into higher tiers of RBT. These findings support notions that engagement and higher-order thinking rather than the critical thinking skills of participants (Mauriano 2006) are directly linked to the structure of the learning environment and the role of the instructor (Jarosewich et. al 2010; Krentler & Willis-Flurry 2005; Offir, Lev & Bezalel 2008; Schellens & Valcke 2006). Although requirements to engage in online discussions existed in the asynchronous environment, this did not produce the level of interaction desired (Buraphadeja & Dawson 2008; Dennen 2005; McLoughlin & Mynard 2009). Rather, it was the absence of authority and the freedom to self-direct and collectively explore observations that led to higher levels of cognitive questioning and engagement. The idea that candidate questioning would improve when given the opportunity to interact with one another affirmed what educators know about collaborative learning, especially in online environments (Garrison & Anderson 2003; Shea 2006). We infer that the context in which communication opportunities are being offered may be evolving to reflect societal changes in terms of preferences for immediate, synchronous forms of communication.

Furthermore, a primary objective of early field experiences in teacher preparation programs is to allow candidates to watch without concern over judgment, and be given the freedom to question for the purpose of understanding. In accordance with earlier research by Hannah (1995), early field experiences need to embody a "safe environment where candidates can explore their beliefs about teaching" (p. 276). Many clinical experiences fall short of this objective, as candidates are left without the opportunity to deeply examine the teaching they observe, either in partnership with a mentor teacher or with their peers as confirmed by our asynchronous findings (Darling-Hammond, 2010). Engineers of online learning environments stand to gain important insights into student interaction from this project. The objective should be to provide clinical experiences, like those actuated through WiTL, that create interactive, collective viewing experiences. These structures allow candidates to analyze and critique the pedagogy they observe in constructivist environments that are removed from the teacher and unobstructed by the presence of authority. Moreover, the use of synchronous text chat permits candidates to freely express their learning, explore their questions, and to draw upon the different perspectives that a collective, democratic learning environment engenders. Successful facilitators of online learning can design interactive, constructivist environments that allow candidates to take the lead and construct their own path to learning objectives. Online course instructors may best serve their students when they remember that effective learning occurs when it is student-directed and student-centered (Sewell, Frith, & Colvin 2010). Given large numbers of students enrolled in online courses and the rapidity with which institutions of higher education have expanded online coursework, the structure of courses that promote optimal learning experiences are important considerations for future and ongoing research.

References

Allen, I., & Seaman, J. (2010). *Learning on demand: Online education in the United States, 2009*. The Sloan Consortium: Babson Survey Research Group, USA. Available: http://sloanconsortium.org/publications/survey/learning_on_demand_sr2010.

Anderson, L., & Krathwohl, D. (2001). *A taxonomy for learning, teaching and assessing: A revision of Bloom's Taxonomy of Educational Objectives*. New York: Longman.

Buraphadeja, V., & Dawson, K. (2008). Content analysis in Computer-Mediated Communication: Analyzing models for assessing critical thinking through the lens of social constructivism. *American Journal of Distance Education, 22*, 130-145.

Brannon, R., & Essex, C. (2001). Synchronous and asynchronous communication tools in distance education. *Tech Trends, 45*(1), 36-42.

Bonk, C., Hanson J., Grabner-Hagan, M., Lazar, M., & Mirabelli, C. (1998). Time to 'connect': Synchronous and asynchronous case-based dialogue among preservice teachers. In C. J. Bonk, and K. S. King, *Electronic Collaborators: Learner-centered Technologies for Literacy, Apprenticeship, and Discourse* (pp. 289-314). Mahwah, NJ: Lawrence Erlbaum Associates Publishers.

Charmaz, C. (2006). *Constructing grounded theory: A practical guide through qualitative analysis.* Thousand Oaks, CA: Sage.

Darling-Hammond, L. 2010. *The flat world and education: How America's commitment to equity will determine our future*. New York: Teacher's College Press.

Dennen, V. P. (2005) From message posting to learning dialogues: Factors affecting learner participation in asynchronous discussion. *Distance Education, 26*(1), 125-146.

Ertmer, P. A., Sadaf, A., & Ertmer, D. J. (2011). Student-content interactions in online courses: The role of question prompts in facilitating higher-level engagement with course content. *Journal of Computing in Higher Education, 23*, 157-186.

Garrison, R., & Anderson, T. (2003). *E-learning in the 21st century: A framework for research and practice*. London: Routledge Falmer.

Hannah, L. (1995). Self-study: Students evaluate the use of video "cases" in an educational psychology course with a field component. *Journal of Technology and Teacher Education, 3*(2/3), 267-279.

Im, Y., & Lee, O. (2003). Pedagogical implications of online discussion for preservice teacher training. **Journal of Research on Technology in Education, 36**, 1R55-170.

Jarosewich, T., Vargo, L., Salzman, J., Lenhart, L., Krosnick, L., Vance, K., & Roskos, K. (2010). Say what? The quality of discussion board postings in online professional develpoment. *New Horizons in Education, 58*(3), 118-132.

Krippendorf, K. (1980). **Content analysis: An introduction to its methodology** Beverly Hills, CA: Sage Publications.

Krentler, K. A., & Willis-Flurry, L. A. (2005). Does technology enhance actual student learning? The case of on-line discussion boards. *Journal of Education for Business, 80*(6), 316-321.

Levin, B., He, Y., & Robbins, H. (2006). Comparative analysis of preservice teachers' reflective thinking in synchronous versus asynchronous online case discussions. *Journal of Technology and Teacher Education, 14*, 439-460.

McLoughlin, D., & Mynard, J. (2009). An analysis of higher order thinking in online discussions. *Innovations in Education and Teaching International, 46*, 147-160.

Mauriano, P. (2006). Looking for critical thinking in online threaded discussions. *E-Journal of Instructional Science and Technology, 9*, 1-18.

Murchú, D., & Muirhead, B. (2005). Insights into promoting critical thinking in online classes. *International Journal of Instructional Technology and Distance Learning, 2* (6). Available: http://itdl.org/Journal/Jun_05/article01.htm.

Ng'Ambi, D. (2006). SMS collaborative questioning: Convergence of task, interactivity and outcomes. *IADIS International Conference Mobile Learning*, 26-33.

Offir, B., Lev, Y., & Bezalel, R. (2008). Surface and deep learning processes in distance education: Synchronous versus asynchronous systems. *Computers & Education, 51*(3), 1172-1183.

Schellens, T., & Valcke, M. (2006). Fostering knowledge construction in university students through asynchronous discussion groups. *Computers & Education, 46*(4), 349-370.

Sewell, J. P., Frith, K. H., & Colvin, M. M. (2010). Online assessment strategies: A primer. *MERLOT Journal of Online Learning and Teaching, 6*(1), 297–305.

Shea, P. (2006). A study of students' sense of community in online learning environments. *Journal of Asynchronous Learning Network, 10*(1), 35-44.

Szabo, Z., & Schwartz, J. (2011). Learning methods for teacher education: The use of online discussions to improve critical thinking. *Technology, Pedagogy & Education, 20*(1), 79-94.

Valcke, M., De Wever, B., Zhu, C., & Deed, C. (2009). Supporting active cognitive processing in collaborative groups: The potential of Bloom's Taxonomy as a labeling tool. *The Internet and Higher Education*, 12165-172.

Students Being Teachers:
Foucault's Eventalization in an Authentic E-Learning Hybrid Course

Christopher Worthman
DePaul University, Chicago, Illinois, USA
cworthma@depaul.edu

Abstract: In this article, I describe the development and teaching of an authentic e-learning hybrid English language arts (ELA) methods course that drew on Foucault's (1984; 1991) concept of *eventalization* and Gee's (1996; 2004) sociocultural theory of learning. Questions about what is worthwhile and who benefits guided the teacher-candidates' (TCs') quarter-long authentic learning project. They researched and developed online curricular modules and considered issues of pedagogy. As a self-study, I used discourse analysis (Gee, 2009) to analyze blog entries and TC weekly discussion board posts. TCs, working in collaboration, challenged taken-for-granted understandings of the ELA within a framework of identifying who benefits from particular theories and practices and what is worthwhile and why in ELA. They demonstrated an understanding of the complexity and ambiguity that defines ELA as contextualized practice. I conclude by considering how the course design facilitated TCs learning.

"Maybe the target nowadays is not to discover what we are but to refuse what we are."

The quote comes from Michel Foucault (1983, p. 216). And like much of what Foucault wrote, it speaks to issues of ontology, or issues of being and who it is we become and why. I present it at the outset to make evident Foucault's influence on my teaching and research and the nature of the project I describe in this article.

As a teacher educator, I prepare teacher-candidates (TCs) to teach high school English. Last year I developed and taught a hybrid course for the first time in nearly 22 years of teaching middle school, high school, undergraduate, and graduate students. The course, a new course in a new degree program, sought to introduce students to the history of teaching reading, writing, and language, the main components of the English language arts (ELA). A course goal was to position students historically within ELA and provide them a context to begin to define their teaching pedagogies. I strived to do this by engaging TCs in a quarter-long authentic learning project that put them in teacher roles of researching and developing curriculum and pedagogical practices.

In this article, I describe how I set out to meet this goal and to what effect. As a self-study, I draw on data collected through weekly blog posts I wrote. These posts describe course development efforts and the theories that informed it, and my subsequent teaching of the course. I also draw on students' weekly discussion board reflections as a source for understanding course efficacy. Two questions informed my work:

1. How does a hybrid course designed as one authentic e-learning experience influence pre-service teachers' understanding of curriculum development and pedagogy?
2. How does an implicit emphasis on Foucault's method of *eventalization* influence pre-service teachers' understanding of teaching?

The next section provides theoretical grounding for both course development and the study.

Course Development and Eventalization

New to online learning, I drew course development inspiration from the work of Herrington, Reeves, and Oliver (2009). They expanded the concept of authentic learning, in which students are immersed into activities that simulate real-world scenarios, to include extended online projects. My goal was to create a course that had TCs using digital technology to create learning modules for components of ELA. I wanted them to use digital technology to develop curriculum that subsequently could be used to teach other in- and pre-service teachers.

Authentic e-learning, as described by Herrington, et al., is part of the larger endeavor of project-based learning (PBL). As its name suggests, PBL requires a project, typically designed to have students do something they have never done before and often requiring them to start from a novice perspective. The expectation is that students will do more than just learn content and procedures. They will develop a level—admittedly often introductory—of expertise on how to use content and procedures in their lives in meaningful ways.

In designing my course-long PBL project, I also drew on James Gee's self-study (2004) of his experience playing video games. Gee, relying on his earlier theoretical work around Discourses and situated learning (Gee, 1996), outlined a number of principles of effective teaching and learning that, he believed, were definitive of the best video games. He suggested that video games combine the right balance of purpose, difficulty, and support to keep gamers interested and willing to take risks and learn from mistakes. The gamers begin with a task and often with little instruction. They jump in and work at it, using exploration, creativity, and critical thinking to move forward. When necessary, they search the user's manual for help. They also call on the expertise of other gamers for guidance. In this regard, knowledge itself is shared among a community of gamers, or within the Discourse or *semiotic domain* of video games, so that the collaboration supports learning in timely and meaningful ways. Gamers rely on the semiotic domain for in-time support as they play and, at times, re-invent the games. My goal was to structure the course along the principles of teaching and learning that Gee outlined, including immersing TCs into the world of teachers and providing timely and relevant scaffolding to minimize frustration and redirect efforts when necessary.

Inherent in my hybrid course design were socio-constructivist theories of learning (Fosnot, 1996). These theories suggest that learning begins with perturbations and is fostered by an individual's ability to draw on experience and motivation to return to equilibration. An individual integrates the learning experience into existing experience. As a social process, informed both by inner speech and human interaction, learning is scaffolded by prior experience and the support mechanisms available. I saw digital technology and student field experiences as potential scaffolding tools. I also saw small group, whole class, and instructor mentoring as essential collaborative tools that could foster the requisite social interaction needed to support learning and alleviate frustration.

I understood collaboration as essential to helping TCs move beyond their experiences and consider other perspectives and possibilities that could potentially lead to new knowledge. The link between PBL and new knowledge development, however, is not seamless. The latter does not necessarily follow from the former. Linda Harasim (2011) wrote that "active learning [PBL included] as it is defined and practiced falls short in addressing social issues and real problems" (p. 81), or falls short of creating new knowledge that can transform practice. She suggested that, unless pushed to think beyond the context in which what they already know exists—beyond past and present experiences—students settle somewhere along the continuum of what is already known. Although they may learn something during the process, what students learn may not challenge existing knowledge and push it in new directions.

Harasim believed collaboration, particularly through the use of online tools, could facilitate conceptual learning through students' active engagement with content and with others. Collaboration fosters idea generation across a community that can lead to intellectual convergence. New knowledge can be created through this convergence. The role of the instructor is to introduce students into the disciplinary community that values the content they are learning. The instructor represents that community but holds back on content teaching, offering instead vocabulary, concepts, guidance, and, most important, explicit examples of the community or semiotic domain that values that content.

Harasim's theory resonated with my evolving teaching goals, which drew inspiration from Foucault's (1991) concept of eventalization. Foucault defined eventalization as

> making visible a singularity at places where there is a temptation to invoke a historical constant, an immediate anthropological trait, or an obviousness which imposes itself uniformly on all… [C]onstructing around the singular event…a 'polygon' or rather a 'polyhedron' of intelligibility, the number of whose faces is not given in advance and can properly be taken as finite" (p. 76-77).

As a process, eventalization does not in and of itself lead to transformative thinking. And it is not a process that one can do for another and hope to share or impart new understanding. Instead, it is an understanding that arises from individual existence in the world that leads to "no longer know what they do, so that the acts gestures, discourses which up until then had seemed to go without saying become problematic, difficult, dangerous" (Foucault, 1991, p. 84). For Foucault (1984), eventalization is transgressive, or a consciousness that things can be done differently, even if we are not quite sure how. This consciousness gives "a new impetus… to the undefined work of freedom" (p. 46), suggesting that once realized the revelation fosters critical inquiry and praxis.

I knew as a teacher educator, however, that I could not offer TCs established plans of action or normative prescriptions. Action plans and normative direction must arise idiosyncratically from TCs' collaborative work. Thus, the purpose of eventalization as a guiding concept in my course development was not to offer advice or guidelines for what must be done to free TCs from bad practices or to justify good ones. Instead, it was to interrogate historical ELA discourses to reveal points of rupture or fissure points—places where the truth of a discourse is disrupted or brakes down—so that what was self-evident to or taken for granted by the TCs is breached.

Thus, in the hybrid course design, eventalization was a guiding concept that helped me identify processes for breaching taken-for-granted understandings about reading, writing, and language teaching. In practice, it centered on an ongoing questioning of the costs of taking one position over another. It led me to scaffold TCs' module design efforts around questions of what is worthwhile and who benefits from what we do as teachers. In this regard, eventalization as a process was to challenge, and not to embrace nor dismiss, existing knowledge and to suggest that what we know and do can be different.

Research Methods

Self-study, as a method of practitioner inquiry, recognizes the reciprocity of teaching and research and the intractable role of the educator in both (Hamilton, 1998). As a research method, it uses narrative to explore issues in teacher education, including the role of the teacher educator in the preparation of future teachers (Bullough & Pinnegar, 2001). The overview provided in the previous section provides a theoretical framework for the hybrid course and the grounding for how I wanted to define myself as a teacher educator and researcher. As part of a self-study, the course design and subsequent TCs' experiences in the course serve to illuminate my teaching practice and its effect.

This article draws on two data sources: my weekly blogs and TCs' discussion boards. The data on course design was culled from weekly blogs I wrote while designing the course and capture my design process and rationale. Data from TC discussion boards reveal the effect of the course on TCs' understanding of curriculum and pedagogy and their efforts to answers the questions about what is worthwhile and who benefits. I analyzed the discussion board responses using critical discourse analysis (Gee, 2009), which as a method provided me a structure for coding data and identifying themes and topic related to the two questions that guided my work. The findings presented in this article represent the predominant themes I found related to curriculum and pedagogy understanding and the questions of what is worthwhile and who benefits.

Each TC contributed at least 6 posts to a discussion board forum on ELA history and module development. I asked TCs to reflect on previous weeks' work, what they had learned and how they would take up the knowledge discovered in their learning modules. I also asked that they consider what is worthwhile and who benefits in the ELA practices and theories discovered. I coded posts for evidence of curriculum and pedagogical understanding, as demonstrated in how TCs would take up content in their modules, and for evidence of eventalization or efforts to breach the self-evident understandings that shaped ELA. In this article, I present three post excerpts that represent TCs thinking about curriculum and pedagogy and what is worthwhile and who benefits. The excerpts are examples of what Graham (1989) called "nodal moments," which are moments—in this case, texts—that reveal new thinking that could potentially be built on and used to create new knowledge and practice. Because they are inherently idiosyncratic and contextualized, these moments are not generalizable. They do, however, provide a source for interpreting the effects of the hybrid course on TCs' professional development and suggest possible directions for future study.

The Hybrid Course

The hybrid course had two foci:

1. an authentic project that had students researching ELA components and deciding how best to present and teach them to others; and
2. built-in scaffolds that positioned TCs to address two questions through their project development: (1) Who benefits from particular approaches to teaching and learning and an emphasis on particular knowledge? And (2) What is worthwhile in the ELA and why?

The 11-week quarter began with two face-to-face sessions. I designed these 3-hour sessions to orient and introduce TCs to the content and structure of the course. I broke the remaining nine weeks into three 3-week blocks of two weeks online and one face-to-face. During online sessions, TCs researched topics, developed modules, and shared progress through VoiceThread, discussion board forums, and bi-weekly self-assessment rubrics. Key parts of the project were due every module, such as group-identified readings and group-generated quizzes that served as course content for other groups.

I set up face-to-face meetings as workshops during weeks 5 and 8—a chance for students to share content they were finding and progress they were making toward creating the modules. During these sessions, students met in groups, which allowed me to offer group feedback in response to specific needs. We then met as a whole class and delved into content more deeply and formulated next steps in content research and module creation. Week 11, a face-to-face session, was a presentation and final in-class written reflection day.

The authentic e-learning project required TCs to do what I believe teachers do when they are at their best, and that is research content; create learning objectives, guiding questions, and curriculum; identify how best to introduce and deliver content; and support and assess student learning. The TCs worked collaboratively, although individuals had specific responsibilities and were assessed on the work they completed and on their role in their group. My role was to provide feedback and give direction when needed, as well as to assess student progress.

I designed the course knowing how difficult of a proposition it would be for TCs and me to take on roles. I knew, however, that we had lived through parts of each component's history. Knowing this, I wanted TCs to realize that what they had experienced as high school and college students arose from a complicated, ambiguous, and arbitrary history, but it was not my role to tell them that. I wanted to come to their own conceptualizations through research and collaborations. From the outset, I did not know what TCs would find and create. I did not know what they would ultimately see as beneficial for those students with whom they hoped to work or what they would determine to be worthwhile in ELA. I had expectations, however, that their work would be grounded in research of ELA history and their modules would engage others.

Findings

Ten TCs enrolled in the course, and I divided them into three groups. Each group narrowed its component focus over a 4-week period after realizing that the components were too broad and complex to address entirely in less than 11 weeks. The reading group chose to focus on the history of the teaching of young adult literature (YAL); the language group on the history of English as a second language (ESL); and the writing group on how the writing process had been implemented over the past 30 years.

All three groups had an easy time identifying the history of their refined component and what perspectives and beliefs predominated at different times. They found written and digital resources. They also supplemented their research with student and teacher interviews and with curriculum and teacher materials from field experience sites. All three groups, however, had difficulty making evaluative claims and, beyond that, naming other possibilities.

They struggled to interrogate and critically analyze the content they were finding, including to compare different trends and truth claims. It was only with my continually emphasizing the questions about what is worthwhile and who benefits that they began to raise questions about content and what they were learning.

My analysis of the data showed that the course's project-based structure and my role as instructor resonated with most of the TCs' generative understandings of curriculum development and pedagogy. For example, their research led them to make claims about the topic that (1) revealed its complexity and ambiguity; (2) connected it to social, political, and economic events; and (3) problematized their prior ELA experiences. The structure also immersed TCs in professional communities that extended beyond the course format to include interviews of teachers and students outside the class and to include, in some cases, integration of what a TC was learning about his or her topic with what other groups were presenting about their topics.

The data also suggest that by the end of the term, TCs were beginning to breach the self-evident knowledge that defined their components and to challenge commonly held beliefs or what is often take for granted. They were also beginning to identify, albeit abstractly, possible avenues of continued research and knowledge development that could lead to new knowledge and critical teaching practices. In this rest of this section, I take up these last two findings—breaching the self-evident and creating new knowledge—as nodal moments, while touching on how the findings in the previous paragraph supported the development of these moments.

Breaching the Self-Evident

Darrel, a member of the writing group, wrote in week 9 about how the writing process when translated into practice was often detrimental to student writing development:

One of the things that has interested me as we explore the process method is the era during the 60s and 70s when the shift was being made from rote learning of grammatical methods to focusing on the process of creating ideas. While I actually believe in this (at least theoretically), it seems that like so many other methods of teaching, once it becomes standardized, there is less concern for the individual student or classroom. Instead, the method becomes rigid and designed for mass consumption, two things that I feel signal the end of successful teaching. However, as I researched responses to the process method I found a school of thought known as "post-process," which posits that writing cannot be defined with a generalization and instead must be an interpretive act and it must be situated in a specific context.

Darrell began the excerpt by noting how his research revealed a shift in writing instruction in the 1960s and 1970s from an emphasis on form to an emphasis on writing process. Earlier in the post, he had said that his high school instruction echoed the rigid implementation of the writing process. He suggested that translating writing process research, which often involved looking at what individual writers did, into practice fostered the creation of standardized writing curriculum "designed for mass consumption." Darrell's analysis suggested that his role as teacher would be the antithesis of what he had experienced and what his research revealed about the research-to-practice shift.

Similarly, Mark, a member of the reading group, revealed the ambiguity of his YAL topic. He wrote during week 10:

The project has been running smoothly, I am hoping to do more with the book *Disturbing the Universe: Power and Repression in Adolescent Literature* [Trites, 1998] I am enjoying the book, and various aspects of the literature itself that I have never considered are discussed at length. As I was saying in class on Monday, I am interested in the function of power and society in Young Adult literature as a genre. I found this quote particularly interesting: "Social institutions are determined by discourse, and they exist for the purpose of regulating social power… They use language simultaneously to repress and to empower their constituents; they gain power from the very people whom they regulate" (22). In relation to our topic, this notion has profound implications; Trites calls into question the source of adolescent literature, which is written by adults for children. She notes how this will impact the student's interpretation of events, topics, and themes in the narrative... I am very interested in pursuing this aspect of Young Adult literature further...

I am also interested as to whether the writing group has found any information with regard to the use of literature in the classroom as a foundation for writing topics. There was much discussion of this aspect of English classrooms throughout history in the Applebee [1974] article we read the first week. I was concerned with the fact that it was noted that this practice was widely done for the fact that (and I am paraphrasing) student had nothing of worth to say. This is also an interesting fact of the purpose of literature in the English classroom in light of the topic I discussed above...

Mark quoted from a self-selected book to suggest that YAL serves a normalizing role in society. Although it is about adolescents and their experiences and challenges, and typically written in the first person, the literature, as a social institution, regulates behavior by defining what an adolescent is. Mark, like Darrel, was not dismissing the worthiness of content he found but was raising questions about who benefits from it. In his case, Darrel implicitly suggests that those who produce and teach curriculum designed for mass consumption benefit at the expense of students. However, he claimed that the writing process as a research-based instructional approach was still worthwhile; it needed, however, to be problematized, which he was doing with his post-process research. For Mark, adults benefit from YAL's regulating (defining) of adolescent behavior, possibly at the expense of adolescents' critical thinking development. His analysis does not dismiss YAL as content but suggests its worth and how it is used are ambiguous.

Creating New Knowledge

Mark and Darrell indicated that they planned to continue to research their topics. Darrell suggested that in his post-process research he had found a counter-voice that articulated concerns about teaching context and student idiosyncrasy. Mark noted his interest in pursuing further his group's topic. He also commented on the work of the writing group, connecting some of the same issues (power and whose voice and language are valued) with which he was grappling in his YAL group with the writing group's work.

The connections Mark and Darrell were making to other research and to other groups, respectively, demonstrated not only an understanding of their topics but also a process of moving toward more complex and critical understandings that come through continuous work with the content and with collaboration and engagement with others' perspectives. Jackie, a member of the language group, recognized the complexity of her topic and attributed it to larger social and political forces. She wrote:

Finding a clear focus for our project and research has been difficult because, both politically and socially, ESL education in the US today is a very controversial topic. There are seemingly unlimited amounts of information and materials available, and I have found it often to be interwoven with other dialogues on immigration, non-mainstream students, public education, and budgeting. Possibly the most significant trend that I have seen in my research, that has focused on the historical context and development of dual language programs in the US, and that resonates with many of the other pedagogical conversations we have had so far, is that the theory of ESL education seems to be much more ideal than the actual practice of it that I have seen so far in my field observations.

Jackie concluded that practice is always complex and ambiguous and that theory can never fully capture or define it. She recognized the discursive flows that infiltrate any ESL pedagogical theory and render it too simplistic for a classroom context.

Jackie's claim about ESL instruction, similar to Darrell's and Mark's about their topics, is not new. However, their claims arise from their group work. Although the claims resonate within the academic community that focuses on ESL instruction, writing instruction, and YAL, for these three TCs, they arose from content they discovered, which was new to them. Because I left them to make sense of the content and only responded to claims they made (usually with more questions), they were positioned to evaluate its meaning and identify possibilities, albeit abstractly, that could inform their own teaching.

As the course concluded, TCs talked about the lack of direction they felt throughout the quarter. They talked about how they grappled with figuring out, first, what they wanted to do and how, and second, what they were going to create. They all found content that I would have used if I were teaching the topics. They all came to conclusions about content that put them in the company of the community of practice that finds that content important. More important, they began to challenge or problematize the content and not accept it as truth *per se*.

I stressed throughout the course that the modules had to be curriculum-like and engage pedagogically those who viewed them. By pedagogically, I meant that content needed to solicit participant response that reflected engagement and understanding. My feedback on the learning modules encouraged TCs to move from only presenting content (research, interviews, timelines, videos, etc.) to presenting it purposefully so as to convey both their burgeoning understanding of it *and* to invite others to make sense of it based on their own experiences. They struggled with this, and I struggled with withholding directives of what should be done. Knowing that they would be taking English methods courses in subsequent quarters, I used our culminating discussion to reiterate the need for their growing critical understanding to be used to foster real possibilities for their own teaching.

Discussion

The hybrid course de-centered traditional content and instructional authority by positioning students as content experts and curriculum developers who are responsible for making pedagogical decisions. Drawing on Foucault's eventalization, I theorized that the de-centering of authority and positioning of students can only happen if the onus of identifying and naming content is on TCs and they are given the responsibility and ancillary support necessarily to take up the role of teachers. In this regard, I strived to breach self-evident and taken-for-granted ideas about my role as instructor and the role of students. Teaching online, whether it comes in the form of a completely online course or a hybrid course, made these efforts of de-centering possible by establishing a framework for extended student-centered collaboration and feedback. The online instruction, marked by demonstrable weekly expectations and support mechanisms, breached traditional and even more progressive instructional contexts by creating scenarios where students had to practice what it is they aspired to be.

Face-to-face meetings, however, were invaluable for the opportunities they provided for shared debriefing and reflection on divergent perspectives that only being in the same place at the same time affords. These meetings served as catalysts for critically analyzing group curriculum and pedagogical decisions and for making immediate the questions of what is worthwhile and who benefits. This has nothing to do with face-to-face intimacy or interaction *per se*. It has everything to do with structured collaborative time to take stock of not only our own learning but of others' learning and recalibrate our own understandings. Together, the online and face-to-face activities fostered authentic engagement with content in the design of curriculum and the consideration of pedagogy. As their first introduction to curriculum and pedagogical issues, TCs were immersed into the complexities and ambiguities of deciding what is worth knowing and why and who benefits from teacherly decisions. In the end, TCs were raising the type of questions that demonstrated an understanding of the complexity and ambiguity teaching itself.

Conclusion

I tacitly asked students "to refuse what we are" as students and teachers. That is, I asked them not to let the refrain of teachers as technocrats and students as lacking requisite skills and experiences necessary to take up meaningful and critical work shape their thinking and efforts. Instead, I asked that they look for possibilities in the history of ELA and begin to visualize through their own work how these possibilities might play out in curriculum and pedagogy. That is a lot to ask for in 11 weeks, and no amount of time is enough to draw firm conclusions about teaching and learning, but it was in the words of Foucault (1996) a chance to "multiply the paths and the possibility of comings and goings..." (p. 306). And for TCs and me, it was an opportunity to practice and contemplate teaching and learning differently, with the realization that, as important work, it is never-ending.

References

Applebee, A. N. (1974). *Tradition and reform in teaching of English: A history.* Urbana, IL: National Council of Teachers of English.

Bullough, R. V., & Pinnegar, S. (2001). Guidelines for quality in autobiographical forms of self-study research. *Educational Researcher, 30*(3), 13-21.

Fosnot, C. T. (1996). "Constructivism: A psychological theory of learning." In C. T. Fosnot (Ed.) *Constructivism: Theory, perspectives, and practice* (pp. 8-33). New York: Teachers College Press.

Foucault, M. (1984). What is Enlightenment? in P. Rabinow (ed.), *The Foucault reader.* New York: Pantheon.

Foucault, M. (1991). Questions of method. In G. Burchell, C. Gordon, & P. Miller (Eds.). In *The Foucault Effect: Studies in Governmentality* (pp. 73-86). Chicago: University of Chicago Press.

Foucault, M. (1996). 'The Masked Philosopher'. In Sylvère Lotringer (ed.) *Foucault Live (Interviews, 1961-1984).* Tr. Lysa Hochroth and John Johnston. 2nd edition. New York: Semiotext(e).

Gee, J. (1996). *Social linguistics and literacies: Ideology in discourses* (2nd ed.). London: Falmer.

Gee, J. (2004). *What video games have to teach us about learning and literacy.* New York: Palgrave Macmillan.

Gee. J. (2009). *How to do discourse analysis.* London: Routledge.

Graham, R. J. (1989). Autobiography and education. *Journal of Educational Thought, 23*(2), 92-105.

Hamilton, M. L. (Ed.). (1998). *Reconceptualizing teaching practice: Self-study in teacher education.* London: Falmer.

Harasim, L. (2011). *Learning theory and online technologies.* London: Routledge.

Herrington, J., Reeves, T.C., & Oliver, T. (2009). *A guide to authentic e-learning.* London: Routledge.

Trites, R. S. (1998). *Disturbing the universe: Power and repression in adolescent literature.* Iowa City: IA: University of Iowa Press.

Parent Involvement and Student/Parent Satisfaction in Cyber Schools

Dennis Beck
University of Arkansas, U.S.A.
debeck@uark.edu

Robert Maranto
University of Arkansas, U.S.A.
rmaranto@uark.edu

Wen-Juo Lo
University of Arkansas, U.S.A.
wlo@uark.edu

Abstract: There is evidence that in traditional public schools the school satisfaction of students and parents varies by parent involvement. Prior studies suggest that multiple factors influence parental involvement, including race, socioeconomic status, parents' educational status, and student gender and age. Although prior research has studied parental involvement and its impact on student achievement in a cyber environment, no prior research has studied its impact on student and parent school satisfaction. Here parental involvement and school satisfaction in a cyber charter school are investigated, using a student (n=269; 53.7% response rate) and parent (n=232; 48.7% response rate) survey. Results show that increases in reported parent involvement are associated with higher levels of student school satisfaction. Save regarding race, no statistically significant differences in school satisfaction across demographic groups are found. Implications are discussed.

Parent involvement

Much research has explored parent involvement in traditional K-12 schools. Parent involvement leads to numerous positive school related outcomes for students including positive attitudes toward school, improved work habits, reduced absenteeism, a decreased risk of dropping out, and increased academic achievement (O'Bryan, Braddock, & Dawkins, 2006). In fact, parent involvement in education is a better predictor of academic success than parent income (What research says about parent involvement in children's education, 2002). Multiple factors influence levels of parent involvement, including race, socioeconomic status, parents' educational status, and students' gender and age. Involved parents tend to be of higher socioeconomic status, highly educated, and have elementary aged students (O'Bryan et al., 2006). Parents with lowest level of involvement are parents of African American and minority students (O'Bryan et al., 2006; Thompson, 2003). In a meta-analysis totaling nearly 12,000 subjects, Jeynes (2003) concluded that parent involvement has a considerable positive impact on all minority groups, with African American students benefitting more than Latino and Asian students.

Among general education students, parent involvement has been found to help mediate a child's developmental trajectory in schools and is consistently linked to positive academic and social outcomes (Fan & Chen, 2001; Hill & Taylor, 2004; Topor, Keane, Shelton, & Calkins, 2010). Parents who are involved in their child's education are more likely to see their child graduate high school while reducing the likelihood of their child receiving disciplinary actions, including suspensions and expulsions (Astone & McLanahan, 1991; Sheldon & Epstein, 2002). Furthermore, parents who are involved and invested in their children's schooling are less likely to have children with behavioral problems (Powell, Son, File, & San Juan, 2010; Rogers, Wiener, Marton, & Tannock, 2009). For these reasons, among others, parent involvement is considered to be a best practice for children by the National Research Council (2001). Further, there is much schools can do to foster parent involvement (Henderson, Mapp, Johnson, & Davies, 2007). The literature suggests that parents are more likely to participate in their child's homework when their child or their child's teacher expresses that the involvement is expected or needed (Balli, Demo, &Wedman, 1998; Hoover-Dempsey & Sandler, 1997).

Regarding special education, the law requires parent involvement for parents of special education children. The Individuals with Disabilities Education Act (IDEA) states that parents must be on decision-making teams in all special education services, and that parents should have various due process mechanisms to pursue if they believe they are not receiving needed services for their children (Turnbull & Turnbull, 2001). Yet in practice, schools vary enormously in the degree to which they foster or discourage parent involvement, both in the Individualized Education Plan (IEP) process and in day to day implementation of IEPs (Ong-Dean, 2009).

Regarding their children's education, parents of special education children differ from parents of the general population in some important ways. For instance, parents of special education children are more likely to attend parent–teacher conferences, meet with the school guidance counselor, and help their children with their homework. Furthermore, they are less likely to be satisfied with the level of communication from the school regarding their child's placement in a given classroom or group (Benson, Karlof, and Siperstein, 2008).

Another study of 45 families of special education children conducted by Spann, Kohler, and Soenksen (2003) further illuminates the need to assess the impact of parent involvement on a child's education. Although the majority of parents, who were recruited from support groups, reported relatively high levels of participation in their child's education, with 51% reporting communicating with their child's school daily and 56% reporting at least moderate involvement with the individualized education program (IEP), the level of involvement, as well as school satisfaction, decreased as the children's age increased. When asked how well the school was addressing their child's needs, 83% of parents whose children were between the ages 15 and 18 reported that the schools were inadequate, as opposed to 36% of parents whose children were from 4 to 5 years of age.

Heller, Spooner, Anderson, and Mims (1988) observed that homework completion for students receiving special education services may be directly related not only to parent attitudes toward homework completion but also to the willingness of parents and teachers to work together. Further confounding the relationship between parents and homework involvement, Bryan and Nelson (1994) observed that parent involvement in homework is the greatest during elementary school while diminishing into junior high school for children with special education needs. Wolf (2007) found that charter schools typically have higher levels of parent involvement. In part, this may reflect the fact that a disproportionate number of charter schools are relatively new schools, many of which were founded in order to work better with parents. In addition, charter schools typically receive fewer resources than traditional public schools, encouraging them to make use of parent resources. Finally, disproportionate numbers of charter school students had serious academic or social problems in traditional public schools, leading their parents to become more involved (Kayes & Maranto, 2006).

Race and parent involvement/satisfaction

Friedman, Bobrowski and Geraci (2006) state that safety is the most significant predictor of parent satisfaction. Interestingly, African Americans and Hispanics are least satisfied with their child's school; which in the case of African American parents sharply contrasts with the perceptions of their children. Perhaps the more negative parent perceptions reflect interactions with school authorities who may not welcome input from African American (Buck, 2010; Delpit, 2012) and Hispanic parents (Valdes, 1996). In general, parent experiences with their child's school influence their satisfaction (Friedman et al., 2006).

Although there has been little research examining how race affects parent involvement, Shah (2009) argues that parents who see other members of their race in positions of authority will feel more empowered to participate. This helps make sense of results that show that parent participation in school is lower for African American and Hispanic parents than it is for White parents (O'Bryan et al., 2006; Thompson, 2003), since a large percentage of school administrators are White (Buck, 2010; Delpit, 2012).

Gender and parent involvement/satisfaction

Gender differences in student school satisfaction have been found among adolescents (Eamons, 2002; Okun, Braver, & Weir, 1990). Females are generally more satisfied with school than males (Okun et al., 1990; Verkuyten and Thijs, 2002; Huebner et al., 2000; Ding & Hall., 2007). Many argue that schools as they currently operate are not "boy friendly" in that they underemphasize dialectical storytelling and interactive learning (Willingham, 2009; Institute for Education Sciences, 2009; Whitmire, 2011). Unfortunately, prior work has not examined the role of gender and parent satisfaction.

Hypotheses

The literature review above suggests the following hypotheses, which will be tested in this paper.
H1: Reported student school satisfaction will increase with reported parent involvement.
H2: Female students will have higher reported parent involvement than male students.
H3: African American students will have lower reported parent involvement than Whites.
H4: Latino students will have lower reported parent involvement than Whites.
H5: Special education students will have higher reported parent involvement than general education students.
H6: Reported parent school satisfaction will increase with reported parent involvement.
H7: Parents of female students will have higher reported involvement than parents of male students.
H8: Parents of African American students will have lower reported involvement than parents of Whites.
H9: Parents of Latino students will be have lower reported involvement than parents of Whites.
H10: Parents of special education students will have higher involvement than parents of general education students.

Background

There is no empirical work regarding student and parent school satisfaction within cyber schools. In general, there is little empirical work making use of the opinions of special education students and parents. This may be due to an underlying presumption that the views of parents and students are neither expert, nor objective (Descry & Martin-Bemer, 2001; Henderson, Mapp, Johnson, & Davies, 2007; Valle, 2009). SunTech was selected because it is a cyber charter secondary school (grades 7-12), 26% of whose students are categorized as needing special education services, roughly 60% more than the state mean. SunTech is an online cyber charter high school with about 700 students, originally founded by the leader of a social services non-profit serving at-risk youth in the state's largest city. Like other charter schools in the state, SunTech cannot selectively admit students. The school has never had a wait list but instead has admitted all students who apply. The founder intended to use online technology to teach and tutor students who had dropped out or were at risk of dropping out of high school. Though the school was founded to serve urban young people, informants report that within two years of its opening a disproportionate share of students came from rural and small town settings, which had previously lacked educational options.

Methods

Participants

Two hundred sixty nine students (53.7% response rate) and 232 parents (48.7% response rate) participated. These response rates provide confidence in the internal validity of findings (Dillman, 2010). Survey results indicate that SunTech families are slightly less educated and somewhat more Caucasian, but otherwise similar to state population. Only 15.1% of SunTech parents identified themselves as college graduates, compared to 24.8% of state residents over 25. Similarly, 18% of SunTech parents reported never having completed a high school degree or GED, compared to 13.5% of state residents. SunTech students self identified as 85% White, 15% African American, 7% Hispanic, and 2% Asian. The state's students are 73% White, 15% African American, 8% Hispanic, and 3% Asian. (SunTech figures sum to over 100% since some students self-identified as more than one race).

As noted above, SunTech serves roughly 60% more special education students than the state mean. Self-identified special education students (though not parents) are slightly under-represented among respondents. 30% of parent respondents, answering on behalf of their children, and 19% of student respondents indicate diagnosed special education needs. Contrasting research suggesting that low incidence disabilities are under-represented in charter schools, 20.6% of SunTech special education students required psychological assessment, as compared to 8.6% for the state. Combined mental retardation and Autism rates among special education students were 15% for both the sample and the state. Learning disabilities were higher among SunTech special education students (68%) than for the state (46.9%), while the incidence of speech therapy, which typically requires fewer resources, was essentially identical, 15.9% for SunTech and 16.2% for the state. In short, there is little evidence that SunTech "creams" easy to educate special education students. While SunTech reports virtually equal numbers of male and female students (as does the state), respondents were 65.8% female. SunTech staff report that female students do slightly better and thus might be more likely to fill out the survey, as indeed fits the broader literature on gender and schooling (Clark, Oakley, & Adams, 2006; Burns & Bracey, 2001; Kafer, 2004; Willingham, 2009; Whitmire, 2011). Also, special education respondents were 53% male and 47% female.

	Parents		Students	
	Overall ($n = 232$)	No Missing ($n = 117$)	Overall ($n = 269$)	No Missing ($n = 208$)
Gender*				
Male	45.6%	46.2%	34.2%	38.0%
Female	54.4%	53.8%	65.8%	62.0%
Race**				
White	82.4%	82.9%	85.0%	77.9%
Latino	3.2%	3.4%	15.0%	8.7%
African American	12.8%	12.0%	7.0%	13.5%
Asian	1.6%	1.7%	2.0%	0%
Special Education***				
Yes	23.2%	20.5%	32.0%	38.0%
No	76.8%	79.5%	68.0%	62.0%

* *For parents this question refers to their child's gender.*
** *Columns add up to more than 100% due to respondents selecting multiple categories.*
*** *For parents this question refers to their child's special education status.*
Table 1: Demographics of SunTech Respondents

Procedures

For deployment, the researchers sent out notification emails to the potential respondents who had been at SunTech for at least one year (Dillman, 2010). SunTech administrators emailed the population of parents and students in early September, 2011, asking them to participate in an online survey, and promising $10 gift cards in exchange. Surveys were emailed a week later. Non-participating subjects were emailed two follow-up reminders, followed by an automated call from the school. A small number of parents who lacked email access were mailed paper surveys with stamped, addressed return envelopes. Participants were assigned individual identifier numbers to ensure that researchers could not identify individual respondents. In all communications to subjects, both the researchers and SunTech administrators made it clear that individual respondents could not be identified by school staff. SunTech employees did not receive access to the raw data to assure respondent confidentiality.

Measurements and Instruments

Parent surveys had 67 items; student surveys, 66 (29 items on each survey were analyzed for this study). Questions relating to parent involvement were taken from Liu, Black, Algina, Cavanaugh, and Dawson (2010). An online survey tool, Qualtrics, was used. Once developed, the surveys were sent to seven expert reviewers. Based on their suggestions, the items were revised for consistency of terminology, specificity of questions and responses, and additional items that should be included. The Parent Involvement Scale (PIS) representing parent involvement consisted of 12 items on both parent and student surveys. Items were rated on a 6-point Likert-type scale from 1 to 6 and the score range for the PIS was from 12 to 72, with higher scores indicating greater parent involvement. The satisfaction scale is a 14-item measure of their satisfaction toward school on a 5-point Likert-type with score range from 14 to 70.

Data Analysis

From September through December 2011, data were obtained from the surveys and were recorded in Qualtrics. SPSS 20 was used to conducted descriptive statistics for closed items and to perform a one-way analysis of variance (ANOVA) to test all hypotheses.

Results
Students

Based on the satisfaction score, students had been divided into three groups to represent low, medium, and high satisfaction toward to their school. The dependent variable was the PIS score. With regard to group differences between student school satisfaction and parent involvement, the ANOVA was significant, $F(2, 205) = 12.71$, $p < .001$. The effect size, as assessed by η^2, indicated that 11% of the variance of the parent involvement was accounted for by student satisfaction levels. Follow-up tests were conducted to evaluate pairwise differences among groups. Because the variances ranged from 79.57 to 214.33, we chose not to assume equal variance among groups and used Dunnett's T3 test as post hoc comparisons. There were significant differences in the means between low and medium satisfaction group ($p = .005$) as well as between low and high satisfaction group ($p < .001$), but no significant differences between medium and high satisfaction group ($p = .370$). The 95% confidence intervals for the pairwise differences, as well as the means and standard deviations for the three groups, are reported in Table 2. In short, results confirm H1. Higher levels of reported parent involvement are associated with higher levels of student school satisfaction.

Satisfaction	n	M	SD	Low	Medium
Low	59	57.00	14.64		
Medium	71	64.11	9.45	[1.74 – 12.48*]	
High	78	66.33	8.92	[4.09 – 14.58*]	[-1.43 – 5.87]

*The difference in means is significant using Dunnett's T3 procedure.
Table 2: Descriptive Statistics and 95% Confidence Intervals of pairwise differences in Mean Changes in Student Satisfaction.

In term of evaluating the differences between male and female students on feeling about parent involvement, the PIS raw scores had been used as dependent variable. The ANOVA was not significant, $F(1, 206) = .11$, $p = .73$, and the effect size was small ($\eta^2 = .001$). In short, H2 is not confirmed as females and males show uniform levels of parent involvement.

Considering student race with parent involvement, we only included three categories (i.e., White, African American, and Latino) in this study because other racial category contained an insufficient number of cases. The ANOVA was not significant, $F(2, 205) = 2.48$, $p = .086$. The effect size was between small and medium range, with the student race factor accounting for 2.7% of the variance in parent involvement. In short, results tend to disprove H3 and H4.

Comparing special education and non-special education students (i.e., based on student's self-report) with parent involvement, the ANOVA result was not significant, $F(1, 206) = .62, p = .43$, with small effect size ($\eta^2 = .003$). H5 was disproved – there is no difference between special education statuses in parent involvement.

Parents

Similar with student's data, parent's satisfaction had been divided into three-level (i.e., Low, Medium, and High) as well. The ANOVA was not significant, $F(2, 114) = 1.17, p = .313$, and the effect size was small ($\eta^2 = .020$). Therefore, the results were not support H6.

Again, a one-way ANOVA was conducted to evaluate whether there are differences between parents' indication of their student's gender while parent report their involvement. The result was not significant, $F(1, 115) = .019, p = .89$; and the effect size was close to zero. Not surprisingly, we were failing to confirm H7.

Due to insufficient number of cases with all minority groups, student race reported by parent was divided into White and Other ethnic minority. The ANOVA was not significant, $F(1, 115) = 3.44, p = .066$. The strength of relationship between the student's race and parent involvement, as assessed by η^2, was between small and medium range, with the student race factor accounting for 2.9% of the variance in parent involvement. Again, the results were disproving H8 and H9.

Finally, comparing special education and non-special education students (i.e., based on parent's self-report) with parent involvement, the ANOVA result was not significant, $F(1, 115) = .39, p = .53$, with small effect size ($\eta^2 = .003$). H10 was disproved.

Discussion

Results indicated that there was a significant difference between student school satisfaction and parent involvement in the student sample. This confirms much of the prior research on the topic (What research says about parent involvement in children's education, 2002; O'Bryan et al., 2006). However, the novelty of this paper is its extension of that prior work to a cyber schooling environment. As field work, and student and parent comments on the survey show, parents are able to take part in their students schooling in a cyber environment, in some respects even more than in a traditional public school environment. At SunTech, because education takes place within the home and often in a synchronous manner, parents are able to monitor student participation in ways that would be difficult, if not impossible, in a traditional public school. Further, parents are able to monitor email and synchronous electronic communication. Accordingly, much of the literature on parent involvement may not only apply, but apply more intensively in a cyber environment.

At the same time, a cyber charter school, may have notable differences. Parents or students had to make an active choice to attend SunTech. Prior work (Beck, Maranto & Jacob, submitted), suggests that these choices were often driven by bullying and academic failure at their prior schools. Accordingly, the population attending SunTech may differ in important ways from the populations attending traditional public schools. Such differences may explain why demographic factors such as gender, special education status and race do not have the predicted impacts. In short, while parent involvement plays an important role in both traditional and cyber settings, the novelty of cyber schooling may result in important demographic and other differences in the exact character of parent/school relationships. Given the growth of cyber schooling and the importance of parent involvement in schooling, this is an area that demands more research.

References

Astone, N. M., & McLanahan, S. S. (1991). Family structure, parent practices and high school completion. *American Sociological Review, 56*, 309–320.

Balli, S. J., Demo, D. H., & Wedman, J. F. (1998). Family involvement with children's homework: An intervention in the middle grades. *Family Relations, 47*(2), 142–146.

Beck, D., Maranto, R., & Jacob, A. (submitted). "Not having to be judged for who I am, but what I do": Comparing special education and general education cyber school students

Benson, P., Karlof, K. L., & Siperstein, G. N. (2008). Maternal involvement in the education of young children with autism spectrum disorders. *Autism: The International Journal of Research & Practice, 12*(1), 47–63.

Bryan, T., & Nelson, C. (1994). Doing homework: Perspectives of elementary and junior high school students. *Journal of Learning Disabilities, 27*, 488–499.

Buck, J. S. (2010). *Acting White*. New Haven: Yale University Press.

Burns, J. & Bracey, P. (2001). Boys' underachievement: Issues, challenges and possible ways forward. *Westminister Studies in Education, 24*(2), 155-66.

Clark, M.A., Oakley, E. & Adams, H. (2006). The gender achievement gap challenge." *ASCA School Counselor*, 43(3), 20–25

Delpit, L. D. (2012). *Multiplication is for White People: Raising expectations for other people's children.* New York: New The Press.Descry, C. & Martin-Bemer, A. (2001). *Unscrewed!: The Education of Annie.* Prescott: SRES.

Dillman, D. A. & Messer, B. L. (2010). Advice in surveying the general public over the Internet." *International Journal of Internet Science, 5*(1), 1-4.

Ding, C., & Hall, A. (2007). Gender, ethnicity, and grade differences in perceptions of school experiences among adolescents. *Studies in Educational Evaluation, 33*, 159–174.

Eamons, N. K. (2002). Influences and mediators of the effect of poverty on youth and adolescent depressive symptoms. *Journal of Youth and Adolescence, 31*, 231–242.

Fan, X., & Chen, M. (2001). Parental involvement and student's academic achievement: A metaanalysis. *Educational Psychology Review, 13*(1), 1–22.

Friedman, B. A., Bobrowski, P. E., & Geraci, J. (2006). Parents' school satisfaction: Ethnic similarities and differences. *Journal of Educational Administration, 44*(5), 471.

Heller, H. W., Spooner, F., Anderson, D., & Mims, A. (1988). Homework: A review of special education practices in the Southwest. *Teacher Education and Special Education, 11*, 43–51.

Henderson, A. T., Mapp, K. L., Johnson, V. R. & Davies, D. (2007). *Beyond the Bake Sale*. New York: The New Press.

Hill, N. E., & Taylor, L. C. (2004). Parental school involvement and children's academic achievement. *Current Directions in Psychological Science, 13*(4), 161–164.

Hoover-Dempsey, K. V., & Sandler, H. M. (1997). Why do parents become involved in their children's education? *Review of Educational Research, 67*, 3–42.

Huebner, E. S., Drane, J. W., & Valois, R. F. (2000). Levels and demographic correlates of adolescent life satisfactory reports. *School Psychology International, 21*, 218-292.

Institute for Education Sciences (2009). *Early Implementation of Public Single-Sex Schools: Perceptions and Characteristics.* U.S. Department of Education, Washington, D.C.

Kafer, K. (2004). Girl power: Why girls don't need the women's educational equity act. Washington DC: Heritage Foundation. http://www.heritage.org/research/reports/2004/09/girl-power-why-girls-dont-need-the-womens-educational-equity-act

Kayes, M. S. & Maranto, R. (2006). *A guide to charter schools.* Lanham: Rowman and Littlefield Education.

Jeynes, W. H. (2003). A meta-analysis the effects of parental involvement on minority children's academic achievement. *Education and Urban Society, 35*(2), 202-218.

Liu, F., Black, E., Algina, J., Cavanaugh, C. & Dawson, K. (2010). "The validation of one parental involvement measurement in virtual schooling." *Journal of Interactive Online Learning, 9*(2): 105-132.

National Research Council. (2001). *Educating children with autism.* Washington, DC: National Academy Press.

O'Bryan, S. T., Braddock, J. H., II, & Dawkins, M. P. (2006). Bringing parents back in: African American parental involvement, extracurricular participation, and educational policy. *The Journal of Negro Education, 75*(3), 401.

Okun, M. A., Braver, M. W., & Weir, R. M. (1990). Grade level differences in school satisfaction. *Social Indicators Research, 22*, 419–427.

Ong-Dean, C. (2009). *Distinguishing Disability: Parents, Privilege, and Special Education.* Chicago: University of Chicago Press.

Powell, D. R., Son, S. H., File, N., & San Juan, R. R. (2010). Parent–school relationships an children's academic and social outcomes in public school pre-kindergarten. *Journal of School Psychology, 48*(4), 269–292.

Rogers, M. A., Wiener, J., Marton, I., & Tannock, R. (2009). Supportive and controlling parental involvement as predictors of children's academic achievement: Relations to children's ADHD symptoms and parenting stress. *School Mental Health, 1*(2), 89–102.

Shah, P. (2009). Motivating participation: The symbolic effects of Latino representation on parent school involvement. *Social Science Quarterly, 90*(1), 212.

Sheldon, S. B., & Epstein, J. L. (2002). Improving student behavior and school discipline with family and community involvement. *Education and Urban Society, 35*(1), 4–26.

Spann, S. J., Kohler, F. W., & Soenksen, D. (2003). Examining parents' involvement in and perceptions of special education services: An interview with families in a parent support group. *Focus on Autism and Other Developmental Disabilities, 18*(4), 228–237.

Thompson, G. L. (2003). Predicting African American parents' and guardians' satisfaction with teachers and public schools. *Journal of Educational Research, 96*(5), 233-247.

Topor, D. R., Keane, S. P., Shelton, T. L., & Calkins, S. D. (2010). Parent involvement and student academic performance: A multiple meditational analysis. *Journal of Prevention & Intervention in the Community, 38*(3), 183–197.

Turnbull, A. P. & Turnbull, H. R. (2001). *Families, professionals, and exceptionality: A special partnership.* Columbus, OH: Merrill.

Valdes, G. (1996). *Con Respeto.* New York: Teachers College Press.

Valle, J. W (2009). *What Mothers Say About Special Education.* New York: Palgrave/Macmillan.

What research says about parent involvement in children's education (2002). Retrieved October 14, 2012, from http://www.michigan.gov/documents/Final_Parent_Involvement_Fact_Sheet_14732_7.pdf

Whitmire, R. (2011). *Why Boys Fail: Saving Our Sons from an Educational System That's Leaving Them Behind.* New York: Amacom Books.

Willingham, D. T. (2009). *Why Don't Students Like School?* San Francisco: Jossey Bass.

Wolf, P. J. (2007). Civics exam: Schools of choice boost civic values. *Education Next, 7*(3), 66-72.

Pre-Service Mathematics Teachers' Growth in Incorporating Technology into their Teaching Practices

Barbara Ann Swartz
University of Virginia, United States
bswartz@virginia.edu

Joe Garofalo
University of Virginia, United States
jg2e@virginia.edu

Abstract: The purpose of this study is to document improvements in pre-service mathematics teachers' (PSMTs) use of technology in their standards-based teaching over a two-semester mathematics pedagogy course through the use of a multidimensional instructional observational tool, the Mathematics Scan (M-Scan). This tool is based on the NCTM's vision of quality mathematics instruction, and its' *Multiple Representations* and *Students' Use of Tools* dimensions specifically focus on the PSMTs' decisions to incorporate multiple representations and utilize tools to develop the mathematics content, most easily facilitated via technology. All of the PSMTs grew in both of these dimensions and this paper describes aspects of the PSMTs' improved instructional practices incorporating technology.

Introduction

The National Council for Teachers of Mathematics (NCTM, 1991; NCTM, 2000) presents a vision for school mathematics that mathematics educators believe reflects high-quality mathematics instruction. In the *Professional Standards for Teaching Mathematics,* NCTM (1991) presents six standards for teaching mathematics that highlight the creation of worthwhile tasks, the teacher's role in discourse, the student's role in discourse, tools for enhancing discourse, and the learning environment. The NCTM's (2000) *Principles and Standards for School Mathematics* includes six *principles* advocating for educators to set high expectations and provide support for *all* students, to create coherent challenging curricula and appropriate assessments that support learning with understanding, as well as to integrate technology in order to enhance students' mathematical thinking. Their *Technology Principle* states that "Technology is essential in teaching and learning mathematics; it influences the mathematics that is taught and enhances student learning" (NCTM, 2000, p. 24), and furthermore, the Council advocates that "teachers should use technology to enhance their students learning opportunities by selecting or creating mathematical tasks that take advantage of what technology can do efficiently and well – graphing, visualizing and computing" (p. 25). Similarly, the Association of Mathematics Teacher Educators' TPACK Framework (AMTE, 2009) calls for teachers to: (1) combine their knowledge of technology, pedagogy, and content to design and develop technology-enhanced mathematics learning environments and experiences; (2) integrate technology to maximize mathematical learning and creativity; (3) assess and evaluate technology-enriched mathematics teaching and learning; and (4) enhance their technological pedagogical content knowledge through ongoing professional development (p. 1). Furthermore, the International Society for Technology in Education (ISTE) *National Technology Standards for Teachers* (2008) advocates that "Teachers use their knowledge of subject matter, teaching and learning, and technology to facilitate experiences that advance student learning, creativity and innovation… (p. 1). The Mathematical Sciences Education Board and National Research Council (MSEB & NRC, 1990) also affirm the benefits of using technology in the mathematics classroom.

In order to be prepared to teach well with technology, the Association of Mathematics Teacher Educators (AMTE) believes that pre-service mathematics teachers should have: "(1) a deep, flexible, and connected conceptual understanding of K-12 mathematics that acknowledges the impact of technology on what content should be taught; (2) a research-based understanding of how students learn mathematics and the impact technology can have on learning; (3) a strong pedagogical knowledge base related to the effective use of technology to improve mathematics teaching and learning; and (4) appropriate experiences during their teacher preparation program in the use of a variety of technological tools to enhance their own learning of mathematics and the mathematical learning of others" (AMTE, 2009, p. 1). The Mathematical Association of America (MAA) and the Committee on the Mathematical Education of Teachers (1991) list "Using Technology" as a standard for the preparation of mathematics teachers, and the Conference Board of the Mathematical Sciences (CBMS, 2001) asserts that prospective teachers need to understand that technology can be used to eliminate complicated computations allowing students to focus more on mathematical thinking and problem solving.

Studying changes in pre-service secondary mathematics teachers' (PSMTs) teaching practices can help identify ways in which teacher preparation programs can better serve these future teachers by helping them develop into high-quality teachers. Juersivich, Garofalo, and Fraser (2009) found that two cohorts of PSMTs who frequently used a variety of technology to both do mathematics and practice teach mathematics in their pre-student teaching course and field experiences regularly used technology in their student teaching to facilitate their pupils' conceptual and procedural understanding. Fraser (2010) subsequently found that those same PSMTs continued to teach with technology when they became novice teachers, largely because they had extensive experience teaching with technology prior to their student teaching. These findings are evidence that it is possible to successfully prepare pre-service mathematics teachers to effectively utilize technology in their instruction. This present study focuses on the growth of pre-service teachers' use of technology in their pre-student teaching experiences.

Research Question

This paper reports on data taken from a larger study of the growth of pre-service teachers' (PSMTs) quality of teaching practices during a yearlong secondary mathematics pedagogy course that is consistent with the NCTM vision (Swartz & Garofalo, under review). The course included peer-teaching with feedback and a concurrent pre-student teaching field placement. That study examined PSMTs' overall growth in standards-based mathematics teaching practices, as measured by M-Scan (Berry, Rimm-Kaufman, Ottmar, Walkowiak, Merritt, & Pinter 2012). This particular report focuses on the evolution of the PSMTs' teaching practices related to their use of technology. The specific research question addressed in this paper is: *To what degree did the PSMTs' incorporation of technology into their teaching practices improve over the course of an academic year?*

Design and Methodology

Site and Participants

The setting of this study was a two-semester secondary mathematics pedagogy course taught at a mid-Atlantic state university. The eight students in the course were enrolled in a five-year teacher education program that leads to a BA in mathematics and an MT in education at the end of the program. During their fourth year of study, students complete this yearlong mathematics pedagogy course taught by the second author prior to their student teaching, which takes place in the first semester of their fifth year. These eight students are all white, from the United States, and in their early twenties, with all but one being female.

Course and Teaching Assignment Overview

The two-semester secondary mathematics pedagogy course is consistent with the NCTM's *Principles and Standards for School Mathematics* (2000). Throughout the entire year, the course emphasizes problem solving and mathematical behavior (Polya, 1945; Schoenfeld, 1992), conceptual understanding (Hiebert & Lefevre, 1986), applications of mathematics, and use of technology to generate multiple representations and perform calculations not otherwise feasible (Garofalo, Drier, Harper, Timmerman, & Shockey, 2000). The course addresses the development of teaching strategies to facilitate students' mathematical sense making and ability to apply mathematics; it also includes peer-teaching episodes and is coupled with a year-long field experience in which PSMTs observe and teach lessons at a local public middle or high school. In essence, one goal of the course and field experience is to help PSMTs develop mathematics TPACK (Mishra & Koehler, 2006).

Course Activities

Every week the PSMTs are assigned homework tasks and readings. The tasks are typically non-routine problems, which elicit different problem solving strategies and contextual tasks which involve application of mathematics. Applications of mathematics explored in class or assigned for homework often involve different types of functions and usually include modeling. These tasks address topics from astronomy, earth science, business, economics, political polls, projectile and periodic motion, etc. Many tasks require the creation of technology files. These tasks are meant to help the PSMTs further develop and utilize their content knowledge, develop better problem solving strategies, think about pedagogy, and use technology effectively. For samples of course activities, see Garofalo et al. (2000), Garofalo & Trinter (2012), Garofalo & Trinter, (in press), and Trinter & Garofalo (2011). When completing these tasks, PSMTs are often prompted to revisit some mathematics content they may have forgotten, never fully understood, or never applied.

Technology experiences emphasize the use of *content-focused technology applications*, including both content-specific technologies (e.g., graphing calculators, dynamic geometry, math-specific applets) and more generic technologies used in content-specific situations (e.g., Excel, digital cameras). PSMTs are exposed to *model lessons* incorporating appropriate technologies to enable them to see the potential of technology and develop a vision for their own technology uses. These experiences include *multiple opportunities* to explore mathematics concepts and applications with technology and to practice teaching mathematics with technology. Throughout the pedagogy course and student teaching, PSMTs have *ready access* to technology to gain experience in planning, implementing, and evaluating technology use.

Teaching Episodes

Over the course of the academic year, the PSMTs created and taught four video-recorded lessons to their peers in the pedagogy course, and they averaged about two hours a week in their field experience observing, assisting the classroom teacher or teaching lessons. For the peer-teaching episodes, each PSMT created a full-period lesson, but were only asked to teach a portion of it to the other PSMTs in the pedagogy course and authors of this study. They set up their teaching episode by telling the class "who they were supposed to be" (i.e. an eighth-grade geometry class), and then, after teaching their lesson, explained how they would complete the lesson when their timed portion ended. After each peer-teaching episode, the PSMTs were asked to evaluate themselves on their lesson plans and teaching actions and discuss what changes they would make to improve their lessons. Other PSMTs in the class then offered their feedback, along with the authors of this study. The PSMTs also received written comments as a condensed and formal version of the feedback provided to them during the debriefing discussion that immediately followed his or her teaching episode. After their third peer-teaching episode, PSMTS were assigned, as homework, to watch the videos of all three of their lessons, review the written feedback for each of them, and then revise the lesson plan for their third episode, with the feedback and what they observed in their videos in mind. They were asked to incorporate what they learned from this assignment into their teaching of subsequent lessons.

Data Collection Methods and Procedures

This study focused on the *four* lessons the PSMTs taught to their peers in the pedagogy course and the *one* lesson taught out in their field placement. The four peer-teaching episodes were taught over the course of the year, with the first and second teaching episodes in November and February (10-15 minutes), and the third and fourth ones at the end of March and April, respectively (20-25 minutes). Between the third and fourth peer-teaching episodes, each PSMT created and taught a full-period lesson to the pupils in their public school field placement.

The peer-teaching lessons taught in the pedagogy course were observed by the researchers and were also videotaped. The lessons taught in the field were not observed live, but were videotaped and submitted by the PSMTs. The four live observations allowed the researchers to experience the lessons first-hand and give feedback on each. In the semester subsequent to the end of the course, the videos of all five lessons of each PSMT were coded, in no particular order, using M-Scan (described below) by the first author. The first author was certified as an M-Scan master coder prior to the commencement of the study. To become an M-Scan master coder, the first author attended an M-Scan training workshop that consisted of a full week of reading relevant literature, practice coding sessions, and discourse with M-Scan authors to ensure reliable baseline coding. Then she coded eight videos of mathematics teaching and satisfied the required criteria of scoring within one point of the master codes at least 80% of the scores and within two points 90% of the scores, for each dimension for all videos (for more details on the reliability process see Berry, Rimm-Kaufman, Ottmar, Walkowiak, Merritt, & Pinter, 2012). The coding of the videos provided numerical scores on each of the nine dimensions of M-Scan for each of the lessons.

Mathematics Scan (M-Scan)

M-Scan is a multi-dimensional observational measure developed specifically to focus on standards-based mathematics teaching quality after an exhaustive search of existing instruments to measure quality mathematics instruction (Berry et al., 2012). It is made up of nine dimensions and its format is based on of the Classroom Assessment Scoring System (Pianta, LaParo, & Hamre, 2005) with identical scoring: "a seven-point scale that is divided into three sections: low (1–2), medium (3–5), and high (6–7)" (Walkowiak et al., in press, p. 20). It uses key word descriptors to characterize the three levels of performance.

The nine dimensions measured by M-Scan are the *Structure of a Lesson*, the teacher's and students' use of *Multiple Representations*, the S*tudents' Use of Mathematical Tools*, the *Cognitive Demand* of the activities in the lesson, the *Mathematical Discourse Community* in the classroom, the *Explanation and Justification* of the students' mathematical thinking, *Problem Solving* by the students, *Connections and Applications* of the mathematics taught to other mathematics topics and to the real world, and the *Mathematical Accuracy* in which the teacher presents the material (Berry et al., 2012). These dimensions measure the quality of mathematics teaching, as they are based on NCTM's *Principles and Standards* and also because researchers in mathematics education have identified their importance (NCTM, 2000, 2007; Walkowiak et al., in press; Weiss & Pasley 2004). M-Scan has an inter-coder reliability coefficient of 0.84 and was validated by content experts (Walkowiak et al., in press).

> The experts agreed that the dimensions of the M-Scan represent components of mathematics instructional quality. After the experts determined whether each coding guide descriptor was indicative of low, medium, or high mathematics instructional quality, their responses were analyzed for matches to the coding guide. The mathematics educator matched 79.7% and the university mathematician matched 82.7% of the descriptors. (Walkowiak et al. p. 27, in press).

The dimensions of *Multiple Representations* and the S*tudents' Use of Mathematical Tools* most directly correspond to the PSMTs' use of technology in their lessons because many PSMTs used Geometer's Sketchpad, TI Smartview, PowerPoint or Smart Notebook to create representations of mathematical content, and/or had students use an interactive whiteboard, graphing calculator, or Geometer's Sketchpad as a tool. *Connections and Applications*, *Problem Solving* and *Cognitive Demand* are also related to the PSMTs technology use, but not as strictly, for some utilized the technology to incorporate real-world data or connections in their lessons but the activities posed did not always utilize technology.

Results

The results are reported in two sections. The first section provides a brief glimpse of PSMTs' technology implementation issues in their first three peer-teaching episodes, along with the types of feedback they were given. In the second section, M-Scan scores are presented to demonstrate improvements in the PSMTs' technology use in their lessons over the course of the academic year.

Technology Use in PSMTs' First Three Teaching Episodes

Here we briefly comment on PSMTs' technology use in their *first three* peer-teaching episodes, because it is important for the reader to get a feel for the kind of mistakes they made in their initial teaching practices and the feedback they received. We believe this feedback helped them improve in their teaching practices over the course of the year. The PSMTs exhibited some quality teaching practices such as good overall planning of lessons, posing good questions, trying to engage all students, bringing in some useful representations and applications of the content, and using appropriate technologies. However, they also demonstrated what the authors refer to as "rookie" mistakes, with and without technology, some of which pertain to implementation difficulties.

Most of the PSMTs *did not incorporate technology in their first* episode, even though they had access to technologies that could have been used to enhance their lessons. Prior to that first teaching episode, PSMTs had several course sessions, which included work with graphing utilities, spreadsheets, dynamic geometry, and digital images, but they still did not incorporate any of these technologies. Feedback given to one PSMT illustrates one type of implementation issue each of them had when trying to represent the mathematics content without using available technology: "You can use the grid feature in Geometer's Sketchpad and the interactive whiteboard to plot points accurately." Later, when they began to incorporate technology, all had *difficulties with implementation at one time or another*. Sample comments to PSMTs about their use of technology included: "The interactive chart was good, but you should refer back to it during the discussion." "Pictures were confusing – use Geometer's Sketchpad to create accurate figures" and "The PowerPoint slide was too wordy…" The PSMTs had good intentions for different representations of mathematics content, but they did not utilize them well. The comments provided individualized feedback and suggestions for how to improve their lessons and use of technology to generate representations.

Improvements in PSMTs' M-Scan Scores Over Time

The increase in PSMTs' M-Scan scores provide empirical evidence that their teaching with technology improved over the academic year. Table 2 displays the average scores the eight PSMTs earned for their first and last teaching episodes in the *Multiple Representations* and *Students' Use of Mathematical Tools* dimensions, the numeric gain from first to last episode, and how many PSMTs had improved by two or more points in each dimension.

M-Scan Dimensions	First	Last	Gain	PSMTs with Gain ≥ 2
Multiple Representations	2.75	4	1.25	3
Students' Use of Mathematical Tools	1.25	3.75	2.5	6

Table 1: Average Growth in M-Scan Dimensions for the 8 PSMTs from their First to Last Teaching Episode

All PSMTs started out with low to medium scores in the *Multiple Representations* dimension, and ended with a range of medium scores. Seven out of the eight gained at least 1 point, with three gaining at least 2. Almost all PSMTs started with low scores in the *Students' Use of Mathematical Tools* dimension, but showed considerable growth in this dimension, with 6 PSMTs gaining at least 2 points and the other two gaining 1 point. Tables 2 and 3 below show how many PSMTs scored at each point-value in their first and last teaching episodes.

Multiple Representations

M-Scan Score	1	2	3	4	5
Number PSMTs scoring for first episode	0	3	4	1	0
Number PSMTs scoring for last episode	0	0	1	6	1

Table 2: Number of PSMTs receiving each score for *Multiple Representations* Dimension

In their first peer-teaching episodes, three PSMTs (Lauren, Jordan, and Dana) received a low score of 2, four PSMTs (Sara, Liz, Nicole, and Chelsea) received a low-medium score of 3, and Margaret had a medium score of 4 in the *Multiple Representations* dimension. All of these PSMTs used at least *two* traditional representations (i.e. hand-drawn or computer-generated figures on the white board, hand-written or typed algebraic equations, or hand-drawn graphs) during their first teaching episodes, but they did not particularly plan for the use of different representations of the mathematics addressed in their lessons. Several of them incorporated three traditional representations, and/or brought in physical shapes, inserted charts or inserted images to provide context for the lesson into a SMART Notebook or PowerPoint presentation file.

By the last episode, all of the PSMTs scored between a low-medium and a high-medium on this dimension. Lauren received a high-medium score of 5, Liz received a low-medium score of 3, and the rest received a medium score of 4. Each PSMT used at least *three* representations. All PSMTs prepared and taught their final lessons using SMART Notebook with a SMART board, and they took advantage of some of its features to bring in different representations of mathematics. Seven of them utilized software like Geometer's Sketchpad and/or specific SMART Notebook features for displaying accurate geometric figures and written notes. They brought in physical shapes, and/ or embedded video, images, three-dimensional figures, and/or maps. Jordan utilized the interactive ability of SMART Notebook and a SMART board to instantly create bar graphs to display data pupils collected in the lesson.

Students Use of Tools

M-Scan Score	1	2	3	4	5
Number PSMTs scoring for first episode	7	0	1	0	0
Number PSMTs scoring for last episode	0	1	3	1	3

Table 3: Number of PSMTs receiving each score for *Students' Use of Tools* Dimension

In their initial teaching episodes, only one PSMT, Margaret, used any type of tool to help illustrate mathematical concepts and she received a score of 3 on the *Students' Use of Tools* dimension; each of the other PSMTs received the lowest possible score (1). During these lessons, many PSMTs simply told the class the mathematics they needed to know, and thus did not plan for students' active engagement in the lesson.

However, by their final teaching episodes, seven of the eight had their pupils use some type of tool. Four of them received a medium or high-medium score in this dimension. Both Margaret and Dana used a combination of physical manipulatives and embedded three-dimensional figures in her SMART Notebook file to teach lessons on volume. Nicole created a Geometer's Sketchpad file that her pupils could manipulate to investigate the relationships between individual data points and the mean and standard deviation of the data set. This dynamic sketch displayed data both numerically and graphically. Lauren combined an interactive Geometer's Sketchpad diagram, with pupils measuring of triangles, in a lesson exploring trigonometric ratios.

Only Liz maintained a "low" score (2) in this dimension because her lesson did not provide the students an opportunity to use the tools; she, as the instructor, was the only one to use any tools.

Figure 1 below shows line graphs of the eight PSMTs' average score in the *Students' Use of Mathematical Tools* and *Multiple Representations* dimensions over each of the five teaching episodes to illustrate their growth trajectories in these dimensions of their technology use.

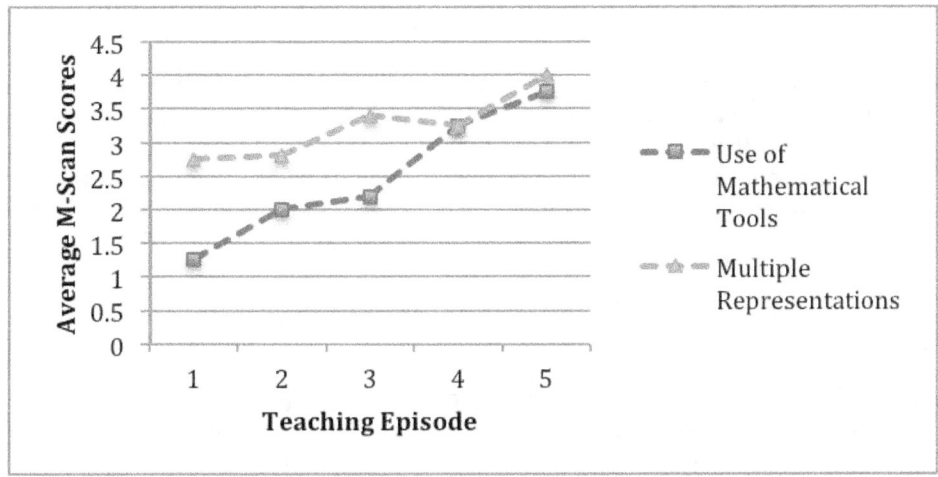

Figure 1: Average Growth by M-Scan Dimensions

In the graph, the growth in scores in the two dimensions is not monotonic, but has upward trends. The graph also depicts the non-linear and non-uniform increases in individual scores, which suggests a potential complex process of incorporating lessons learned from the activities in class and the constructive feedback given to them over time.

Discussion

The increase in the *Multiple Representations* dimension scores can be attributed to many of the activities in the pedagogy course. Regularly, the PSMTs created and worked with multiple representations of concepts for many activities and assignments. They experienced how such representations helped them better understand mathematics concepts and procedures and thus were motivated and able to incorporate such into their own lessons.

The *Students' Use of Mathematical Tools* dimension had a large average increase from the first teaching episode to the last over the eight PSMTs. The growth is not surprising since PSMTs learned to use tools to do mathematics throughout the course, to solve problems and explore applications. PSMTs often commented that using tools to do mathematics gave them new insights and helped them better understand mathematics. When asked what this implied to them, they often mentioned that they would have their own students use tools to learn as well. Clearly by the end they attempted to do this, even when teaching conditions were not conducive (i.e. the final scores could have been depressed due to the short duration of lessons since there was not enough time to fully utilize many tools).

The PSMTs development in these two dimensions is not only due to the course experiences, but also to the feedback that each was given after each teaching episode relative to their implementation of technology. In response to this ongoing feedback, they incorporated more representations, utilized them more effectively, and had students using tools in their lessons.

It is important to note that when the course was taught the researchers did not anticipate using the M-Scan measure on the PSMTs. The course reflects the *Principles and Standards* of NCTM and so does M-Scan, resulting in the congruency between the activities and foci of the course and the researchers' lens for which they evaluated the lessons and gave feedback. The pedagogy course is centered on multiple problem solving opportunities for the PSMTs and focuses on developing understanding of mathematics and its applications. This is achieved with cognitively demanding tasks, making connections and showing the applications of the content, representing the content in multiple ways, and utilizing tools to help develop students' understanding.

Overall, the lessons the PSMTs developed for their final teaching episodes demonstrated a better understanding of appropriate planning for technology use for their pupils' development of mathematical understanding. They utilized technology to generate and incorporate a variety of representations to help illustrate the mathematics concepts to be learned in their lessons. The PSMTs were also able to provide richer problem-solving, discourse opportunities for their pupils, successfully enacted small group work, and had students explain their work and thought processes.

Conclusion

The *Principles and Standards* defined by NCTM (2000) have created a descriptive model for high-quality mathematics teaching including the use of technology to create mathematical tasks and representations. It is important to notice that explicit instruction can help improve pre-service teachers' teaching practices to help them achieve NCTM's vision. Santagata, Zannoni, and Stigler (2007) advocate that pre-service teachers need to practice what they learn in teacher education programs, and activities such as teaching lessons to their peers is just the sort of activity that provides necessary practice for pre-service teachers' developing TPACK. The immediate feedback and opportunities to "re-do" a lesson helped the pre-service teachers practice revising and improving their lessons while simultaneously impelling them to reflect upon what worked in the lesson, what did not, and why. The course also required the PSMTs to write reflection papers on what it means to teach mathematics and to be an effective teacher of mathematics. Activities like these help the pre-service teachers to solidify their own conceptions of teaching mathematics with technology, so they can apply it to their lesson planning and instructional practices.

An important finding to highlight is that *teacher education can help PSMTs improve their teaching and technology incorporation through a combination of classroom activities and practice teaching with feedback.* It also shows that the more time spent on practice teaching, the greater improvements there were in the PSMTs' teaching dimensions. This study suggests that true improvements in teaching practices and technology incorporation do not materialize after a few short weeks, but can take the entire academic year. Teacher preparation programs can incorporate opportunities for PSMTs to practice teaching with technology, coupled with direct feedback, so that these PSMTs are better prepared to take advantage of technology. This will help them develop TPACK and incorporate it in their teaching.

References

Association of Mathematics Teacher Educators. (2009). *Mathematics TPACK (technological pedagogical content knowledge) framework*.

Berry, III, R. Q., Rimm-Kaufman, S. E., Ottmar, E. M., Walkowiak, T. A., Merritt, E. & Pinter, H. H. (2012). The Mathematics Scan (M-Scan): A Measure of Mathematics Instructional Quality. Unpublished measure, University of Virginia.

Conference Board of the Mathematical Sciences. (2001). *The Mathematical Education of Teachers*. Providence RI and Washington DC: American Mathematical Society and Mathematical Association of America.

Fraser, V. (2010). The use of technology-generated representations in mathematics instruction: A study of novice teachers' practices. Doctoral dissertation, University of Virginia.

Garofalo, J., Drier, H., Harper, S., Timmerman, M. and Shockey, T. (2000). Promoting appropriate uses of technology in mathematics teacher preparation. *Contemporary Issues in Technology and Teacher Education, 1*(1), 66-88.

Garofalo, J. & Trinter, C. P. (in press). Using Simulations to Foster Pre-Service Mathematics Teachers' Self-Assessment, Learning, and Reflections on Teaching. *The Mathematics Teacher.*

Garofalo, J. & Trinter, C. P. (2012). Tasks That Make Connections through Representations. *The Mathematics Teacher, 106*, 302-306.

Hiebert, J., & Lefevre, P. (1986). Conceptual and procedural knowledge in mathematics:An introductory analysis. In J. Hiebert (Ed.), *Conceptual and procedural knowledge: The case of mathematics* (pp. 1-27). Hillsdale, NJ: Lawrence Erlbaum Associates.

Juersivich, N., Garofalo, J. & Fraser, V. (2009). Student Teachers' Use of Technology-Generated Representations: Exemplars and Rationales. *Journal of Technology and Teacher Education, 17*(2), 149-173.

Mathematical Association of American & the Committee on the Mathematical Education of Teachers. (1991). *A call for change: Recommendations for the mathematical preparation of teachers of mathematics.* Washington, DC: MAA.

Mathematical Sciences Education Board & National Research Council. (1990). *Reshaping School Mathematics: A Philosophy and Framework for Curriculum.* Washington, DC: National Academy Press.

Mishra, P. & Koehler, M. J. (2006). Technological pedagogical content knowledge: A framework for teacher knowledge. *Teachers college record, 108*(6), 1017-1054.

National Council of Teachers of Mathematics. (1991). *Professional standards for teaching mathematics.* Reston, VA: NCTM.

National Council of Teachers of Mathematics. (2000). *Principles and standards for school mathematics.* Reston, VA: NCTM.

Pianta, R.C., La Paro, K., & Hamre, B. (2005). *The classroom assessment scoring system, Pre-K manual.* Unpublished manuscript, University of Virginia.

Polya, G. (1945). *How to solve it.* Princeton, NJ: Princeton University Press.

Santagata, R., Zannoni, C., & Stigler, J. W. (2007). The role of lesson analysis in pre-service teacher education: An empirical investigation of teacher learning from a virtual video-based field experience. *Journal of Math Teacher Education, 10*, 123-140. DOI: 10.1007/s10857-007-9029-9.

Schoenfeld, A. H. (1992). Learning to think mathematically: Problem solving, metacognition, and sense-making in mathematics. In D. Grouws (Ed.), *Handbook for Research on Mathematics Teaching and Learning* (pp. 334-370). New York: MacMillan.

Swartz, B. A. & Garofalo, J. (under review). Documenting changes in pre-service mathematics teachers' instructional practices.

Trinter, C. P. & Garofalo, J. (2011). Exploring non-routine functions algebraically and graphically, *Mathematics Teacher,* 104 (7), 508-513.

Walkowiak, T., Berry, R.Q., Meyer, J.P., Rimm-Kaufman, S.E., & McCracken, E.R. (in press). Introducing an observational measure of mathematics instructional quality: Evidence of validity and score reliability. *Educational Studies.*

Weiss, I. R. & Pasley, J. D. (2004). What is high-quality instruction? *Educational Leadership, 61*(5), 24-28.

The PBL-TECH Project: Web-Based Tools and Resources to Support Problem-Based Learning in Pre-Service Teacher Education

Thomas Brush
Indiana University, USA
tbrush@indiana.edu

Krista Glazewski
Indiana University, USA
glaze@indiana.edu

Anne Ottenbreit-Leftwich
Indiana University, USA
aleftwic@indiana.edu

John Saye
Auburn University, USA
sayejoh@auburn.edu

Zhizhen Zhang
Beijing Normal University, China
zzz.bnu@gmail.com

Sungwon Shin
Indiana University, USA
shinsung@indiana.edu

Abstract: This paper discusses the PBL-TECH project, which seeks to design, disseminate, evaluate, and sustain an enhanced teacher preparation model that provides teacher educators across the United States with web-based tools and resources to teach future teachers to effectively implement innovative technology-supported problem-based learning (PBL) instructional practices, focusing on two specific research-supported PBL models: Problem-Based Historical Inquiry (PBHI) and Socioscientific Inquiry (SSI). Our project focuses on the design and development of web-based tools and resources to support both the modeling of technology-enhanced PBL activities in teacher education, and the exploration of the best methods for integrating technology-supported PBL practices in teacher education. We also provide a discussion of our current and proposed research efforts to explore the most effective ways to implement technology-enhanced PBL in teacher education.

Introduction

In the most recent national educational technology plan, the U.S. Department of Education (2010) recognizes the critical importance of building 21st century skills (e.g., "critical thinking, complex problem solving, collaboration, and multimedia communication") within all content areas (p. 9). Various researchers have suggested that teachers need to provide authentic, real-world learning experiences to help students succeed in the 21st century (Bell, 2010; Lombardi, 2007; Saye et al., 2013) and most agree that the most powerful uses of technology are those that utilize a student-centered approach (Lai, 2008; Law, 2008). The Department of Education also agrees with the requirements for these types of learning experiences, and purports that technology can help teachers reach this goal: "technology is at the core of virtually every aspect of our daily lives and work, and we must leverage it to provide engaging and powerful learning experiences and content, as well as resources and assessments that measure student achievement in more complete, authentic, and meaningful ways" (p. 7). However, some have found that teachers do not integrate technology in these student-centered ways (Project Tomorrow, 2008, 2009). Therefore, in order to achieve the kinds of technology uses required to maximize learning (Lai, 2008; Law, 2008), we need to help teacher education faculty and pre-service teachers conceptualize how technology may be used to facilitate more authentic and collaborative student learning (Brears, MacIntyre, & O'Sullivan, 2011).

One of the most highly recommended best practices that supports authentic and collaborative student learning is problem-based learning (PBL). Problem-based learning (PBL) is a student-centered instructional approach that anchors the curriculum in ill-structured, authentic problems (Barrows & Kelson, 1995; Hmelo-Silver, 2004; Savery, 2006). Several meta-analyses suggest that PBL experiences are more effective than traditional instruction with regards to increased student achievement (Ravitz, 2009; Strobel & Barneveld, 2009; Walker & Leary, 2009; Wirkala & Kuhn, 2011). For example, Wirkala and Kuhn (2011) examined the effectiveness of PBL with middle school students and found that those students demonstrated significantly better performance on a wide range of outcomes when they engaged in PBL instruction versus lecture-based instruction. In addition, Pedersen and Liu (2002) found that PBL was an effective method for students to transfer their knowledge to not only similar problems but also to different situations. The authors argued that "if we are able to enhance students' thinking during PBL, thus helping them to participate more effectively in the work required in the PBL environment, then we may also see enhanced problem solving in other situations" (Pedersen & Liu, 2002, p. 318).

New technology tools have the capacity to make the implementation of PBL in both university and K-12 classrooms much more effective. Collaboration is a large component of PBL, and many "Web 2.0" technology tools have recently been developed to facilitate collaboration among learners. For example, one vocational teacher education course used wikis to facilitate PBL. Pre-service teachers were provided a case and used a template wiki page that included guidance for each section that needed to be addressed (e.g., design considerations, recommendations, record of meetings, references) (Robertson, 2008). Other teacher education programs have used online resources such as electronic resources, threaded discussion, PBL scenarios, videoconferencing, and distance tutorial support to facilitate PBL (Wheeler, Kelly, & Gale, 2005).

K-12 schools are beginning to recognize the achievement of technology-enhanced problem-based learning curriculums. Several models such as High Tech High (11 schools) and New Tech High (86 schools) use a technology-enhanced PBL approach to learning. Some teacher education programs have attempted to address the need for teachers prepared to meet the instructional needs of these new school models by incorporating more PBL into their courses. A study of one program that introduced technology integration in a PBL environment found that pre-service teachers' intentions to use technology for PBL increased (Park & Ertmer, 2008). In another study, 96 pre-service teachers collaborated on PBL lessons that integrated technology (So & Kim, 2009). Results indicated that the pre-service teachers demonstrated increased knowledge of PBL theory and practice.

Problem and Purpose

Unfortunately, many teacher education programs still approach pre-service classrooms with conventional practices (Feiman-Nemser, 2008; Kiggins & Combourne, 2007), and few pre-service teachers have clear conceptions of designing and implementing technology-enhanced PBL instruction (So & Kim, 2009). However, more teacher education programs are beginning to recognize the potential for PBL and the need for support in order to integrate PBL into their programs (Edwards & Hammer, 2006; Murray-Harvey & Slee, 2000). In order for PBL to be successfully adopted by pre-service teachers, teacher education faculty need to be comfortable with technology-enhanced PBL (Vannatta & Beyerbach, 2001). Thus, there is a need to both identify and/or develop web-based tools and resources that teacher educators and pre-service teachers can utilize to develop effective PBL curricula, and provide opportunities for teacher educators to collaborate with experts in the integration of Web 2.0 tools and PBL strategies to use these resources to implement curriculum reform in their own teacher education programs.

The purpose of this paper is to discuss the PBL-TECH project, which seeks to design, disseminate, evaluate, and sustain an enhanced teacher preparation model that provides teacher educators across the United States with web-based tools and resources to teach future teachers to effectively implement innovative technology-supported PBL instructional practices, focusing on two specific research-supported PBL models: Problem-Based Historical Inquiry (PBHI) and Socioscientific Inquiry (SSI). Our project focuses on the design and development of web-based tools and resources to support both the modeling of technology-enhanced PBL activities in teacher education, and the exploration of the best methods for integrating technology-supported PBL practices in teacher education. In addition to discussion of the PBL-TECH tools and resources we have designed to support PBL, we will also provide a discussion of our current and proposed research efforts to explore the most effective ways to implement technology-enhanced PBL with both teacher educators and pre-service teachers.

Description of PBL-TECH

In order to maximize the potential that Web 2.0 tools can provide to support problem-based curriculum in teacher education, all of the barriers described above need to be addressed. The overall goal of PBL-TECH is to design, disseminate, evaluate, and sustain an enhanced teacher preparation model that will provide teacher educators with web-based resources to prepare future teachers to effectively implement technology-enhanced PBL instruction. Each component of the project design is discussed in more detail below.

Our PBL Models: PBHI and SSI. The PBL-TECH project has specifically focused on the content areas of social studies and science to promote and integrate our PBL models in teacher preparation programs: Problem-based Historical Inquiry (PBHI) and Socio-Scientific Inquiry (SSI). The two PBL models both emphasize students to not only engage in the inquiry process to investigate and examine historical or scientific issues, but also to reflect on social, ethical, and moral values of those issues when solving problems or making decisions (KolstØ, 2001; Sadler & Zeidler, 2005; Sadler, Barab, & Scott, 2007; Saye & Brush, 2004). In both contexts, students confront complex and ill-structured societal problems that are authentic, and they are expected to develop content knowledge, critical reasoning, problem solving and collaboration skills, diverse perspectives, and most importantly, civic competence to make informed and reasoned decisions regarding those problems through inquiry process.

Both PBHI and SSI models require a sufficient amount of scaffolding and collaboration efforts of teachers and students since problems are inherently complex and ill-structured as they are embedded within social and ethical contexts (Sadler & Zeidler, 2005; Saye & Brush, 2004). Hard scaffolding such as embedded hyperlinks, student activity guides, and annotation tools, as well as teachers' soft scaffolding to engage students more deeply in the problem, are crucial components to support the student inquiry process (Hannafin, Land & Oliver, 1999; Saye & Brush, 2002). Furthermore, as such problems have no single and straightforward solutions and involve multiple sources of knowledge, students need to engage in collaboration to address the complexity and challenges they face during the process with positive interdependence, multiple intelligences, and collective rationality (Saye & Brush, 2004). Hence, scaffolding, authenticity, and collaboration are emphasized in the two disciplined inquiry approaches, as well as the need for technology-enhanced PBL environments to promote and support such inquiry approaches.

Development of web-based tools and resources to support technology-enhanced PBL. Over the past 15 years, we have explored how technology can support the implementation of PBL strategies for both teachers and K-12 students. Our research has led to several recommendations for the types of tools that need to be developed to assist teacher education faculty with implementing and modeling PBL with their students (see Brush & Saye, 2009; Saye & Brush, 2009). Through the PBL-TECH project, we planned to assess the potential of available Web 2.0 tools for facilitating PBL, design new technology tools to address needs not met by current tools, organize new and existing technology tools into a conceptually-integrated authoring suite, and make them available to the teacher educator community. These tools are designed to facilitate the critical processes of PBL: scaffolding, authenticity, and collaboration. In addition, the tools are embedded in PBL environments for each subject area: *Persistent Issues in History Network* (PIHNet: http://www.pihnet.org) and *Socio-Scientific Inquiry Network* (SSINet: http://www.ssinet.org).

Scaffolding tools. Examinations of teachers attempting PBL in their classrooms reveal the tremendous cognitive burdens that this teaching practice places upon both students and teachers (Brush & Saye, 2001, 2004; Onosko, 1991; Rossi, 1995; Rossi & Pace, 1998; Saye & Brush, 2002). Teachers must be able to monitor and spontaneously support students as they struggle with complex material and ill-structured problems. Implementing PBL also requires substantially more preparation time to develop deep content knowledge and rich instructional materials necessary to support student inquiry. Web 2.0 technologies can ease the cognitive burdens that dissuade many from inquiry practice. Providing teacher educators with scaffolding tools to facilitate development and implementation of PBL activities may facilitate integration of problem-based teaching methods into teacher education programs. Some of these tools we explored and developed include the following:

(1) *Tools with hyperlinking and annotation capabilities in web-based documents.* These tools can be used with online digital resources by teacher educators to provide students with conceptual guidance about what knowledge to consider (definition), metacognitive guidance to monitor their thinking (background information), or strategic guidance about how to proceed in problem-solving (thinking question) (Hannafin, Land, & Oliver, 1999) (see Figure 1).

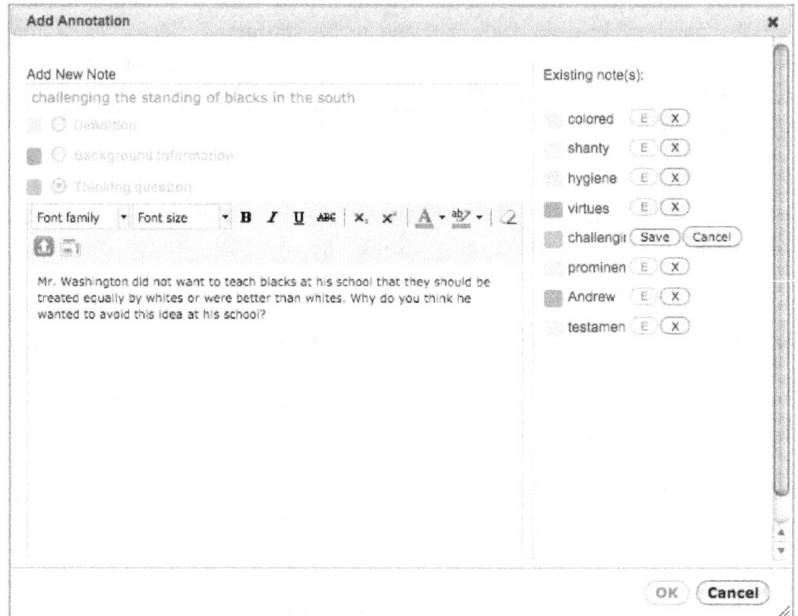

Figure 1. PBL-TECH Annotation Tool

(2) *Online templates of common tasks involved in implementing PBL.* To address other challenges associated with PBL, we also provide online templates of scaffolds for common problem-based tasks. For example, one common task faced by teachers is developing a central (or driving) question that is broad enough to cover multiple content goals, but appropriate in scope for the target learner. In our suite of web-based tools, we included a resource for developing the central question as well as determining if it meets the instructional setting and goals (see Figure 2).

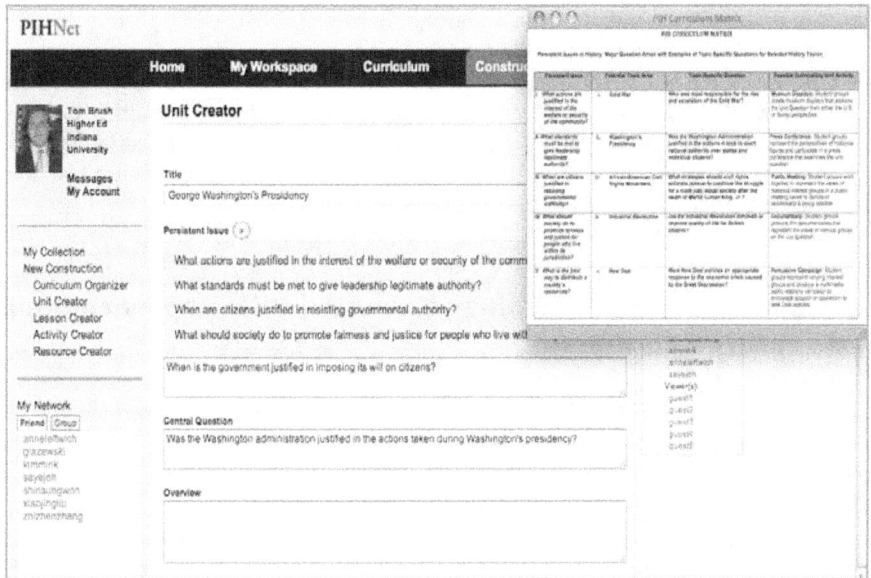

Figure 2. Curriculum Matrix

Authenticity tools. Technology tools can support the authenticity and conceptualization of problems. Our suite of web-based tools includes the capacity to deliver model PBL cases (both video and text-based), as well as tools to easily develop new cases that fit the context and needs of individual teacher education programs. Model PBL cases provide further examples of scaffolding and other inquiry strategies that may stimulate teacher thinking and streamline the preparation process (Krueger, Boboc, Smaldino, Cornish, & Callahan, 2004). Teachers have found that these tools and resources provide some relief from the heavy burdens of preparing, organizing, and implementing PBL lessons and that such models encourage reflective dialogue and richer conceptualizations of PBL practice (Saye & Brush, 1999, 2002, 2004; Saye, Kohlmeier, Brush, Mitchell, & Farmer, 2009).

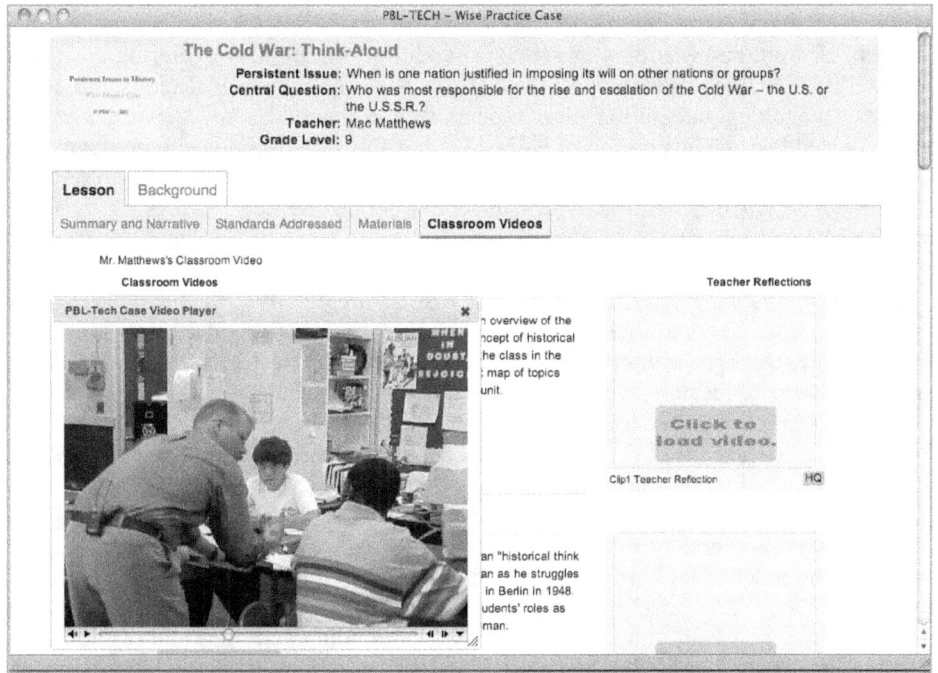

Figure 3. PBL-TECH Wise Practice Case Database

Collaboration tools. One important instructional process in PBL is supporting collaboration (Saye & Brush, 2004). Our suite of tools includes resources for mediating collaboration through organizational and communication structures. These tools enable teacher educators, practicing teachers, and pre-service teachers to chat online, add collaborators for their work, and create and manage groups. We also plan to add other collaborative features such as wiki capabilities to support faculty-faculty collaboration, faculty-student collaboration, and student-student collaboration. These collaborative spaces will facilitate both faculty and pre-service teachers' development of rich models of technology-enhanced PBL practice.

Research Agenda: Exploring Technology-Enhanced PBL Implementation with Pre-Service Teachers and Teacher Educators

Throughout the PBL-TECH project, we have been collaborating with both teacher educators and practicing teachers to determine the best ways to leverage the affordances Web 2.0 tools and resources towards effective implementation of PBL in a variety of educational settings. Our major research efforts have focused on two interrelated areas specifically relevant to technology and teacher education:

- Examining how pre-service teachers integrate PBL practices into their teaching models and beliefs, and specifically how they utilize the PBL-TECH tools and resources to support PBL curriculum design and implementation.
- Examining how teacher educators integrate PBL strategies into their methods courses, and how the PBL-TECH tools and resources support their efforts.

Examining how pre-service teachers integrate PBL practices into their teaching, and how they can use PBL-TECH tools and resources to support these efforts. For the past several years, we have been exploring how pre-service teachers have integrated specific PBL practices (particularly our PBHI model) into their teaching beliefs and curriculum design. These efforts have led to several studies in which we examined the overall research question "How does participation in a teacher education program that integrates technology-enhanced PBHI practices impact pre-service teachers' instructional decision-making?" Our findings suggest that pre-service teachers completing a program that fully integrates PBHI as an overall conceptual framework for the program (namely the social studies education program at Auburn University) demonstrate instructional decision-making (in both curriculum design and implementation) that aligns with the key components of the PBHI model (Brush and Saye, in press; Saye, Kohlmeier, Brush, Howell, and Maddox, in press). In addition, we are also exploring how pre-service teachers are utilizing the new PBL-TECH tools to support their efforts to design model PBL units and activities in key methods classes (e.g., our technology integration class, social studies methods, and science methods). Our preliminary findings have indicated that the integration of embedded scaffolds that support the implementation of our PBHI and SSI models within the PBL-TECH unit creator and resource creator tools have positively influenced pre-service teachers' abilities to design units and activities that incorporate the key features of those models (Shin, Brush, Zhang, Shin, Kim, & Lu, 2013).

Examining how teacher educators integrate PBL strategies into their methods classes. Assisting faculty with integrating PBL strategies into their classes has an ultimate aim to model those strategies for future teachers. This will provide future teachers with opportunities to learn how to effectively implement PBL in K-12 classrooms. By partnering with teacher educators, we are providing pre-service teachers with models of PBL strategies and with first-hand experiences as learners experiencing those PBL activities. Our initial research efforts have focused on the question, "How do teacher educators integrate PBL models (particularly PBHI and SSI) into their teaching methods?" We have initially introduced the PBHI/SSI models and our PBL-TECH tools to specific teacher education faculty in social studies and science education who are interested in exploring PBL strategies. These efforts have led to three different studies in which teacher educators used the PBL-TECH tools to design and implement at least one model PBL unit in their classes. For example, in an elementary science methods course, a faculty member we are partnering with requires her preservice teachers to use the PBL-TECH tools to collaboratively construct one PBL unit complete with corresponding activities and resources. We are continuing to partner with these faculty throughout the implementation process in order to provide insight into how faculty adopt and adapt the PBL models in their classes.

These efforts have also led to an additional research strand exploring how we can use our tools to support collaboration among faculty who are designing PBL units and activities for their methods classes. We plan to examine how the online collaborative tools in PBL-TECH can assist other teacher education faculty interested in PBL and coordinate an online professional development community with the focus of expanding the implementation and modeling of PBL activities in other teacher education programs. This research may provide further insight into how innovative curriculum strategies can be more easily disseminated to other programs, and will lend particular insight as we expand our "recruitment" efforts in an attempt to establish research and development partnerships with additional teacher education programs.

Summary: Significance of the PBL-Tech Project

While PBL is receiving increased support from K-12 educators, it has not yet been broadly adopted at the higher education level (Pierret & Friedrichsen, 2009; Sadler et al., 2007). There are a number of questions that remain when determining the best methods for preparing future teachers to implement these types of innovations that have implications for university-level instruction. The PBL-TECH project is addressing these questions through a collaborative initiative that will provide teacher educators with tools, resources, and a support structure specifically designed to facilitate the development and modeling of PBL curricular initiatives in their classrooms.

First, there are barriers to teacher preparation and adoption that have implications for university practice. The lack of research regarding adoption of PBL approaches in K-12 education reflects a more systemic issue in the transfer of university-generated, research-based innovations and their adoption by teachers. This gap between research-based innovations developed by teacher education faculty and "feet-on-the-ground" practitioners has been discussed by several researchers (Anderson, 2002; Foti & Ring, 2008; Hiebert, Gallimore, & Stigler, 2002; Sadler et al., 2007). They note that teachers are concerned with "what works" at the practical level. Researchers have demonstrated that collaborative communities of practice that incorporate extensive use of modeling to support discussion and reflection of innovative teaching practices are highly effective in disseminating those practices (Saye et al., 2009). Through this project, we will provide faculty and pre-service teachers the opportunity to view demonstrations and models through online cases examples, mentoring, and consistent feedback.

An additional set of barriers to adoption of new teaching methods is the conflict between teaching content as a set of facts and verbal information (the way that it is often presented in textbooks) versus a process with controversy, conflicts, and uncertainty, as well as lack in confidence in dealing with instructional content in this manner (Davidsson, 2009; Tal & Morag, 2009), Thus, our project will provide faculty and teachers with a method to engage students, and more confidence in presenting content as a process with conflicts, rather than a static set of facts.

Finally, there is a need for online communities that support university faculty and pre-service teachers' efforts at new innovations. It is generally recognized that faculty and teachers need support and mentoring throughout the adoption process. Appleton (2008) describes an intensive one-on-one mentoring approach for elementary teachers working with their curriculum, which boosted teacher confidence in implementing innovative classroom practices in education. However, this is not amenable to a scale-up practice. In response, many have started to support faculty and pre-service teacher development through collaborative online communities (Saye & Brush, 2009), which can afford scalability and sustainability. What is unique about our approach is that faculty and their pre-service teachers will participate in the same online community. This places everyone in a position to access the knowledge base within the community, such as case examples, lesson plans, and discussion forums. This approach ensures steady communication across all levels of expertise and roles within the environment and, as a result, will inform how to build such online settings to maximize participation, knowledge gain, and contribution.

References

Anderson, R. D. (2002). Reforming science teaching: What research says about inquiry. *Journal of Science Teacher Education, 13*(1), 1-12.

Appleton, K. (2008). Developing science pedagogical content knowledge through mentoring elementary teachers. *Journal of Science Teacher Education, 19*(6), 523-545.

Bell, S. (2010). Project-based learning for the 21st century: Skills for the future. *The Cleaning House: A Journal of Educational Strategies, Issues, and Ideas, 83*(2), 39-42.

Brears, L., MacIntyre, B., & O'Sullivan, G. (2011). Preparing teachers for the 21st century using PBL as an integrating strategy in science and technology education. *Design and Technology Education. 16*(1), 36-46.

Brush, T. & Saye, J. (in press). An instructional model to support Problem-Based Historical Inquiry: The Persistent Issues in History Network. *Interdisciplinary Journal of Problem-Based Learning, 8*(1).

Brush, T., & Saye, J. W. (2001). The use of embedded scaffolds in a technology-enhanced student centered learning activity. *Journal of Educational Multimedia and Hypermedia, 10*, 333-356.

Brush, T., & Saye, J. W. (2004, April). *The effects of multimedia supported problem-based historical inquiry on student engagement, empathy, and historical reasoning.* Paper presented at the annual meeting of the American Educational Research Association, San Diego, CA.

Brush, T., & Saye, J. W. (2009). Strategies for preparing preservice social studies teachers to integrate technology effectively: Models and practices. *Contemporary Issues in Technology and Teacher Education, 9*(1), 46-59.

Davidsson, E. (2009). Enhancing visitors' interest in science- a possibility or a paradox? A study of what scientific content staff members focus on when planning a new exhibition. *Research in Science Education 39*, 197-213.

Edwards, S. & Hammer, M. (2006). Laura's story: Using problem based learning in early childhood and primary teacher education. *Teaching and Teacher Educator, 22*(4), 465-477.

Feiman-Nemser, S. (2008). From preparation to practice: Designing a continuum to strengthen and sustain teaching. *Teachers College Record, 103*(6), 1013-1055.

Foti, S. & Ring, G. (2008). Using a simulation-based learning environment to enhance learning and instruction in a middle school science classroom. *Journal of Computers in Mathematics and Science, 27*(1), 103-120.

Hannafin, M., Land, S., & Oliver, K. (1999). Open learning environments: Foundations, methods, and models. In C. Reigeluth (Ed.), *Instructional Design Theories and Models* (pp. 115-140). Mahwah, NJ: Lawrence Erlbaum Associates.

Hiebert, J., Gallimore, R., & Stigler, J. W. (2002). A knowledge base for the teaching profession: What would it look like and how can we get one? *Educational Researcher, 31*(5), 3-15.

Hmelo-Silver, C. E. (2004). Problem-based learning: What and how do students learn? *Educational Psychology Review, 16*(3), 235-266.

Kiggins, J., & Cambourne, B. (2007). The knowledge building community program: A partnership for progress in teacher education. In T. Townsend & R. Bates (Eds.), *Handbook of Teacher Education* (pp. 365-380). NewYork: Springer.

KolstØ, S. D. (2001). Scientific literacy for citizenship: Tools for dealing with the science dimension of controversial socioscientific issues. *Science Education, 85*, 291-310.

Krueger, K, Boboc, M., Smaldino, S., Cornish, Y., & Callahan, M. (2004). INTIME impact report what was INTIME's effectiveness and impact on faculty and preservice teachers? *Journal of Technology and Teacher Education, 12(2),* 185-210.

Lai, K. (2008). ICT supporting the learning process: The premise, reality, and promise. In J. Voogt & G. Knezek (Eds.), *International handbooks of information technology in primary and secondary education* (pp. 315-230). New york: Springer.

Law, N. (2008). Teacher learning beyond knowledge for pedagogical innovations with ICT. In J. Voogt & G. Knezek (Eds.), *International handbooks of information technology in primary and secondary education* (pp. 425-434). New York: Springer.

Lombardi, M. (2007). *Authentic learning for the 21st century: An overview.* Report of the EDUCAUSE Learning Initiative. Retrieved March 1, 2013 from: http://net.educause.edu/ir/library/pdf/eli3009.pdf.

Murray-Harvey, R., & Slee, P. (2000. December). *Problem based learning in teacher education: Just the beginning.* Paper presented at the Australian Association for Research in Education, Sydney, Australia.

Onosko, J. J. (1991). Barriers to the Promotion of Higher Order Thinking in Social Studies. *Theory and Research in Social Education*, 19, 341-366.

Park, S. H., & Ertmer, P. A. (2008). Impact of problem-based learning (PBL) on teachers' beliefs regarding technology use. *Journal of Research on Technology in Education, 40*(2), 247-267.

Pedersen, S., & Liu, M. (2002). The transfer of problem-solving skills from a problem-based learning environment: The effect of modeling an expert's cognitive processes. *Journal of Research on Technology in Education, 35*(2), 303-320.

Pierret, C., & Friedrichsen, P. (2009). Stem cells and society: An undergraduate course exploring the intersections among science, religion, and law. *CBE - Life Sciences Education, 8*, 79-87.

Project Tomorrow (2008). *Selected National Findings of the Speak Up 2007 Survey.* Retrieved March 1, 2013 from: http://www.tomorrow.org/speakup/speakup_congress_2007.html.

Project Tomorrow. (2009*). Learning in the 21st century: 2009 trends update.* Retrieved March 1, 2013 from: http://www.tomorrow.org/speakup/learning21Report_2009_Update.html.

Ravitz, J. (2009). Summarizing findings and looking ahead to a new generation of PBL research. *The Interdisciplinary Journal of Problem-based Learning, 3*(1), 4-11.

Robertson, I. (2008). Learners' attitudes to wiki technology in problem based, blended learning for vocational teacher education. *Australian Journal of Educational Technology, 24*(4), 425-441.

Sadler, T. D., Barab, S. A., & Scott, B. (2007). What do students gain by engaging in socioscientific inquiry? *Research in Science Education, 37*, 371-391.

Rossi, J. A. (1995). In-depth study in an issues-centered social studies classroom. *Theory and Research in Social Education*, 23(2), 88-120.

Rossi, J. A. & Pace, C. M. (1998). Issues-centered instruction with low achieving high school students: The dilemmas of two teachers. *Theory and Research in Social Education*, 26(3), 380-409.

Sadler, T. D. (2004). Informal reasoning regarding socioscientific issues: A critical review of research. *Journal of Research in Science Teaching, 41*, 513-536.

Sadler, T. D., & Zeidler, D. L. (2005). Patterns of informal reasoning in the context of socioscientific decision making. *Journal of Research in Science Teaching, 42*, 112-138.

Sadler, T. D., Barab, S. A., & Scott, B. (2007). What do students gain by engaging in socioscientific inquiry? *Research in Science Education, 37*, 371-391.

Savery, J. R. (2006). Overview of problem-based learning: Definitions and distinctions. *Interdisciplinary Journal of Problem-based Learning, 1*(1), Retrieved from http://docs.lib.purdue.edu/ijpbl/vol1/iss1/3

Saye, J. W., & Brush, T. (1999). Student engagement with social issues in a multimedia-supported learning environment. *Theory and Research in Social Education, 27*(4), 472-504.

Saye, J. W., & Brush, T. (2002). Scaffolding critical reasoning about history and social issues in multimedia-supported learning environments. *Educational Technology Research and Development, 50*(3), 77-96.

Saye, J. W., & Brush, T. (2004). Promoting civic competence through problem-based history learning experiments. In G.E. Hamot, J.J. Patrick, & R.S. Leming (Eds.), *Civic learning in teacher education* (Vol. 3, pp. 123-145). Bloomington, IN: The Social Studies Development Center.

Saye, J. W., & Brush, T. (2009). Using the affordances of technology to develop teacher expertise in historical inquiry. In J. Lee & A. Friedman (Eds.), *Research on Technology in Social Studies Education* (pp. 19-36). Greenwich, CT: Information Age Publishing.

Saye, J., Kohlmeier, J., Brush, T., Howell, J., & Maddox, L. (in press). Assessing the effects of a teacher education program on pre-service secondary social studies teachers' instructional decision-making. *International Journal of Social Education, 24*(2).

Saye, J. W., Kohlmeier, J., Brush, T., Mitchell, L., & Farmer, C. (2009). Using mentoring to develop professional teaching knowledge for problem-based historical inquiry. *Theory and Research in Social Education, 37*(1), 6-41.

Saye, J. & the Social Studies Inquiry Research Collaborative (SSIRC). (2013). Authentic pedagogy: Its presence in social studies classrooms and relationship to student performance on state-mandated tests. *Theory and Research in Social Education, 41*(1), 89-132.

Shin, S., Brush, T., Zhang, Z., Shin, S., Kim, M., & Lu, Y. (2013, April). *Evaluation of the new construction tools in Persistent Issues in History Network*. Paper presented at the Annual Meeting of the American Educational Research Association, San Francisco, CA.

So, H. & Kim, B. (2009). Learning about problem based learning: Student teachers integrating technology, pedagogy and content knowledge. *Australasian Journal of Educational Technology*. 25(1), 101-116

Strobel, J. & Barneveld, A. V. (2009). When is PBL more effective? A meta-synthesis of meta-analyses comparing PBL to conventional classrooms. *Interdisciplinary Journal of Problem-based Learning*, 3(1), 44-58.

Tal, T., & Morag, O. (2009). Reflective practice as a means for preparing to teach outdoors in an ecological garden. *Journal of Science Teacher Education, 20*, 245-262.

U.S. Department of Education (2010). *Transforming American education: Learning powered by technology*. Retrieved March 1, 2013 from: http://www.ed.gov/sites/default/files/netp2010-execsumm.pdf

Vannatta, R., & Beyerbach, B. (2001). Facilitating a constructivist vision of technology integration among education faculty and preservice teachers. *Journal of Research on Computing in Education, 33*(2), 132-148.

Walker, A., & Leary, H. (2009). A problem based learning meta analysis: Differences across problem types, implementation types, disciplines, and assessment levels. *The Interdisciplinary Journal of Problem-based Learning, 3*(1), 12-43.

Wheeler, S., Kelly, P., & Gale, K. (2005). The influence of online problem-based learning on teachers' professional practice and identity. *Research in Learning Technology, 13*(2), 125-137.

Wirkala, C. & Kuhn, D. (2011). Problem-based learning in K-12 education: Is it effective and how does it achieve its effects? *American Educational Research Journal, 48*(5), 1157-1186.

TPACK: Exploring a Secondary Pre-service Teachers' Context

Petrea Redmond,
University of Southern Queensland, Australia,
redmond@usq.edu.au
Jennifer Lock,
University of Calgary, Canada,
jvlock@ucalgary.ca

Abstract: Twenty-first century teacher educators need to design learning experiences integrating technology for transformative learning. Bringing together the power of deep content knowledge, pedagogical knowledge and technological knowledge in an integrated manner is critical in the design of today's learning experience. The TPACK framework assists educators to gain competency and confidence to design technology-enhanced learning in ways that transform the learning experience for both students and teachers. This paper describes the TPACK findings of secondary pre-service teachers who have just completed their second professional experience placement in conjunction with a curriculum and pedagogy course. Pre-service teachers reported that they were developing the necessary confidence in working with the technology and designing learning using a TPACK framework. From the data, it was apparent that teacher educators are able use the framework to design, model and explore innovative teaching *with* technology to design TPACK learning experiences that are mindful and thoughtful.

Introduction

Pre-service teachers have difficulty finding appropriate information and communication technology (ICT) integration models both within their professional experience placements in schools and in their university courses. Without a robust model or framework, they struggle to develop the knowledge, skills and practice in relation to technology management, content, and pedagogies in conjunction with discipline content and pedagogy.

Further, Niess (2008, 2011) argued that teacher preparation courses need to emphasize the understanding of learning design skills to provide teaching and learning experiences for a diverse range of learners with differing learning needs in a technology-mediated classroom. As teacher educators, our role is to provide pre-service teachers with the knowledge, skills and experiences to be able to design and teach in today's and tomorrow's technology-enhanced learning environments. For pre-service teachers to be able to be designers of learning in these technology-enabled environment, Niess (2008) suggested effective experiences that can be integrated in courses include "exploring students' thinking and understanding when learning with technology" (p. 228).

ICT in classrooms can no longer be viewed as being an "option or a fun activity that is added to daily work" (Redmond & Lock, 2008, p. 4295). Rather, Redmond and Lock (2008) argue for a shift from ICT being viewed as "cute (e.g., something new or different) to being convenient (e.g., increase productivity) to being complementary (e.g., additional) to being core (e.g., integral and necessary to extend and enhance learning)" (p. 4295). The shift in thinking in terms of ICT in teaching and learning being *core* requires a change in how teachers and pre-service teachers view and value digital technology in their personal and professional lives. It also requires them to develop the necessary knowledge and skills in digital technology used, teaching with digital technology, technology supporting the pedagogy, and using technology to support the teaching and learning of content. It is important that the professional development and educational opportunities for teachers and pre-service teachers are not 'technocentric' (Harris, 2005) emphasising the tool rather than how it can support effective learning and teaching.

Koehler and Mishra (2008) described traditional pedagogical technologies as being characterized by *specificity, stability, transparency of function* and *transparency of perception*. The ever changing nature of digital technology may result in teachers feeling a lack of expertise and confidence in the use of emerging technology for teaching and learning. As such, "[l]earning to become flexible, creative educators who can transcend functional fixedness and other barriers is an ongoing and complicated process and must be confronted at both pre- and in-service levels" (Koehler & Mishra, 2008, p. 9). No longer can teacher educators and pre-service teachers see the use of ICT as being the domain of some other educational professional (e.g., ICT lead teacher, computer teacher or ICT technician). Rather, it is for them to develop the capacity to meaningfully integrate digital technology to support teaching and learning in knowledge creation environments.

Designing and facilitating rich learning within technology-enabled learning environments is complex. Harris, Mirshra, and Koehler (2009) argued:

> Understanding that introducing new educational technologies into the learning process changes more than the tools used – and that this has deep implications for the nature of content-area learning, as well as the pedagogical approaches among which teachers can select - is an important and often overlooked aspect of many technology integration approaches used to date (p. 395).

In today's teacher preparation programs, teacher educators are confronted with the challenge of how to design learning experiences for pre-service teachers that give them the experience of developing content, pedagogical, and technological knowledge through the integration of technology in their teaching practice. This paper reports on the learning experience *with* technology resulting from secondary pre-service teachers self-reporting on their TPACK competencies early in their program and prior to completing an ICT required course.

TPACK

Shulman (1986) introduced the concept of pedagogical content knowledge (PCK). He advocated that effective teachers need to integrate multiple domains of knowledge in the areas of pedagogy and content. He identified the following three distinct content knowledge categories: "(1) subject matter content knowledge, (b) pedagogical content knowledge, and (c) curricular knowledge" (p. 9). The complex nature of teaching and learning has been further complicated by the introduction of new and emerging digital technologies.

Mishra and Koehler (2006) built on Shulman's (1986) PCK concept in the development of TPACK (initially TPCK). "TPACK emphasizes the connections among technologies, curriculum content, and specific pedagogical approaches, demonstrating how teachers' understandings of technology, pedagogy, and content can interact with one another to produce effective discipline-based teaching with educational technologies" (Harris et al., 2009, p. 396). TPACK is an evolving construct to frame the complex and dynamic nature of learning and the knowledge required for teaching in technology enhanced learning environments (Doering, Veletsianos, Scharber, & Miller, 2009). Effective technology integration requires the intersection among the three key interdependent knowledge areas: pedagogical content knowledge, technology content knowledge and technological pedagogical knowledge. At the intersection of all these knowledge areas is technological pedagogical content knowledge (Koehler & Mishra, 2008). The TPACK framework provides an approach "to examine a type of knowledge that is evident in teachers' practice when they transform their own understanding of subject matter into instruction in which technology and pedagogies support students' understanding and knowledge creation" (Kinuthia, Brantley-Dias, & Clarke, 2010, p. 647).

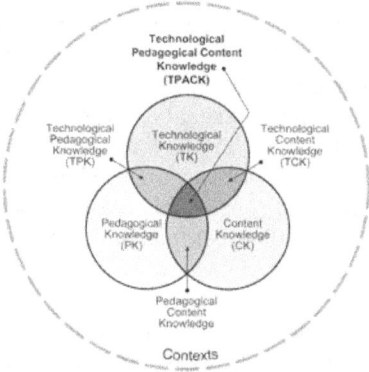

Figure 1. The TPACK Framework and Its Components. (http://www.tpck.org/)

Context

Internationally, there has been greater an emphasis placed on how ICT is being used to support and enhance learning and teaching in all educational contexts. Within Australia, the Federal Government funded the *Teaching*

Teachers for the Future (TTF) project which is designed to enable all pre-service teachers "to become proficient in the use of ICT in education" (Australian Government, n.d.). The project included all 39 Australian teacher education institutions and involved capacity building activities for pre-service teachers and teacher educators. As part of this work, the TPACK framework was used to track and report on pre-service teachers' development of knowledge in using ICTs to transform teaching and to provide new ways to engage learners. In addition to this national project, the Queensland and Australian Professional Standards for Teachers have clearly articulated explicit expectations that support the need for pre-service teachers to develop strong understandings of ICT integration. For example, teachers need to "Use ICT safely, responsibly and ethically" (Australian Institute for Teaching and School Leadership, 2012) and "use teaching, learning and assessment strategies and resources in which ICT is embedded" (Queensland College of Teachers, 2006).

In this study, the participants (*N*=55) were secondary pre-service teachers in their second year of a four year program or in their first semester of a one year after-degree graduate diploma program at a regional university in Australia. At the end of the semester, the pre-service teachers completed their second professional experience placement in schools. Further, the participants were enrolled in a curriculum and pedagogy course for Middle Years learners. The course was designed to model the integration of digital technology to support self-directed and collaborative learning. While inquiring into the issues for middle years learners and investigating curriculum and pedagogy for middle years learner, pre-service teachers participated in an international online collaborative activity to explore issues related to today's diverse and digital classroom, for example, inclusivity, Indigenous perspectives, cyber bullying, ESL and ICT integration. The course was offered in face-to-face, blended and online modes.

Method

Towards the end of the semester, pre-service teachers were asked to complete the online TPACK survey. The survey was modified from earlier studies found at http://www.tpack.org/. The survey originally had an elementary focus rather than secondary. It was modified to include a range of disciplines that secondary pre-service teachers could teach beyond Social Studies, Mathematics, Science and Literacy which were included the initial survey. The following disciplines were added: Languages other than English (LOTE), Computing, The Arts, and Health and Physical Education (HPE) and Business. Given the secondary pre-service teachers were required to teach in two different disciplines, this enabled them to self-report in two discipline areas.

It was a three-part survey: Part A elicited demographic information (10 questions); Part B was related to specific components of TPACK; and Part C included open ended questions regarding ICT for teaching and learning (6 questions). In Part B the questions asked pre-service teachers to self-rate their competency related to TPACK and the six other sub-elements of the TPACK construct (i.e. technology knowledge, content knowledge, pedagogical knowledge, pedagogical content knowledge, technological content knowledge, technological pedagogical knowledge) and also explore where they see models for TPACK in their teacher education program and while on field experience. The survey used a 5-point Likert scale (1 – Strongly Disagree to 5 – Strongly Agree). The survey was selected because the original survey had been revised based on previous research and included reliability score for each TPACK domain.

Findings and Discussion

Fifty-five (N=55) pre-service teachers completed the online survey. Forty-two percent who completed the survey were male and 58% were female. The majority of the participants (51%) were between the ages of 32 – 50. The next highest group was aged between the ages of 18 – 22 (22%); with 13% between the ages of 27-32; 11% between the ages of 23 – 26; and only 3% were over 50 years of age. The secondary disciplines represented within the study included: English, Mathematics, Sciences, Social Sciences, Computing, LOTE, HPE, The Arts and Business. In Queensland, high school teachers must select two disciplines to teach in. The most number of participants for the study were in the Sciences and Mathematics disciplines, followed by the Social Sciences and Business. Further, 67% of the participants were in the first semester of a one year graduate diploma program and 33% were in their second year of a four year Bachelor of Education. None of the participants had yet to complete a course related to integration of digital technology and learning and only 31% had participated in any professional development or other learning opportunities to assist them with the integration of ICTs in teaching and learning.

Table 1 presents the mean rating and standard deviation data for the seven inter-related TPACK components for this study based on the survey responses.

TPACK Components	Mean Rating (M)	Std Dev (SD)
Content Knowledge (CK)	4.31	0.62
Technology Knowledge (TK)	3.66	0.75
Pedagogical Knowledge (PK)	3.89	0.68
Pedagogical Content Knowledge (PCK)	4.24	0.52
Technological Content Knowledge (TCK)	4.13	0.71
Technological Pedagogical Knowledge (TPK)	4.02	0.51
Technological Pedagogical and Content Knowledge (TPACK)	4.10	0.71

Table 1: Mean and Standard Deviation Score Responses for TPACK Components

Overall, the pre-service teachers self-reported confidence in their knowledge in all seven components of TPACK with limited variance. The highest confidence was in their CK ($M = 4.31$, $SD = 0.62$). In the CK component those pre-service teachers who had Social Sciences as a teaching area had the highest confidence levels ($M = 4.48$, $SD = 0.57$) and HPE had the lowest ($M = 4.00$, $SD = 0.82$.). This is a similar result to Lee, Chai and Koh (2012) whose research found in the pre-service teachers first teaching area that CK was the component with the highest value of self-report.

In this study, the pre-service teachers' self-report indicated that their lowest confidence was in TK ($M = 3.66$, $SD = 0.75$) from a 5 point scale. This result aligns with the research outcomes of Schmidt, Baran, Thompson, Mishra, Keohler and Shin (2009) who found that TK had the second lowest level of confidence at 3.82 ($SD = 0.57$). In contrast, Lee, Chai and Koh (2012) found that PCK had the lowest mean and TK was rated mid-range across the seven TPACK components. Pre-service teachers reported they were confident in their abilities to learn to use technology with 82% reporting at the combined agree and strongly agree score. On the other hand 24% of them did report that they did not frequently play with technology and did not know about a lot of different technologies.

Pedagogical knowledge (PK) had the second lowest mean of the seven TPACK components ($M = 3.89$, $SD = 0.68$). Again, Schmidt et al., (2009) had lower levels of self-reporting ($M = 4.0$, $SD = 0.44$). The survey question where they had the lowest confidence was in their ability to identify common student understandings and misconceptions. All other question responses had a combined confidence (agree and strongly agree) at or above 79% with 96% self-report for their ability to adapt their teaching based on what students currently understand or do not understand.

Pedagogical Content Knowledge (PCK) had the highest mean in the self-report at 4.24 ($SD = 0.52$) within a five point scale. Those pre-service teachers who had LOTE as a teaching area had the lowest levels of comfort in PCK, with 32% of them suggesting they would have difficulty selecting effective teaching approaches to guide student thinking and learning in LOTE. The highest confidence in PCK was in the discipline of Business with over 80% agreeing or strongly agreeing they can select teaching approaches to guide student thinking and learning. The next highest were in Math, English and Social Science all with over 70% agree and strongly agree responses. Although the LOTE pre-service teachers did not report a low confidence in their content knowledge when combined with pedagogical knowledge they self-reported much lower than all of the other disciplines.

The pre-service teachers self-reported a Technological Content Knowledge (TCK) mean of 4.13 ($SD = 0.71$). Again the LOTE pre-service teachers reported lowest in their confidence to know about technologies that can be used to enhance understanding in their discipline (33%). HPE pre-service teachers also reported low with 21%

unsure about technologies for their discipline. The low TCK is not unexpected given they reported the lowest mean for CK. The disciplines with the highest levels of confidence with TCP were Business and Computing having over 70% with a combined agree/strongly agree self-rating. This should not be unexpected given high levels of technology in both disciplines.

The mean for Technological Pedagogical Knowledge (TPK) was 4.02 ($SD = 0.51$). The self-report from pre-service teachers in the Schmidt et al, (2009) study was 4.3 ($SD = 0.48$). The weakest element the pre-service teachers reported was in their confidence to provide help to others in TPK. All other components of TPK had a combined agree and strong agreement at over 80%.

The participants mean score for Technological Pedagogical and Content Knowledge (TPACK) was 4.1 ($SD = 0.71$). Figure 2 below provides the percentage responses for all nine disciplines for each of the five response options.

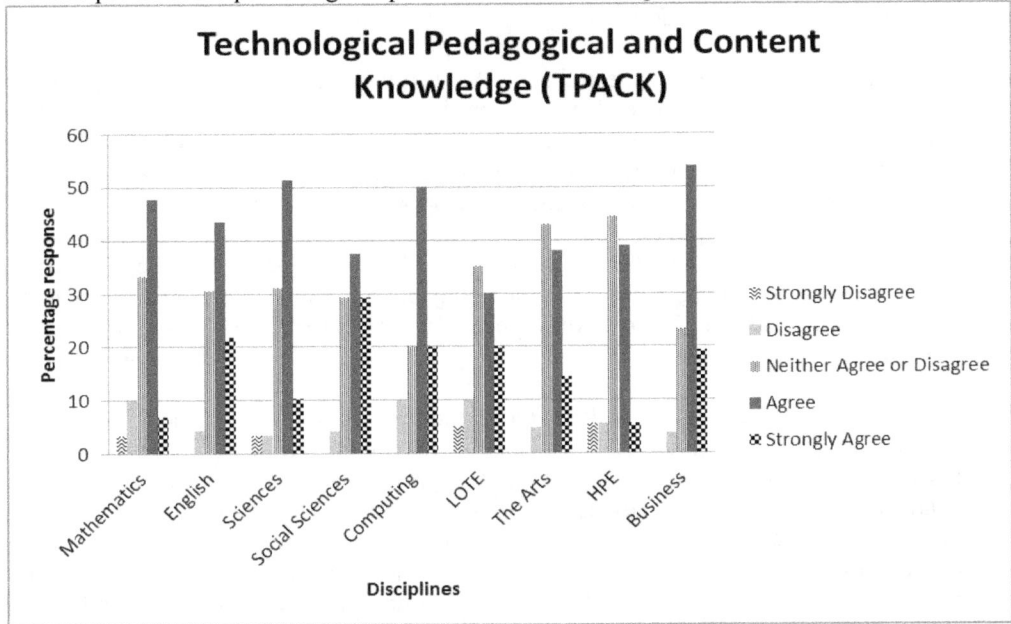

Figure 2: Self report TPACK according to disciplines

As indicated in Figure 2, the lowest level of confidence in TPACK was for pre-service teachers in the Mathematics discipline and the highest levels of strong agreement was in English (21.7%) and Social Sciences (29%). The highest level of agreement was for Business (53.8%). In all disciplines there were low levels of disagreement and strong disagreement about their TPACK confidence.

Pre-service teachers acknowledged strong support of modelling of TPACK by both their faculty instructors and their mentor teachers. More than 65% of the pre-service teachers indicated that their instructors in foundation courses and curriculum and pedagogy courses modelled various approaches of teaching and learning *with* technology. In open ended responses, the pre-service teachers explicitly provided examples from a range of courses that demonstrated the TPACK model by making the following statements: "In [course name] we used SimSchool. We were taught about differentiating tasks for students"; and "[course name] consistently focused on the combination of teaching strategies alongside of ICTs and content. Every lesson that was taught by her was sufficiently detailed and acted as an excellent reminder for the implementation of these areas into our planning and teaching".

The percentage of modelling was lower (45%) for instructors in other faculties. This is concerning because the majority of pre-service teachers will have 43% of their courses for the four year program completed in other faculties as they gain their content knowledge for their teaching areas. During their professional experience placement, 75% of the pre-service teachers indicated that their mentor teacher provided modelling of TPACK. The majority of pre-service teachers provided examples that went beyond the traditional use of PowerPoint, Internet searching and students using MS Word. They shared many examples of online collaboration, and the use ICT devices such as interactive whiteboard, iPods, probes, and graphic calculators used in various disciplines. Disappointingly several pre-service teachers commented that they did not see any modelling of TPACK during their professional experience with one pre-service teacher stating "No mentor has modelled any IT".

The majority of pre-service teachers self-reported high levels of comfort with regard to using and teaching with digital technology. One pre-service teacher stated "I'm quite comfortable using ICTs within my classes, as long as I've had time to play around with it and understand its functions". They were able to provide an example of how they have already done so on one of their professional experience placements. Most of the examples were discipline specific which positively emphasised the relationship between content, pedagogy and technology. For example, when "teaching natural disasters in SOSE I combined theory with a virtual national geographical natural disaster survival game"; and "I was teaching a senior art class and we used an Interactive whiteboard and located websites, images (artworks) and virtual tours of galleries".

What was disappointing was that it appeared from the data they have limited knowledge of what is possible using ICT for teaching and learning beyond what has been demonstrated or modelled to them within their teacher education program or on professional experience. For example, when they are asked to collaboratively create a wiki as part of assessment within their teacher education program and then on professional experience they have their students do the same. There was an acknowledgement by one pre-service teacher that

> "What is possible only relates to what is available in the school and class. To learn a bunch of technologies you are never going to use is disheartening and time consuming. This course teaches that knowledge is evolving and so my current knowledge of what is possible in terms of teaching with ICT depends on what is available".

However, within teacher education, as well as during their professional experience, pre-service teachers need to explore possibilities of how they can use ICTs beyond duplicating what they have already seen. This is affirmed by Harris and Hofer (2011) whose research suggest that professional development should not focus on the affordances of hardware and software but provide opportunities for exploring and sharing technological possibilities and consider "how best to select and combine them to match the student's standards-based learning needs" (p. 228). One pre-service teacher commented "Many things are possible with ICT and as technology continues to expand so does the numerous opportunities to integrate ICT in student learning. It is clear that ICTs can be used in all subject areas and enhance them".

Implications

Teacher education programs strive to create rich learning experiences and model effective practices using technology to enhance teaching and learning. Irrespective of location, the mandate to integrate technology to enhance learning and teaching requires teachers to have strong content knowledge, pedagogical knowledge and technological knowledge and practice. In the Queensland (Australia) context the recently funded *Teaching Teachers for the Future* project placed additional pressure on Australian teacher education providers to further develop the knowledge and experience of both teacher educators and pre-service teachers in the area of technology enhanced learning. The National and Queensland professional standards for teachers demand pre-service teachers demonstrate levels of knowledge and practice in this area also.

The pre-service teachers' self-perceptions of their confidence of the TPACK elements were high not only at the individual content, pedagogical and technology levels but also improving learning at the TPACK level. The course provided a lived experience of working in a technology-enhanced environment to develop content, pedagogical and technological knowledge and skills that pre-service teachers can draw from for their professional practice and was supported by learning in other courses and their professional experience placements. Further, pre-service teachers were able to provide specific examples from different courses where TPACK was effectively modelled for them and this is prior to them completing a specific course focusing on ICT integration.

Although this paper reports on a snapshot of data from one course within teacher education, working in a TPACK framework has a number of consequences for educators at all levels.

1) Teaching teacher educators. "[T]houghtful pedagogical uses of technology require the development of a complex, situated form of knowledge" (Mishra & Koehler, 2006, p. 1017). Teacher educators often see themselves as content experts or even pedagogical content experts. Very few would consider themselves technological pedagogical content experts. As such, teacher education programs require the right mix of experts and expertise to speak to content, speak to pedagogy, speak to technology, and to speak to TPACK.

2) Modelling and exploring options. Angeli and Valanides (2008) recommended that "teachers need to be explicitly taught how tool affordances can be used to transform content into powerful pedagogical forms" (p. 19). Practicing teachers and teacher educators need to provide these models and also opportunities for exploration and implementation of innovative learning experiences for pre-service teachers to integrate technology as part of their everyday teaching practices.

3) Designing for TPACK learning experiences. When designing learning experiences, teachers guide their thinking and decision-making based on their theoretical knowledge, contextual knowledge, epistemological beliefs, and practical experiences. In preparing to design TPACK experiences in teacher education, it must take into account teachers' current knowledge but also extend their knowledge about how to teach with technology (Angeli & Valanides, 2008).

4) Knowledge and context impact on practice. Doering et al, (2009) remind us that in terms to TPACK "teachers do not use all three of the knowledge domains equally" (p. 336). The level of content, pedagogical or technological knowledge used in practice is related to the individual context at the time and also an educator's personal knowledge of each domain. "[C]ontext influences both teacher knowledge and practice. In turn, teacher knowledge influences practice, and practice influences which types of knowledge are used more in the classroom" (p. 336).

Limitations and Conclusion

A limitation of this study was that the data were limited to one course in one regional university in Australia. This limits the ability to generalise beyond the initial context. A second limitation is that the data were collected through pre-service teachers self-rating their competencies for each of the elements of TPACK. Data collected through self-rating is subjective, although the impact of this is reduced through the use of a previously validated survey instrument. A third limitation is the fuzzy boundaries related to TPK, TCK and PCK. Researchers have difficulty articulating the boundaries around these areas (Graham, 2011) and it may be that the pre-service teachers similarly had difficulties distinguishing between these components and the questions related to them in the survey may be misleading. Future research in this area could include a longitudinal study tracking pre-service teachers over time. Further, the use of pre- and post-test within a course or over a program would provide additional information with regard to growth and change areas.

TPACK is a "unique body of knowledge that is constructed from the dynamic interaction of its constituent knowledge bases namely knowledge of content, pedagogy, learners, context, and technology" (Angeli & Valanides, 2008, p. 16). It provides a framework to build learning opportunities to enhance both the individual components of TPACK and TPACK overall. This paper forms part of an ongoing dialogue around the use of TPACK as we explore and embrace new possibilities of teaching and learning *with* technology. Specific teaching and modelling is required so that pre-service teachers adopt and use TPACK as part of their repertoire of practice, as well as, for teacher educators to be able to design and implement such a framework within their course contexts.

Teacher education programs can no longer teach basic technology skills in isolation from content and pedagogical contexts. The development of TPACK in teacher educators, practising teachers and pre-service teachers is a messy and ill-structured problem. The content, pedagogy and technology knowledge of teacher education are dynamic, complex and interrelated. The complexity of developing the next generation of teachers is compounded with the infusion of technology in both homes and in classrooms. TPACK provides a framework to unpack and repack the parts and the whole so to design and facilitate meaningful learning and teaching *with* technology. Our challenge as teacher educators is to design and model robust learning experiences using TPACK as a way to provide pre-service teachers with a lived experience to best inform their professional practice.

References

Angeli, C., & Valanides, N. (2008). *TPCK in pre-service teacher education: Preparing primary education students to teach with technology*. Paper presented at the Annual Meeting of the American Educational Research Association, New York City, NY.

Australian Government. (n.d.). Teaching Teachers for the Future. Retrieved October 15, 2012, from http://www.ttf.edu.au/

Australian Institute for Teaching and School Leadership. (2012). National Professional Standards for Teachers - Graduate Teachers. Retrieved October 15, 2012, from http://www.teacherstandards.aitsl.edu.au/CareerStage/GraduateTeachers/Standards

Doering, A., Veletsianos, G., Scharber, C., & Miller, C. (2009). Using the technological, pedagogical, and content knowledge framework to design online learning environments and professional development. *Journal of Educational Computing Research, 41*(3), 319-346.

Graham, C. R. (2011). Theoretical considerations for understanding technological pedagogical content knowledge (TPACK). *Computers & Education, 57*(3), 1953-1960.

Harris, J. (2005). Our agenda for technology integration: It's time to choose. *Contemporary Issues in Technology and Teacher Education, 5*(2), 116-122.

Harris, J., & Hofer, M. J. (2011). Technological pedagogical content knowledge (TPACK) in action: A descriptive study of secondary teachers' curriculum-based, technology-related instructional planning. *Journal of Research on Technology in Education, 43*(3), 211-229.

Harris, J., Mishra, P., & Koehler, M. (2009). Teachers' technological pedagogical content knowledge and learning activity types: Curriculum-based technology integration reframed. *Journal of Research on Technology in Education, 41*(4), 393-416.

Kinuthia, W., Brantley-Dias, L., & Clarke, P. A. J. (2010). Development of pedagogical technology integration content knowledge in preparing mathematics preservice teachers: The role of instructional case analyses and reflection. *Journal of Technology and Teacher Education, 18*(4), 645 – 669.

Koehler, M., & Mishra, P. (2008). Introducing TPCK. In AACTE Committee on Innovation and Technology (Ed.), *Handbook of Technological Pedagogical Content Knowledge (TPCK) for Educators* (pp. 1-29). New York, NY: Routledge.

Lee, K. S., Chai, C. S., & Koh, J. H. L. (2012). *Fostering Pre-service Teachers' TPACK Towards Student-centered Pedagogy*. Paper presented at the Society for Information Technology & Teacher Education International Conference.

Mishra, P., & Koehler, M. J. (2006). Technological Pedagogical Content Knowledge: A Framework for Teacher Knowledge. *Teachers College Record, 108*, 1017-1054.

Niess, M. L. (2008). Guiding preservice teachers in developing TPCK. In AACTE Committee on Innovation and Technology (Ed.), *Handbook of Technological Pedagogical Content Knowledge (TPCK) for Educators* (pp. 223-250). New York, NY: Routledge for the American Association of Colleges for Teacher Education.

Niess, M. L. (2011). Investigating TPACK: Knowledge growth in teaching with technology. *Journal of Educational Computing Research, 44*(3), 299-317.

Queensland College of Teachers. (2006). Professional Standards for Teachers. Retrieved October 15, 2012, from https://www.qct.edu.au/Publications/ProfessionalStandards/ProfessionalStandardsForQldTeachers2006.pdf

Redmond, P., & Lock, J. (2008). *Investigating Deep and Surface Learning in Online Collaboration*. Paper presented at the Society for Information Technology & Teacher Education 19th International Conference Las Vegas, Navada.

Schmidt, D., Baran, E., Thompson, A., Koehler, M., Punya, M., & Shin, T. (2009). *Examining preservice teachers' development of technological pedagogical content knowledge in an introductory instructional technology course*. Paper presented at the Society for Information Technology & Teacher Education International Conference.

Shulman, L. S. (1986). Those who understand: Knowledge growth in teaching. *Educational Researcher, 15*(2), 4-14.

Pen Casting in a Teacher Education Program

Nancy B. Sardone
Georgian Court University
United States
nsardone@georgian.edu

Barbara Cordasco
Georgian Court University
United States
cordascob@georgian.edu

Abstract: This study examined the use of a recording tool as a way to develop reflective practice of teacher candidates ($n=16$), who recorded a portion of their lesson plan content for future dissemination to K-12 students. Descriptive and frequency statistics were used to examine participant pretest/posttest data. Findings indicate that candidates recorded pen casts an average of 2.68 times, indicating metacognition was activated as they paid attention to the pen cast upon replay, identified areas for improvement, performed those improvements, and were concerned about the accuracy of information. Candidates offered their perspectives on the use of the tool and K-12 students and their parents provided commentary about this form of content delivery.

Introduction

Rehearsal strategies are cognitive processes used to learn and perfect skills and help students "think about a task prior to beginning it, while working at it, and upon its completion" (Polloway, Patton, & Serna, 2008, p.394). Metacognition activates when cognition fails, such as when a person recognizes that they did not perform a task correctly or understand what they just read or heard. Simply, it means thinking about *thinking*. Metacognitive processes are invoked when the learner attempts to rectify a situation (Roberts & Erdos, 1993). Metacognition is a thinking process that teacher educators work to instill in their candidates, as it is a critical skill of reflective practitioners. Yet, it is often elusive because it is difficult to explain, rather, it is a process to experience. This paper presents findings from an exploratory study where teacher candidates' used a new technology tool, smartpen, to record a portion of their lesson plan content, which captured both the audio and handwritten strokes (Figure 1). Candidates recorded a pen cast, reviewed it, identified errors, and made improvements. The pen cast recording was shown during lesson delivery and the URL was shared with students to review, as needed.

The more an item is rehearsed, the greater possibility that it will be retained. There are two types of rehearsal strategies - covert and overt. Covert rehearsal is defined by Levin, Guttmann, and McCabe (1977) as "internal verbal rehearsal or imagery generation" (p.339), a process in which the individual mentally visualizes and uses imagery to practice the skill to be performed. There is no outward physical movement associated with covert rehearsal, often used by athletes in preparation for a game or competition. For example, a freestyle swimmer will visualize the correct and efficient execution of the freestyle stroke. Silent rehearsal is another form of covert practice. Often referred to as 'talking to yourself', it includes approaches such as silently reading, rereading, or silently reciting information to be learned. In his research on rehearsal and the acquisition of a second language, Smith (1983), discussed the value of silent rehearsal and found it a useful strategy in helping people prepare for what they would like to say. More recently, Carrier (2003) in his study of college students' rehearsal strategies stated that although silent rehearsal is the most frequently selected method, it is not the most effective.

The second rehearsal strategy, overt rehearsal, is the "direct enactment of a desired behavior" (Kazdin & Mascitelli, 1982, p.251). It occurs when the individual practices the skill or information to be learned in an outwardly active manner. Verbal rehearsal is a prime example of overt practice. This may be accomplished by reading aloud, role-playing, or writing notes followed by reading them aloud and reviewing video tapes of the rehearsal. In their research on the study habits of college students, Justice and Dornan (2001) state that there are positive correlations between active study strategies and academic success. Past research has demonstrated that low-achieving students who listened to a lecture in class and then reviewed the same lecture on videotape not only completed their notes, but also brought the accuracy and wholeness of their notes up to the level of the highest achieving students (Kiewra et al., 1991). These studies demonstrate that review is needed in the learning process.

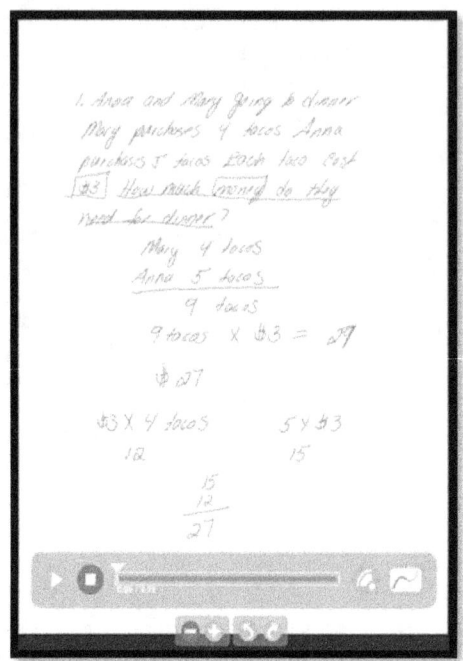

Figure 1. Image of handwriting capture

Metacognition is a critical skill of reflective practitioners. In their work on reflective teaching, Zeichner and Liston (1996) note the zeal for this topic has been adopted by "teachers, teacher educators, and educational researchers all over the world" (p.4) as an analytical mind tool designed to evaluate one's professional effectiveness. They describe the reflective process as teachers questioning their values and assumptions about what they are teaching, how they are teaching, and why they are teaching it. Skilled classroom technicians may present well-crafted lessons that meet required standards, but if they never stop to consider why they do what they do or how effective the lesson was, the possibility for deep and meaningful professional development is limited.

In the college of education where this study took place, the conceptual framework and associated knowledge base identifies four components candidates are expected to accomplish as they progress through the preparation program: acquire content knowledge, create effective learning environments, focus on learners, and develop as professionals. To foster candidate development as professionals, candidates are asked to reflect on their beliefs, values, and behaviors through writing (e.g. a paper espousing their personal philosophy of education) and be evaluated through observation of their classroom behaviors while student teaching (i.e. clinical supervisors and cooperating teachers). Content knowledge is measured via cumulative grade point average, scores on tests of basic reading, mathematics and writing skills (Accuplacer /Praxis 1), and Praxis II examinations in the discipline of the certification title. To best fit Zeichner and Liston's (1996) description of the reflective process, candidates need opportunities to investigate their own knowledge of content and develop a plan for correction prior to evaluation by others.

Classroom uses for pen casting to support instructional strategies are numerous, including procedural or rule-based knowledge needed for mathematics and writing. The use of pen casts to demonstrate mathematical procedures brings to light an important body of research related to math anxiety. Stereotypes that females lack mathematical ability persist and are widely believed by parents, teachers, and female college students themselves who have the highest levels of math anxiety of any college major (Furnham, Reeves & Budhani, 2002; Hembree, as cited in Beilock, Gunderson, Ramirez, & Levine, 2010). This is disturbing, as 83 percent of elementary school teachers in the United States are female and the elementary level of education is where a sound educational foundation for student learning is expected (National Education Association, 2010). Findings of a recent University of Chicago yearlong study of first and second grade teachers reveal a positive relationship between female teachers' high math anxiety and young female students' low math achievement (Beilock et al., 2010). Authors of this study suggest one way to strengthen elementary teacher preparation is to address issues of math anxiety. Further, results of a recent study (Taylor, 2008) suggest that underprepared students can learn math from different means of instruction as a way to address issues of math anxiety and achievement.

Review of the rehearsal strategies literature as a way to activate metacognition leads us to believe that a new technology tool, specifically smartpens, may be particularly useful in helping teacher candidates to more effectively practice their upcoming lesson by focusing on the content associated with that lesson. This method may ensure that accurate content knowledge is realized by teacher candidates before delivery to K-12 students. If the use of smartpens allows for the same type of active study strategies acknowledged as successful by Justice and Dornan (2001), where college students benefitted by recording and later reviewing course content, it would be expected that teacher candidates would benefit from making their own content recording, reviewing it for accuracy, and developing a plan for improvement. If pen casts activate metacognition, then teacher educators might consider smartpens for candidates' use as a rehearsal strategy as a way to foster the development of reflective practice. Further, working with technology tools helps teacher candidates learn how to integrate technology into the curriculum while experiencing their own processes of content investigation (Chua & Wu, 2005).

The Study

This study examined the use of a recording tool as a way to develop reflective practice of teacher candidates ($n=16$), who recorded a portion of their lesson plan contents for future dissemination to K-12 students. Descriptive and frequency statistics were used to examine participant pretest/posttest data. Candidates offered their perspectives on the use of the tool. K-12 students and their parents provided commentary about this form of content delivery. Institutional consent for conducting the study was obtained.

Participants

College juniors ($n=16$) enrolled in a private university in New Jersey participated in this study. They were enrolled in education course, Co-Planning and Co-Teaching for Inclusive Settings, which has a 15-week internship component consisting of 90-hours of classroom experience (one day per week for 15 weeks). It is the last course that candidates complete prior to student teaching. Gender split in the sample was 15 female; 1 male.

Research Questions

At the outset of this research study, we were interested in if pen casting could activate metacognition to ensure the accuracy of lesson content through reflective practice. In addition, we were interested if K-12 students and their parents thought the pen casts were helpful to their learning. The study was framed by the following research questions:

1. Do pen casts used for the purpose of reflective practice encourage metacognition in lesson development of teacher candidates?
2. Are the developed products (pen casts) helpful to students and their parents? If so, how so?

Modes of Inquiry

Two modes of inquiry were used in this study. In the first, data describing students' experiences were collected using a pre and posttest survey instrument, which was constructed using guidelines outlined by Gall, Borg, and Gall (1996). The pretest asked participants four questions. Question one asked for name and gender; question two about their familiarity with pen casting and the smart pen tool. Question three asked candidates if they liked to learn via video format, and question four provided an opportunity to offer an opinion about the effectiveness of pen casts as an instructional tool. The last two questions were asked to measure preconceived notions about learning through pre-recorded formats. K-12 students and their parents were asked to comment on the usefulness and perceived effectiveness of the pen cast created to teach a portion of a lesson. Comments were collected by the teacher candidate and/or cooperating teacher in the internship setting. Participants completed the five-question posttest survey upon course close. Question one asked candidates which subject they taught; question two asked how many K-12 students' reported viewing the pen cast after the lesson; question three asked candidates to report on their own observations of K-12 students while viewing the pen cast; question four solicited comments on student perceptions of their learning via pen cast; and question five asked candidates the opportunity to offer an opinion about the effectiveness of pen casts as an instructional tool.

The second mode of inquiry involved a two-step analysis of the final pen cast recording and notebook contents. The notebook contained a running record of each and every recorded pen cast. An analysis of the notebook would determine the existence of errors as well as provide the number of re-recordings made due to errors. Evidence of both - errors and re-recording - would indicate that metacognition was activated. Metacognitive training consists of coaching students in thinking skills that allow them to monitor their own learning (Thompson & Thompson, 1998). Candidates can practice, or rehearse, listening skills, active reading skills, and organizational skills via the smartpen tool.

Materials

Four *LiveScribe* ™ Smart Pen computers and associated micro-dot notebooks were purchased for this study. These small pen-sized computers contain built in microphones, speakers, and cameras needed for handwriting capture and audio recording. Using microdot technology, the written text is synchronized with audible voice. Computer desktop software was installed on each of the four laptop computers in preparation for the study. The *LiveScribe* ™ Smart Pen platform consists of a smartpen, microdot notebook, USB connection, desktop software, and the Web-based online community.

Procedures

In the course, Co-Planning and Co-Teaching for Inclusive Settings, candidates co-plan, design, and deliver lessons to K-12 students. Sixteen participants were shown how to create a pen cast using the smartpen during one class session. They were instructed to include a pen cast of content contained in one of their required eight lesson plans for future delivery in their student teaching internship. Both formal and ongoing informal discussions about this assignment were noted by one of the researchers, who also taught a section of the course.

When candidates were ready to record their pen cast, an equipment-ready office was provided. The candidate recorded themselves talking to fictitious students, while writing their lesson processes in the provided notebook. A transcript of a first-grade lesson on how to add two-digit numbers together is found below to get an idea of what candidates recorded in their pen cast. The pen cast can be heard and watched via the following URL: [http://tiny.cc/8dz1m]. "Today we are going to learn about adding two digit numbers. For example, 23 plus 51. First we need to stack the numbers. 23 is placed on top of 51. Since we're adding, don't forget the addition sign. Make sure the numbers are lined up. That way, it makes adding a lot easier. We are then going to add the ones column. The ones column consists of the numbers 3 and 1. Always remember that the ones column is on the right-hand side. So, the numbers 3 plus 1 gives us the result of 4. Next we are going to add the tens, which is the 2 and the 5. Always remember that the tens column is on the left-hand side. The numbers 2 and 5 gives us the result of 7. So, if the tens column gives us 7 and the ones column gives us 4, the result of the problem is 74. Good job. We just completed adding two-digit numbers."

Through plug and play technology, candidates uploaded the pen cast to the free *Livescribe* ™ host server/Web site (dubbed the "online community"). Once uploaded, candidates reviewed their pen cast and made a decision if it needed to be re-recorded. If yes, they re-recorded the lesson content using the notebook and smartpen and uploaded to the Web site. Once the candidate believed the pen cast was acceptable, they had an URL assigned This URL was viewed during the candidate's lesson delivery. It was disseminated students so they could access and review for homework. For elementary students, candidates wrote a note to parents indicating that a pen cast associated with that day's lesson material was available to help with homework, as needed. In the note, the Web-site address [URL] was provided.**Data Coding and Analysis**

Quantitative data describing students' experiences were collected using the pre and posttest instruments and entered into analytic software, *SPSS* for Windows. *SPSS* functions of frequencies and descriptives were run to analyze the quantitative data based on established coding schemes. Coding schemes for the pretest include: gender (male=0; female=1); familiarity with smartpens and pen casting (yes=1; 2=no); if candidate liked to learn via video format (yes=1; no=2; no experiences=3); and the opportunity to offer an opinion about the effectiveness of pen casts as instructional tools (disagree=1; disagree somewhat=2; not sure=3; agree somewhat=4; agree=5).

The following posttest survey coding was used: the subject taught in the lesson (math=1; science=2; language arts=3; social studies=4); how many K-12 students reported viewing the pen cast after the lesson (did not ask=0; one or two students=12; three or four students=34; five or more=50); the frequency of viewing (never=0; once=1; twice=2; three or more=30); and the opportunity to offer an opinion about the effectiveness of pen casts as instructional tools (disagree=1; disagree somewhat=2; not sure=3; agree somewhat=4; agree=5).

Qualitative data collected via the pre and posttest instruments were entered into analytic software, *Atlas.ti*. These textual data were generated from posttest question three, which asked candidates to report on their own observations of K-12 students while viewing the pen cast and question four, which asked for comments on student perceptions of their learning after the lesson pen cast. Additional comments solicited from parents were also analyzed. Frequently occurring comments made by candidates, K-12 students, and parents were clustered and themes of usefulness, attitude, and uses of pen casts.

Results and Discussion

Results of this study are framed by the research questions. To answer the first question, Do pen casts used for the purpose of reflective practice encourage metacognition in lesson development of teacher candidates, the number of times candidates' re-recorded pen casts was determined by reviewing the notebooks. They recorded and rerecorded their work an average of 2.68 times, (range 1-7 times) indicating that they paid attention to the pen cast upon replay, identified areas for improvement, re-recorded their work, and were interested in delivering accurate information in their lessons through the use of clarity and precision. This is metacognition and it was activated when candidates' recognized that they did not perform the task correctly. These results were similar to Justice and Dornan's study (2001), where college students benefitted by recording and later reviewing course content. Pen casts were helpful to teacher candidates in bringing about metacognition as a way to more efficiently practice lesson content by focusing on the content. Use of the pen computer tool may ensure that accurate content knowledge is realized by the candidate before delivery to K-12 students.

Osterman and Kottkamp (1993; 2004) agree with Zeichner and Liston (1996) noting the need for social interaction to develop reflective practices. Through regular dialogue with peers, teachers gain the opportunity to hear about others' practices, which can enhance personal understanding. Without the opportunity for structured social support and processing, the dark side of reflection can occur, leaving individuals feeling isolated and unsettled (Haddock, 1997). In the education course under study, all students created a pen cast as part of their course requirement. The assignment itself as well as in-class discussion about the assignment offered numerous opportunities for students to discuss their findings. Within teacher education programs, opportunities for students to share their internship teaching experiences in class as well as analyze why they did what they did allows for reflective growth for those participating in the discussion (Syrjala, 1996).

Candidates were asked about their experiences with pen casting at the outset of the study to assess their levels of willingness to engage, as this attribute affects attitude. Results revealed that no candidate in the sample had heard of pen casting prior to this study. The pretest mean was 3.94 on the question asking if the candidate believed that pen casts offered K-12 students with an effective way to learn course material, compared to the mean of 4.56 when asked the same question on the posttest. Nine participants reported an affinity for watching and listening to instructional videos to learn concepts and seven reported no experience with this type of format for learning. After teaching their lesson with a pen cast accompaniment, candidate comments included, "This is an awesome way for students to visually see a lesson" and "This format held student attention during the lesson." One candidate provided a nice summary, "Pen casting is a great teaching and learning tool. Pen casts are easy for the teacher to create and even easier for the students to use." To further answer research question one, a content analysis of the pen casts was performed. Results indicated that candidates had errors in their procedures and/or explanations in their earliest created pen casts. These errors were identified by the candidate and corrected, as evidenced in newer pen cast recordings. This provides evidence that the metacognition rehearsal strategy using the smartpen tool improved lesson content.

The second research question, are the developed products (pen casts) helpful to students and parents? If so, how so was investigated in a few different ways. First, it was determined that the most frequent grade level taught by candidates was 4th grade (31.3 percent), followed by 1st grade (25 percent), 3rd grade (12.5 percent), 5th grade (12.5 percent), 6th grade (12.5 percent), and 9th grade (6.3 percent). Since 81.3 percent of the sample comprised candidates teaching at the elementary level (K-5), the pen casts provided students with the opportunity to review lesson material at home with a parent or caretaker. In addition, most (75 percent) pen casts were created to teach mathematical procedures, 19 percent language arts content, 6 percent science content, and no lessons in social studies were recorded.

Post instruction behavior of the K-12 students clearly indicated that they found the pen casts helpful and took advantage of the opportunity to watch the product after the lesson. Fifty percent of K-12 students reported watching the pen cast after the lesson, indicating that many students needed to review taught material. In a follow-up study, asking K-12 students why they needed to review lesson material or what they gained from such a review would provide another window into the complexity of taught content and may reveal issues in the learning process.

The following information was obtained from parents, who provided notes to the teacher. Elementary students watched the pen cast at home once (50 percent), twice (18.8 percent), or three or more times (12.5 percent). Student comments revealed that they thought it "cool" to hear the teacher's voice in their own home. One comment indicated the significance of such an instructional resource as it addresses dual modalities, "When I listen to and watch the math problem being solved, I understand it better." Another student described the classroom environment where the math lesson was originally taught as disruptive, "Everyone is talking in school and it is hard to focus on the math lesson. At home, I can focus more so the pen cast that my teacher made for us was helpful."

Consistency of vocabulary terms in mathematical processes was a theme noted by parents as a way to reduce confusion at homework time indicated in the following comment, "The pen cast allowed me to hear the vocabulary terms the teacher used for math (i.e. grouping), which is different from the terms I was taught (i.e. borrowing)." Another parent of a student receiving special education said, "The video is a good re-teaching tool because sometimes, no matter how many times the material is covered in school, my son forgets how to solve math problems. If a series of pen casts were available online as an archive of what was taught that day, it would help to remind my son." Perhaps as a sign of environmentally concerned times, two parents noted an appreciation for electronic dissemination of lesson resources versus those in paper format as a way to reduce paper products in a 'green' measure. A sampling of pen casts created in this study is provided in Table 1.

Math Pen Casts	Grade	Topics Covered
http://tiny.cc/8dz1m	1st	How to add two digit numbers.
http://tiny.cc/f0xru	3rd	How to determine the mean, mode, and median of points scored by one player in a basketball game.
http://tiny.cc/ejzy7	4th	How to divide one/two digit numbers and checking work.
http://tiny.cc/mrhs6	4th	How to calculate life expectancy based on gender in the United States.

Table 1. Samples of Teacher Candidate Created Pen Casts

Upon close of this study, we offer some words about the challenges of recording with smartpens and using pen casts in K-12 classroom settings. First, some participants reported problems when trying to disseminate the URL due to district policy regarding access to non-approved Web sites. Further, it was reported that a few cooperating teachers would not allow student teachers to disseminate the pen cast URL out of consideration for K-12 students who do not have home access to the Internet; touting that unevenness in accessible resources as unfair. Paradoxically, most candidates reported that their cooperating teachers were excited about the potential of pen casting, advocating for its use with the school principal. Further, four post-hoc reports from cooperating teachers and teacher candidates alike indicated they purchased a smartpen for future instructional use.

Second, we underestimated the excellent quality of the microphone of the smartpens. Although a quiet office was provided for recording, background sounds were easily picked up. In addition, candidates would have benefitted from a mini-lesson about the importance of voice inflection, using humor, and the importance of providing an authentic context for problem solving. Only two candidates provided such; one taught how to calculate the average life expectancy in the United States; and another taught how to calculate the value of being a 'team player' through statistics.

In terms of uses for teaching and learning, one graduate of the education program under study uses pen casts regularly in his 8th Grade Algebra class. He utilizes a flipped classroom strategy, where students are instructed to watch 10-minute pen casts teaching mathematical procedural knowledge. Students then enter his class with a basic understanding, then reinforced by his guided classroom instruction. His students believe his lessons have value, as evidenced by some of the comments he has received: "…if you forgot your notebook or a problem you can just look at the *Livescribe* online. I use it for notes when I am absent and if I forgot how to do something that was taught in class. My favorite activity that you used it for was when you were at the teacher's convention and you taught us a lesson in class without even being here."

With the increase in popularity of tablet computers for classroom use, we suspect that apps will become more the norm for teacher candidates (and teachers, too) to rehearse lesson content, record lesson procedures for student use, and other forms of visual instruction. Quality apps for the iPad device, such as *Chalk Board* (Conol), *Whiteboard* (Greengar Studios), and *Screen Chomp* (TechSmith) are readily available and free. *ScreenChomp* is the best choice if you plan to combine audible sounds with synchronized key strokes. Further, with *ScreenChomp* you can import photos from the library or take a photo and use as the background for your lesson activity; a feature not available with the current *LiveScribe* ™ smartpen offering.

Chua and Wu's (2005) words are worth repeating - working with technology tools helps teacher candidates learn how to integrate technology into the curriculum while experiencing their own processes of content investigation. Although the smartpen tool and its "APP" cousins offer many classroom applications, our goal was to provide a rehearsal tool to candidates to help them become self-investigators and aid in self-regulation in a non-invasive, non-evaluative way en route to becoming a reflective practitioner.

Limitations

The sample size in this study is small (*n*=16), making it difficult to generalize to the larger population. In addition, pen cast dissemination is far from perfect. The URL that the pen cast renders is exceptionally long and may cause an unintended delay in the taught lesson. We recommend that candidates truncate the URL by using an URL shortening service such as tiny.*URL* (http://tiny.cc/) or bitly (https://bitly.com/).

References

Beilock, S., Gunderson, E., Ramirez, G., and Levine, S. (2010, February 2). Female teachers' math anxiety affects girls' math achievement. *Proceedings of the National Academy of Sciences of the United States of America, 107*(5) 1860-1863.

Carrier, K. A. (2003). Improving high school English language learners' second language listening through strategy instruction. *Bilingual Research Journal, 27*, 383-410.

Chua, B. and Wu, Y. (2005).Designing technology-based mathematics lessons: A pedagogical framework. *Journal of Computers in Mathematics and Science Teaching, 24*(4), 387-402.

Furnham, A., Reeves, E., and Budhani, S. (2002). Parents think their sons are brighter than their daughters: Sex differences in parental self-estimations and estimations of their children's multiple intelligences. *The Journal of Genetic Psychology, 163*(1), 24-39.

Gall, M.D, Borg, W.E., & Gall, J.P. (1996). *Educational research*. White Plains, NY: Longman.

Haddock, J. (1997). Reflecting in groups: contextual and theoretical considerations within nurse education and practice. *Nurse Education Today, 17*, 381-385.

Justice, E. M., & Dornan, T. M. (2001). Metacognitive differences between traditional-age and nontraditional-age college students. *Adult Education Quarterly, 51*(3), 236-249.

Kazdin, A. & Mascitelli, S. (1982). Covert and overt rehearsal in homework practice in developing assertiveness. *Journal of Consulting and Clinical Psychology, 83*, 240-245.

Kiewra, K., DuBois, N., Christian, D., McShane, A., Meyerhoffer,M., and Roskelley, D. (1991). Note-taking functions and techniques. *Journal of Educational Psychology, 83*, 240-245.

Levin. J., Guttman, J., & McCabe, A. (1977). Notes and comments: Distinguishing between two covert learning strategies with elementary school children. *American Educational Research Journal, 14*(3): 339.

National Education Association (NEA). (2010). *Status of the American public school teacher 2005–2006*. Washington, DC: National Education Association. http://www.nea.org/assets/docs/2005-06StatusTextandAppendixA.pdf

Osterman, K. & Kottkamp, R. (1993). *Reflective practice for educators: Improving school through professional development*. Newbury Park: Corwin Press, Inc.

Osterman, K. & Kottkamp, R. (2004). *Reflective practice for educators: Professional development to improve student learning* (2nd Ed.). Thousand Oaks: Corwin Press.

Polloway, E., Patton, J., & Serna, L. (2008). *Strategies for teaching learners with special needs*. Upper Saddle River: Pearson, Merrill, Prentice Hall.

Roberts, M. J., & Erdos, G. (1993). Strategy selection and metacognition. *Educational Psychology, 13*, 259-266.

Syrjala, L. (1996). The teacher as a researcher. In Eeva Hujala (Ed.) *Childhood Education: International Perspectives*. Finland: Association for Childhood Education International, Oulu University. ED 403 069.

Smith, B. (1983). Fundamental problems in phonics. *Studies in Second Language Acquisition, 6* (1), 88-93.

Taylor, J. (2008, September 22). The effects of a computerized-algebra program on mathematics achievement of college and university freshmen enrolled in a developmental mathematics course, **The Free Library**. http://www.thefreelibrary.com/The effects of a computerized-algebra program on mathematics... a0188062763

Thompson, L., and Thompson, M. (1998). Neurofeedback combined with training in metacognitive strategies: Effectiveness in students with ADD. *Applied Psychophysiology and Biofeedback, 23*(4): 243.

Zeichner, K. & Liston, D. (1996). *Reflective teaching: An introduction*. Mahwah: Lawrence Erlbaum Associates, Publishers.

Aspects of an Emerging Digital Ethnicity

Nan B. Adams
Southeastern Louisiana University, United States
Nan.Adams@selu.edu

Thomas A. DeVaney
Southeastern Louisiana University, United States
Thomas.Devaney@selu.edu

Abstract: The Digital Ethnicity Scale (DES), utilizing Longstreet's (1978) model of the Aspects of Ethnicity, was developed to describe the impact human interaction with digital communication technologies is having on cultural development. Longstreet's socio-biological definition of ethnicity focuses on cultural development during the earliest stages of human development, prior to the onset of children's abstract thinking. The ultimate goal for the development of the Digital Ethnicity Scale is to describe those aspects of digital ethnicity and collect these descriptions along with demographic data to achieve profiles of various digital ethnicities. These digital ethnic profiles are intended to provide insight into the social and educational needs of rapidly changing societal groupings by providing guidance for educational leaders, teachers and teacher education programs to prepare candidates who will be able to address the biological, social and cognitive changes brought about by pervasive use of digital communication technologies. A 5-phase development process, including the development and validation of both Likert-type items and semantic differentials, was conducted with more than 2000 respondents. Both theoretical and practical results of this inquiry are presented.

The availability and use of digital communication technologies increasingly pervades every facet of our lives. The influence of these technologies is changing human actions and beliefs; the construction of our social reality appears to be in flux. A growing segment of the population 'text' rather than 'talk'; couples fall in love online and meet after the fact; gender identity is becoming a choice made not by biology but by a screen name or the physical appearance of an avatar. Social groups are formed in virtual space that provides new kinds of common identity to previously disparate individuals. Virtual schools prepare learners worldwide, while having no physical campus for teachers and learners to congregate. Palfrey and Gasser (2008) discuss the development of 'digital natives' whose "culture is global in scope and nature. Whether physically based in Rio de Janeiro, Shanghai, Boston, Oslo, or Cape Town, Digital Natives . . . form part of global culture of their peers. They are connected to each other in terms of how they relate to information, how they relate to new technologies, and how they relate to one another" (p. 13). Schools have always been the institutions that prepare current and future society; they are where organized, formal learning is intended to take place. As virtual learning experiences increasingly replace traditional learning activities, it is critical to study those aspects of society and the resultant ethnicities that are guided by this change in teaching and learning practices.

Marc Prensky (2001a, 2001b) writes of Digital Natives and Digital Immigrants and how children are being socialized in vastly different ways than their parents. He states that "it is now clear that as a result of this ubiquitous [digital] environment and the sheer volume of their interaction with it, today's students think and process information fundamentally differently than their predecessors" (2001a, para 4). When discussing the implications for cultural loss due to the changes that are occurring to children immersed in interaction with digital technologies, Prensky (2001b) cites one key area of loss as the skill of reflection. He defines reflection as the ability to generalize and create mental models from our experiences and suggests that the implication for this loss is to develop educational strategies for developing reflection and critical thinking to counteract this seemingly media-induced loss in children. His most recent writings center on the development of what he terms Digital Wisdom (Prensky, 2009). He calls for concerted efforts to realize the impact on child development both intellectually and socially and calls for teaching 'digital wisdom'. He states that "the digitally wise distinguish between digital wisdom and mere digital cleverness". He concludes that "It is through interaction of the human mind and digital technology that the digitally wise person is coming to be. I believe it is the time for the emerging digitally wise among us . . . to embrace digital enhancement and to encourage others to do so." These aspects of child development are critical issues for teacher educators as they prepare teachers to address student learning styles and needs. Koutropoulos (2011) in his critique of the monolithic assumptions of Prensky's Digital Natives contends that from a social perspective, in contrast to writings about digital natives that portrayed digital natives as masters of their own destiny, Johnson (2006), a digital native herself teaching other digital natives, indicates that digital natives are complacent, actively seek authority figures and are unable to cast a critical gaze on their lives. This provides some argument for the role of teacher and learner in this digital age. Koutropoulos (2011) goes on to suggest that no organized research has been done to identify the real changes to education that should be developed in response to pervasive societal use of digital technology, and complains that we are not talking about pedagogy, and what is really good for the learners, but taking suppositions based on speculation rather than research to drive practice. Exploring the aspect of social value patterns included in this model to describe changes in our rapidly increasing digital society intends to provide insight into the demonstrated needs of learners that may be addressed by informed teaching practices.

Small and Vorgan (2008) discuss the effects of extensive interaction with digital technologies and observe that "as the brain evolves and shifts its focus toward new technological skills it drifts away from fundamental social skills, such as reading facial expressions during conversation or grasping the emotional context of a subtle gesture" (p.2). They talk of an increasing "brain gap" (p.3) resulting separate cultures. Small and Vorgan go on to discuss changes in communication preference style that often affects issues of privacy, how people meet socially, and often how they form loving attachments.

As digital technologies increasingly occupy the lives of young children, influencing their understanding of the world that surrounds them and influencing their development of communication and language skills, it is critical that deliberate analysis of the changes take place. Their engagement with these digital tools is shaping the preferences young children develop for their construction of reality and guides their interaction with their surroundings. The implications for the increased use of digital communication technologies on current and future educational practice are profound, and must be deliberately studied and addressed by education professionals to guide effective educational practice.

Longstreet's (1978) construction of the concept of ethnicity, originally developed to describe patterns, or aspects, that represent areas of social behavior that may exist among members of a social group, appears to provide an appropriate and useful framework for investigating the impact digital communication tools are having on cultures and societies. Her definition of ethnicity focuses on cultural development during the earliest stages of human development, prior to the onset of children's abstract thinking. This focus captures much of the timeframe given schools and teachers to accomplish the task of shaping formal and informal learning activities for students.

The model developed by Longstreet was tested in terms of the digital environment so that we could develop survey items to collect data about the different aspects of ethnicity using a digital lens. The ultimate goal for the development of the Digital Ethnicity Scale is to describe those aspects of digital ethnicity and collect these descriptions along with demographic data to achieve profiles of various digital ethnicities. These digital ethnic profiles may provide insight into the social and educational needs of rapidly changing societal groupings with hopes of providing guidance for future educational practice.

Varying Definitions for the Term Ethnicity

For most, the word 'ethnicity' conjures both abstract and concrete meanings, which are often contextual. In the concrete uses of government and institutions, ethnicity usually denotes race. In the more abstract, it often means a group of humans who are identified through shared characteristics that may be real or assumed. This ambiguity seems to track the lack of agreement among scholars that has ebbed and flowed along with interest in the endeavor of building a consensus for meaning. Isajiw (1974) analyzed 65 sociological and anthropological studies and found that only 13 had definitions for the term ethnicity, with the remaining 52 having no explicit definition at all. With no real resolution in sight, the term has been defined as needed by institutions and individuals to gather data or describe groups of people.

Two major viewpoints guide the issue: objectivists, who regard ethnic groups as cultural and social entities with distinct boundaries that are characterized by lack of interaction and relative isolation, and subjectivists, who describe ethnic groups as culturally constructed categorizations that guide social behavior and interaction and define these groups by subjective self-categorizations (Jones, 1997). This begs the question of whether ethnic groups are based on shared, objective cultural practices that exist independently or the more subjective notion that ethnic groups are constructed by the processes of perception and derived social organization of their members.

Longstreet's Construction of Meaning for the Concept of Ethnicity

Longstreet (1978), unlike other scholars, provides the only constructed model for describing identified aspects of ethnicity. This model provides the socio-biological definition of ethnicity as being "that portion of cultural development that occurs before the individual is in complete command of his or her abstract intellectual powers and that is formed primarily through the individual's early contacts with family, neighbors, friends, teachers, and others as well as with his or her immediate environment of the home and neighborhood" (p.19). This construction of the concept of ethnicity, originally developed to describe patterns that may exist among members of a social group, provides an appropriate and useful framework for investigating the impact digital communication tools are having on educational practices of cultures and societies.

Our children are interacting with computers very young, even as early as 2 or 3 years of age, which puts them into the age when they are powerful learners of languages of all kinds – including the operational languages of computing. Longstreet's aspects of ethnicity are helpful in describing children growing up engaged and often surrounded by digital environments that encompass their early childhood. They are engaged in interactive video and computer games and other forms of digital communication at a time when biological development and ethnic understandings are most influenced, and yet these young children are not yet in command of their full abstract and intellectual powers and there is a lack of conceptual awareness of what is happening to them. The ultimate goal for the development of the Digital Ethnicity Scale is to describe those aspects of ethnicity using a digital lens and collect these descriptions along with demographic data to develop profiles of various digital ethnicities. These digital ethnicity profiles are intended to provide guidance for effective educational practices to serve the needs of a rapidly changing digital world.

Aspects of Ethnicity – The Underlying Theory and Working Model

Longstreet developed a functional model for the 5 aspects that may be used to describe her concept of ethnicity. These aspects are (a) social value patterns, (b) intellectual mode, (c) orientation mode, (d) verbal communication, and (e) nonverbal communication. A brief description of each follows:

1. Verbal communication may be described as the structure a person uses when communicating orally. The rules or patterns for this oral communication are learned by children prior to the development of their abstract intellectual abilities. The ability to learn language seems to be a universal capacity of humankind (Longstreet, 1978, p. 42).
2. Nonverbal Communication may be described as a system of facial expression, body movements and spatial arrangements that communicate meaning to others (Longstreet, 1978, p. 59).
3. Orientation Mode refers to patterns of behavior used, regardless of the presence of others, as ways of orienting oneself to the differing contexts of one's usual environment. It may be described as the way one communicates with themselves (Longstreet, 1978, p. 74). The orientation mode may be the most complex of the described modes. This mode is influenced by the social environment but ultimately becomes the ways one becomes comfortable in their own environment when no communication takes place.
4. Social Value Patterns are based on the sets of persistent behaviors that a group expects from its members and upon which it places certain values and upholds with certain beliefs (Longstreet, 1978, p. 89).
5. Intellectual Modes are described by Longstreet as the most emotionally charged aspect of ethnicity. This mode is not intended to deal with human innate intelligence, but rather reflect the way we externalize our thoughts,

how we approach a problem, what gets our full attention, what details we are most likely to recall. Intellectual modes link intellectual performance to past experiences (Longstreet, 1978, pp. 106-107).

When seeking a model to describe human development through social interaction, and especially social interaction in digital communication environments, the notion of identity often emerges. The authors wish to acknowledge that identity focuses on the individual's definition of self (Erikson ,1968), whereas ethnicity describes an individual's place or believed inclusion within a cultural group. This inquiry focuses on the individuals as they relate to a group.

Digital Ethnicity as A Specialized Form of Ethnicity

When constructing a scale to describe those aspects of ethnicity that may be influenced by early and pervasive interaction with digital communication technologies, consideration of which aspects to investigate was a challenging task. Longstreet predicted a variety of contextual ethnicities that may be distinct ethnicities. These distinct and specialized ethnicities were described as being grounded in one or more of the identified 5 Aspects of Ethnicity. For example, Scholastic ethnicity may be a distinct form of ethnicity grounded in intellectual mode but still related to and having impact upon the other modes identified within this construction of ethnicity. National ethnicity may be a distinct form of social value patterns and communication modes. Gender ethnicity may be a distinct form of orientation mode. In this vein, the current research has sought to describe Digital Ethnicity as a distinct form of the combined Communication Mode, which is a combination of verbal and non-verbal communication mode.

The Digital Ethnicity Scale

Over a period of 2 years, the Digital Ethnicity Scale (DES) was developed and refined to test the construct of Digital Ethnicity using Longstreet's Aspects of Ethnicity Model. The final version of the Digital Ethnicity Scale includes a two-section structure. The first section contains 12 Likert-type items that were retained from the previous analyses. The second section of the survey consists of 16 semantic differentials designed to measure Communication Mode.

Final analysis in the development process was based on an initial sample of 850 participants. Seven respondents reported an age that was less than 18 and were removed from the analyses. Additionally, 14 respondents did not report an age and were removed from the analyses. Of the remaining 829 respondents the majority were female (72.3%) and reported their race as White (69.7%). The age of the respondents ranged from 18 to 80 with a mean of 36.71. The majority of respondents reported using the computer everyday (84.7%) and using the computer for a combination of work and recreation.

Section 1: Intellectual Mode, Orientation Mode, and Social Value Pattern

The final version of the Digital Ethnicity Scale contained 12 items designed to measure the three aspects of Intellectual Mode, Orientation Mode, and Social Value Pattern. Consistent with the previous revision, the scale was analyzed using exploratory factor analysis. The final analysis was conducted by specifying a 3-factor solution with a Varimax rotation. Because of previous refinements to the items, the suppression level for the factor loadings was increased to .50.

The results of the 3-factor solution from the factor analysis are presented in Table 1a. The results indicate that the items loaded as predicted with all items loading above the .50 criterion. The first factor contained the four items related to Orientation Mode and accounted to 17.87% of the variance. Factor 2 contained the Social Value Pattern items and accounted to 15.82% of the variance. The final factor contained the four items related to Intellectual Mode and accounted for 15.57% of variance. Finally, the reliability estimates ranged from .570 to .648.

Item	Factor 1	Factor 2	Factor 3
I respond to emails immediately	.694		
I would rather send email than talk on the phone	.675		
I leave my computer on all of the time just in case I need to get online	.652		
	.600		
I am usually on the internet at the same time every day		.775	
Posting pictures, even misleading ones, on the web doesn't hurt anyone		.736	
		.590	
It is okay if I pretend to be someone else online		.571	
It is okay to talk about my private life online with people I do not know			.701
			.693
It is okay to download or copy music for free			
Using a computer makes me smarter			.656
Because of the internet I am able to solve problems myself that I would not be able to do otherwise			.584
Computers make us question what we know			
The internet helps me make good decisions			
Proportion of variance explained	17.87	15.82	15.57
Reliability	.634	.570	.648
Identified Aspect of Ethnicity	Orientation Mode	Social Value Pattern	Intellectual Mode

Table 1a. Factor Loadings for Revised 15 Item Digital Ethnicity Scale

Section 2: Semantic Differentials to Measure Communication Mode

The initial analyses of the semantic pairs identified a 3-factor structure consistent with the findings of Osgood, Suci, and Tannenbaum (1957). For the final phase of the development, 13 semantic pairs were retained and biased/fair was replaced because it did not load on any factor during initial analyses. Additionally, two pairs were added to the set for a total of 16 semantic pairs. The structure of the 16-item set was examined using a factor analysis with an eigenvalue greater than 1 extraction criterion, Varimax rotation, and .50 display criterion for factor loadings. The results of the analysis are presented in Table 1b.

Pair	Factor 1	Factor 2	Factor 3	Factor 4
hard-easy	-.833			
easy to understand-confusing	.795			
fluent-awkward	.776			
comfortable-anxious	.743			
chaotic-ordered	-.613			
wholly engaging-insufficient	.515			
trustworthy-bogus		.777		
ethical-corrupt		.702		
personal-impersonal		.566		
part of a community-isolated		.522		
informative-entertaining			.682	
public-privacy			.608	
influential-inconsequential			.558	
interesting-boring			.534	
choice-need				.762
text intensive-highly graphic				
Proportion of variance explained	22.28	15.79	10.81	8.20
Semantic Space Dimension	Evaluation	Potency	Activity	

Table 1b. Factor Loadings for 16 Semantic Pair Set

The results of the factor analysis of the 16 pairs indicated a 4-factor solution that accounted for 57.08% of the variance. The first three factors corresponded to the dimensions of Evaluation, Potency, and Activity, respectively, and accounted for 48.88% of the variance. The fourth factor only contained one pair, choice/need, and represented an additional unique dimension. Osgood et al. (1957) acknowledged that semantic spaces would likely have more than the three dominant dimensions. Therefore, the structure of this set of semantic pairs is consistent with the common structure proposed by Osgood et al. Additionally, the failure of the text intensive/highly graphic pair to load on any of the factors suggests that is also represents a unique dimension. However, the variance accounted for by the dimension is not large enough to be extracted as a factor in the solution.

Discussion

As digital communication technologies increasingly replace face-to-face communication and interactions, the experiences that construct human perceptions of reality are altered. Marshall McLuhan (1964) observed that "Everybody experiences far more than he understands. Yet it is experience, rather than understanding, that influences behavior" (p. 277). The Digital Ethnicity Scale seeks to describe those aspects of ethnicity that are influenced by immersive experience with digital communication tools.

When constructing a scale to describe those aspects of ethnicity that may be influenced by early and pervasive interaction with digital communication technologies, consideration of which aspects to investigate was challenging. We were unable to obtain consistent separate sets of data for the aspects of verbal and non-verbal communication. It appears that the digital media, not television but all other digital communication environments, has impacted the verbal forms of communication in ways that cannot be tested separately from nonverbal communication and in ways that do not exist in other environments. This fusion may well be a major characteristic of digital ethnicity, but not one that can as yet be characterized by the instrument we have developed. However, digital influences on those ethnic aspects of Social Value Patterns, Orientation Mode and Intellectual Mode provided distinct descriptions of digital ethnic behavior that appear to be useful for the development of an instrument focused on construction of digital ethnic profiles.

Just because this research did not find a description of the changes occurring to communication modes does not mean that these changes are not occurring. McLuhan's 1967 conception that the *Medium is the Message* provides insight into this media-induced change and is probably more relevant now than when it was originally discussed. Even more relevant may be pursuing the impact of the digital environment on the construction of meaning and even of reality.

Further Exploration and Expansion of the Theoretical Basis of This Research

There exists a large amount of interaction between the world around us and the digital environment – our students are currently experiencing multiple environments that the individual is negotiating. For example, students write on a computer, stop and talk, and they may well send copies of the writing back and forth digitally and then discuss the work verbally. The investigation of this negotiation of a variety of learning environments is not studied with this current inquiry. This should be part of further study, but may be informed by the development of digital ethnic profiles. The ability to understand and accommodate changing orientation and intellectual modes along with an understanding of changing social value patterns that result from interaction with digital media will inform educators and other social scientists as we work to understand this emerging digital society.

Recommendations for Future Research

Through exploratory analyses, the current research has identified the foundations of a scale that reflects Longstreet's aspects of ethnicity applied to the interaction with digital environments. However, the following recommendations should direct future research concerning the development and validation of the DES.

First, the analyses conducted in the present research were based on the total sample, which was skewed with respect to gender (72.3% females) and race (69.7% white), and did not examine the factor structure for subgroups. Future research should examine the scale properties for subgroups based on demographic characteristics such as gender, race, and age through techniques such as confirmatory factor analysis. Because the current research included only respondents who were 18 years old or older, future research should also attempt to sample and examine the scale properties for individuals who are under 18 years. This is particularly relevant based on Longstreet's assumption that ethnicity is developed prior to the onset of abstract thinking in children and the volume of technology to which today's children are exposed.

Second, the current research has provided a foundational set of items related to each of Longstreet's aspects of ethnicity. Although the reliability estimates for the final set of items was acceptable for exploratory analyses, future research should continue to refine and potentially add items to increase the reliabilities of the subscales. Enhancing the reliabilities will also impact usability of the scale for research and practice.

Third, the current research focused on the development of an initial item set related to Longstreet's aspects of ethnicity. However, in order for the scale to have practical applications, procedures to calculating and reporting results must be determined. This is based on the assumption that different profiles will exist based on selected demographic data.

Fourth, future research should undertake the reconceptualization of Communication Modes (as a possible combination of Longstreet's original Verbal and Non-Verbal modes) in terms of the digital environments.

Fifth, because this inquiry has combined all of the different digital environments into one (computers, video games, intelligent phones, webcams, etc.), an investigation into the different types of digital environments should be undertaken.

Finally, it is commonly understood that interaction with digital technologies is changing the structures of society and varying aspects of human nature. Digital environments for work and play will only increase, therefore, the theoretical constructs describing digital ethnicity should be pursued further. McLuhan's work of the 60s and 70s and Hall's undertakings may provide further avenues for investigation.

References

Erikson, E. (1968). *Identity: Youth and crisis*. New York, NY: W. W. Norton.
Isajiw, W. (1974). Definitions of ethnicity. *Ethnicity 1*, 111-24.
Johnson, K. (2006). The millennial teacher: Metaphors for a new generation. **Pedagogy, 6**(1), 7-24. Retrieved from http://muse.jhu.edu/journals/pedagogy/v006/6.1johnson.html
Jones, S. (1997). *The archeology of ethnicity*. London: Routledge.
Koutropoulos, A. (2011). Digital natives: Ten years after. *Journal of Online Learning and Teaching, 7*(4). Retrieved from http://jolt.merlot.org/vol7no4/koutropoulos_1211.htm
Longstreet, W. S. (1978). *Aspects of ethnicity*. New York, NY: Teachers College Press.
McLuhan, M. (1964). *Understanding media: The extensions of man*. New York, NY: McGraw-Hill.
McLuhan, M. (1967). *The medium is the message*. New York, NY: Bantam Book.
Osgood, C., Suci, G., & Tannenbaum, P. (1957). *The measurement of meaning*. Urbana, IL: University of Illinois Press.
Palfrey, J., & Gasser, U. (2008). *Born digital: Understanding the first generation of digital natives*. New York, NY: Basic Books
Prensky, M. (2001a). Digital natives, digital immigrants. *On the Horizon, 9*(5), 1-6. Retrieved from www.marcprensky.com
Prensky, M. (2001b). Digital natives, digital immigrants, part 2: Do they really think differently? *On the Horizon, 9*(6): 1-6. Retrieved from www.marcprensky.com

Prensky, M. H. (2009). Sapiens digital: From digital immigrants and digital natives to digital wisdom. *Innovate Journal of Online Education, 5*(3), 1-9. Retrieved from www.innovateonline.info

Small, G., & Vorgan, G. (2008). *iBrain: Surviving the technological alteration of the modern mind.* New York, NY: Harper Collins.

The Effects of Student Response Systems (SRSs) on Eighth Grade Pre-Algebra Students' Achievement and Engagement

Lauren Happel
Northwestern State University, Unites States
lauren8199@yahoo.com

Sanghoon Park
University of South Florida, Unites States
mot7689@gmail.com

Ron McBride
Northwestern State University, Unites States
mcbride@nsula.edu

Abstract: Student response systems (SRSs) or clickers are used in the classroom to encourage students' participation and further promote active classroom learning. Previous studies have showed mixed results regarding the effectiveness of SRSs in increasing student engagement and further promoting classroom learning. Moreover, many studies have been conducted and focused on the college level courses. In this study, we examine the effects of using SRS on eighth grade pre-algebra students' achievement and engagement. We used two intact pre-algebra classes with 16 students in each class. The study took place over a four week long pre-algebra lesson on measurement. After the four-week unit of study, posttests and engagement surveys were administered, and data were analyzed using independent samples t-tests. The results of the study showed that students in the SRS group showed significantly higher achievement and engagement than the students who did not use SRS in the classroom.

Introduction

Student response systems (SRSs), or clickers, have been used in the classroom in order to create a more active learning environment. The SRS includes both a handheld device and a USB receiver. The handheld device sends a wireless signal to a teacher's computer through the use of a receiver. Penuel, Boscardin, Masyn, and Crawford (2007) suggested a series of pedagogical strategies that can be used with SRSs including "posing conceptually focused questions, requiring students to answer questions, displaying students responses for all to see, and engaging students in discussion" (p. 320). By implementing the strategies constantly, teachers can encourage classroom participation and keep the attention of students. Teachers using SRSs expect students to actively participate in class discussions and perform well on tests because students can instantly send answers to questions the teacher poses through the use of the clickers (Kaleta & Joosten, 2007). With instant formative assessment, the teacher can diagnose the students' knowledge at any given moment, and students are expected to be more engaged and achieve higher (Greer & Heaney, 2004). Previous studies have shown that an average of about 94% of students will attempt to answer a question using clickers when focused questions are given, which is a promising percentage for teachers who strive to have the majority of their students engaged in the lesson (Guthrie & Carlin, 2004). SRSs can be effective technology if teachers make a conscious effort to think about the needs of their students and the goals of the class. Higher order thinking and stimulating discussions are encouraged in order to make the clickers reach their highest potential for student engagement and learning (Dangel & Wang, 2008). SRSs also allow teachers to implement a form of technology that lends itself to interactive learning. The technology is placed into the students' hands, which lends itself to student interaction and engagement (Kaleta & Joosten, 2007).

During the past decades, however, many studies focused on the effectiveness of the SRSs in the college level classrooms. Not much research has been conducted to examine the use of SRSs in the learning process prior to college level (Penuel, Boscardin, Masyn, & Crawford, 2007). We also found that the SRSs related studies also showed mixed results regarding the effects of it on student engagement. Most studies found a positive correlation between the clickers and engagement, yet still some studies showed a negative impact. The negative results were often due to the technical issues associated with technology (Carnaghan & Webb, 2006).

Student Response Systems (SRSs)

SRSs are wireless devices that allow students to send their responses to a computer in the classroom. Numerous varieties of these systems range in color, brand, and size. According to Kaleta and Joosten (2007), the systems can range anywhere from as large as a remote for a television to as small as a credit card. Some of the devices have numerous buttons on them, some only have one button, and some even allow the students to text answers to the computer. The general purposes for all of the devices are the same. They all send wireless information to a receiver that is connected to a classroom computer by a USB port. Once the information is received, the software for the device compiles the information and presents it in a table or graph form. The graph can then be easily displayed to immediately see the classes' responses. According to Lincoln (2007), higher education instructors are the ones who begin to implement the SRSs into their classrooms because it helps them to integrate the system directly into PowerPoint presentations. Since many college instructors rely heavily on these PowerPoint methods, the use of clickers in the classroom allows for an easy transition into this form of technology. The SRSs can be implemented by the instructor in a variety of ways.

The most common way of using SRSs in the classroom is to support active learning by collecting individual responses. Instructors use the SRSs to pose focused questions during the presentation or lecture (Kaleta & Joosten, 2007; Penuel, Boscardin, Masyn, & Crawford, 2007). The questions are content based, opinion based, or application based which would require a deeper understanding of the topic. SRSs can be implemented in a very small class or in a large lecture hall with hundreds of students. The immediate results from the questions asked are then displayed on the projector or interactive white board. The instructor can use the results to discuss the correct answer and address any concerns or misunderstandings the results may have shown. This strategy of implementing the clickers in the classroom has shown to improve classroom discussion by opening up communication between the teacher and students.

Another way of SRS implementation is to promote group discussion. After the question is discussed as a whole group, the instructor can pair up students to discuss the responses they made. During the small group discussion, students have a chance to justify the answer they submitted and decide among their group members about whose answer best addressed the question (Kaleta & Joosten, 2007).

A third way of using SRSs in the classroom is to quiz students. Quiz sessions can be used to review the material that will be tested. This strategy allows the students to see where they stand in comparison to their peers. After each question is posed, the software can bring up a graph that displays the results of the answers for that particular question. Students can see whether or not they answered the question correctly. They can also have the opportunity to see how many others in the class missed the same question. Freeman et al. (2007) found that students who used clickers had lower failure rates and performed better on their exams than the group who used the color-coded cards without SRSs. However, it should be noted that this strategy is only successful if the students' anonymity is kept. The students do not want other students in the class knowing which questions they got right or wrong (Kaleta & Joosten, 2007). Gauci, Dantas, Williams, and Kemm (2009) warned that active learning can be diminished with SRSs if students did not feel a sense of anonymity that the clicker devices provided.

SRSs and Engagement

Many studies have reported positive effects of using SRS on students' engagement when used in different subject areas. Kaleta and Joosten (2007)'s survey study showed that 94% of the university faculty perceived that there was an increase in student engagement as a result of using the clickers. Sixty-eight percent thought the clickers increased student interactions, and 87% of them believed it increased student participation. Also 69% of students believed that they were more engaged as a result of using the clickers, and it helped them pay attention, and 70% found it increased their participation in class (Kaleta & Joosten, 2007). Lincoln (2007) reported that students from a

Principles of Marketing class had similar results in terms of student engagement and attitudes. Based on a survey given to the marketing students, about 66% thought the clickers helped to keep their attention during class. About 63% believed the clickers made the class more enjoyable. High percentages were noted when the students were surveyed about clickers making class fun and whether they would like to use them in other classes. Gauci, Williams, and Kemm (2007) also conducted a study with 175 students who were taking a physiology course by employing various methods such as: student interviews, questionnaires, and participation results. The data suggested that 84% of the students answered the questions with the clickers even though the choice to participate was voluntary. The students reported that 83% of them were engaged and 85% of them were stimulated intellectually. About 89% of them believed that the use of the clickers motivated them to think more. Crossgrove and Curran (2008) conducted a study on the use of clickers in two separate biology courses. Overall, the students had positive comments about the use of the clickers. They found the clickers increased their class participation, helped them to understand the concepts in class, and increased their motivation to learn. However, a difference was found between the answers of the students in the non-major level course versus the major-level course. Students taking the course outside of their major were more likely to report that the clickers contributed to their performance on exams than those students taking the course as part of their major. Many non-majors (81%) believed the instructor should continue to use the clickers during instruction, as compared to the majors (64%).

A study conducted by Preszler, Dawe, Shuster, and Shuster (2007) reported similar findings. The instructors of the six biology courses incorporated the clicker to answer questions throughout their usual form of lecturing. At the end of the semester, the students were surveyed about their use of the clickers. Overall, students in both sets of courses agreed the clickers had a general positive effect on the course and they agreed that clickers were a helpful addition to the class. Eighty-one percent of students also reported that their course interest was increased after using clickers. Even though the general ideas of the students were positive between both sets of classes, the lower-level students had better impressions as compared to the higher-level students. These differences illustrated how the students answered the survey, as shown by the percentages of them who agreed with the statements.

However, Carnaghan and Webb's study (2006) found a contradiction to many of the other studies. Most of the studies prior to this one have shown that student engagement was affected in a positive way due to the use of the SRSs. This particular study shows a different outcome. The study was conducted with four sections of an introductory to management accounting course. The results of this study suggested that students liked the ease of use with the devices. They also appreciated how the instructors could easily clarify the answers when the students were not on the right track. Although the students did find satisfaction with the device, they did not necessarily find satisfaction in the course. Researchers also found that the students did not ask as many questions in class when the devices were used possibly because the questions asked by the instructors were too easy.

SRS and Achievement

Many survey studies found that students believed the instantaneous feedback provided by the clickers contributed to their learning the material. Kaleta and Joosten (2007) reported that immediate feedback allowed the students to self-check their learning progress for the topic they were learning. About 38% of the students reported that the clickers assisted them in earning a better grade in the course than they would have received in the class without the use of the clickers When SRS were used in a quiz session, students reported they tried harder to learn the content in order to do well on the questions asked with the clickers (Prather & Brissenden, 2009). In Lincoln's study (2007), however, 54% of students in the marketing course answered no support of using clickers to better learn the course material. More than half of students believed that clickers did not help to improve the grade in the course.

In a study conducted by Greer and Heaney (2004), four sections of an earth science course were involved. They found that students overall thought the SRSs improved the course quality and allowed for more higher-order thinking questions to occur. The majority of the students, between 65-77%, believed the system helped them to assess their level of understanding in the class. Even more students thought the systems had an impact on helping them learn. The study conducted by Freeman et al. (2007) also examined the effects of student achievement from the use of the clickers by comparing two biology courses. They found that the students who used the clickers had an overall lower percentage failure rate than previous semesters when compared to previous semesters of the same course. With a 400 point exam, the students with the clickers earned on average 14 points higher than the two years previous to that (Freeman et al., 2007). Preszler et al. (2007) conducted a study with four lower-level and two upper-level courses. All of the instructors incorporated clicker questions throughout their traditional lectures. At the end of the semester, over 500 students were surveyed about how the clickers assisted in their learning. Overall, the students in the lower-level courses had a better impression of the clickers than the students in the upper-level courses. About 70% of the students across all of the six courses agreed that clickers helped them understand the course material. Among the six courses, the highest number of students in one of the four lower-level courses reported the positive effect of clickers.

A couple of researchers examined not only the effects of the clickers on student achievement but also on the long-term retention of the course material. Poulis and Massen (1998) used a physics course using SRSs with only one button. This button was used by the students for only answering 'yes' to the questions asked by the instructor. The researchers chose to use a basic system in order to minimize confusion about how to work the devices. At the end of the semester, the students were given a survey based on a Likert scale of 1 to 9 asking whether the lectures helped them to better understand and learn the course material. The students who took the course section without the use of the clickers had an average answer of 5.1 whereas students who took the course with the clickers answered the same question with an average of 6.7. They also examined the long-term pass rates of this course. The clicker courses had an average pass rate over the four years of about 82%. The pass rate for the non-clicker courses were at about 48%. Crossgrove and Curran's study (2008) also showed the students performed better on the exam content where the clickers were used versus the content where the clickers were not used.

Advantages and Challenges of using SRSs

In order to encourage the future use of clickers in the classroom, some studies shared some tips and recommendations on how clickers can be successfully implemented. Lincoln (2007) noted that SRSs kept the students' attention, provided instant feedback, took attendance, and reduced grading. In regards to the feedback, the clickers assisted in two ways. First, they allowed the student to see how their answers compared to others in the class. They were easily able to see whether they were on track with what the instructor was expecting them to get out of the lecture. Second, the clickers allowed the instructor to easily see where the students stood in terms of understanding the material being presented. If the class as a whole was not answering the quiz questions correctly, the instructor could easily identify that and review what was just taught. If student responses are identified correctly, then the instructor would move onto the next topic.

Another major advantage of the SRSs is they assist in providing student-teacher interaction. This is especially true in large lecture classes where traditional style lecturing makes it hard to involve all students. Instructors in large classes attempt to involve the students by quizzing them with various methods. For example, they might ask the class to vote by raising their hand, call on students to answer questions, try small group discussions, or even use color-coded cards as a means of quiz responses. The problem shown with these methods is the anonymity of the students is not kept intact. When the method used in class does not provide for anonymous answers, the students have been shown to not feel comfortable answering using those methods. These methods also do not allow the students to immediately see their responses as compared to those in the rest of the class (Purchase, Mitchell, & Ounis, 2003).

Kaleta and Joosten (2007) suggested five major challenges in their study which included time, cost and use, technical support, the learning curve, and confidence. The first challenge was time. Not only did it take the instructors extra time to prepare the quiz questions, but it also took time to incorporate those questions into their usual lecture. The instructors found they were also not able to talk about as many topics as usual. This was because they found the clickers allowed too much time to go in-depth on topics that should have only been covered slightly. The second challenge was cost and use. In many cases, the students purchased the clicker systems from their university bookstore. The students thought the clickers were expensive. They were willing to pay for such an expensive tool only if the clickers were used enough in the class to make the cost worthwhile. The third challenge was technical support. Especially with large classes, the problem of broken, lost, or defective clickers occurred. The instructors thought this took up too much of their time, and they did not always have the knowledge to remediate the problem. They believed there should be some sort of support from the schools in terms of help when it comes to malfunctioning clickers. The learning curve was seen as the fourth challenge. The instructors realized it took a considerable amount of time for both the teachers and students to learn the clickers and feel comfortable using them on a daily or weekly basis. The instructors believed that taking professional development courses before implementing the clickers is the biggest factor in reducing this learning curve. If instructors can gain necessary skills from trainings and become more familiar with clickers, students will also be likely to use them without much trouble. The final challenge was confidence. Confidence in this case means that the students often thought their responses were not being registered with the receiver, even though the computer showed it was received. This led to some of the students being stressed about using the clickers in the classroom.

The researchers also focused on challenging instructors to move students beyond simply remembering facts and ideas. They referenced the principles for good practice model which showed how the clickers assist students in not only remembering, but also understanding what they learned, applying it to new situations, analyzing, and evaluating their knowledge. They thought the clickers have the potential to touch on all of these learning outcomes if they are utilized in the active learning style (Dangel & Wang, 2008).

In order to help understand the effectiveness of SRSs, we empirically examined the effects of using SRSs on eighth grade pre-algebra students' achievement and engagement. Two research hypotheses were tested in this study.

1. Eighth grade pre-algebra students who use student response systems (SRSs) for four weeks would score higher in their post achievement test than eighth grade pre-algebra students who do not use the SRSs.
2. Eighth grade pre-algebra students who use student response systems (SRSs) for four weeks would report higher perception of engagement in their engagement survey than eighth grade pre-algebra students who do not use the SRSs.

Methodology

A pretest-posttest control group experimental design was used in this study to examine the causal effect relationship between the use of SRSs and pre-algebra students' engagement and achievement. Two intact pre-algebra classes were randomly selected to conduct the study. The students in the experimental group were assessed during lecture presentations using the SRSs: whereas, the students in the control group were assessed using paper and pencil techniques. Other classroom conditions such as teacher, course contents, and the course topics were identical between the two groups only except the use of the SRSs.

The use of ActivExpression response system was considered the independent variable because it was the portion of the study that was controlled by the teacher. The experimental group used the SRSs. The control group did not use the SRSs. The students in the control group were assessed throughout the unit of study with the same questions the experimental group were asked. However, the control group answered the questions through discussion and paper and pencil methods instead of using the SRSs like the experimental group did. Both groups were taught the same information about a pre-algebra related topic. The topic of study came from the state standards and the school district's grade level expectations (GLEs). They were also both taught by the same instructor.

Two dependent variables were used in this experimental research study. The first dependent variable was achievement. The students were given a pretest to ensure the experimental and control groups were equivalent in terms of prior knowledge on the topic being studied. The pretest consisted of ten short answer questions. For example, it asked the students if they knew what surface area and volume meant. One point was assigned for each correct test item. No points were assigned for incorrect answers. There were a total of ten possible points on the pretest. The post achievement test consisted of twenty short answer questions using mathematical problems. For example, the posttest included questions such as: *A rectangular shaped swimming pool has a volume of 100,800 cubic feet of water. The height of the pool is 30 feet and the length is 80 feet. What is the width of the pool?* One point was assigned for each correct test item. The possible total score for the posttest was twenty points. The test questions were directly related to the material being taught by the instructor. The pre and posttests aligned with what was being taught during the four week instructional unit and they focused on the objectives of understanding surface area and volume of rectangular solids and cylinders. The same objectives were being assessed by the instructor through the use of the SRS quizzes.

The second dependent variable was students' perceived engagement. The students in both groups were given a researcher-developed engagement survey. It contained ten questions and assessed the students on a five point Likert scale with a score ranging from one representing 'strongly disagree' to five, representing 'strongly agree.' For example, it asked the students' opinions on questions such as: *I am learning in a way that interests me.* They circled their number response from one to five. The engagement survey assessed the students on their level of engagement with the topic being studied. The total possible mean score was 5 points if all of the answers were 'strongly agree.'

Participants

Eighth grade pre-algebra students participated in this study. There were a total of 32 students participating. Sixteen students were included in the experimental group using the SRSs and 16 students in the control group, not using SRSs. Each group was in a separate class period but received the same instruction with the same teacher. In the experimental group, there were nine female students and seven male students. In the control group, there were six female students and ten male students. All participating students were Caucasian. The ages of the students participating in the study ranged from 12 to 14 years old. There were a variety of ability ranges within the two class groups. They lived in a middle class rural community. The learners all had similar backgrounds and prior knowledge. The school is small enough that they all had the exact same sixth and seventh grade math teachers at this school prior to this eighth grade math class. Therefore, their prior knowledge should be similar due to learning from the same teacher the past two school years.

The classroom where the study took place was equipped with a Promethean Board, interactive whiteboard. The software, ActivInspire, was used by the teachers to create the questions and response answers. The SRSs that were used with the Promethean board are called ActivExpressions. They are handheld devices for each student, labeled with a number.

Procedures

The students in both the experimental and control groups were taught using the same lesson content in a four week unit on a pre-algebra topic of measurement. The topic was chosen based on the state standards and grade level expectations for eighth grade students. Each lesson lasted 52 minutes and took place in the morning. The two groups were given the same instruction except the experimental group used the SRS to respond.

The students were administered a pretest to determine their group equivalence in terms of prior knowledge in algebra. The pretest was administered in the students' classroom the week before the unit of study began. Then the students began their four week unit of study.

As the ActivInspire flipchart was displayed on the Promethean board, the questions were displayed one at a time. The students were given a chance to submit their answers to the question by using the ActivExpression. The devices allowed the students to answer a true/false question, a multiple choice question, and it even allowed them to text an answer to the question in short answer form. Each ActivExpression (clicker) was assigned a number. The students were aware of their own number but not of each others. Only the teacher was aware of this information in order to protect the students' anonymity. To answer the question, the students submitted their answer through the student response system. A signal went to a hub that was attached to the computer. This computer was connected to the Promethean board and immediately displayed the correct answer and included how many students scored the correct answer. The students were able to receive immediate feedback about their answer. The teacher led the students in a discussion about the correct answer, and responded to students' questions about a particular topic.

ActivExpressions (clickers) were used to review the content taught in the unit of study. The teacher used the response systems as a way to gain student attention and to receive immediate feedback from the students in order to check their level of understanding. If the response system answers indicated the students did not understand a topic, then the teacher immediately knew to review the information again. However, if the students were successful on the review questions, then the teacher knew they can move onto the next topic of study and not waste time on the information the students already understand. The teacher used informal assessment with the control group as well such as class discussions and paper and pencil problems in order to assess the control group's understanding of the material being taught. The data quality was assured by following study protocol that was developed and strictly followed by the teacher during the study. The documented study procedures also ensured elimination of possible researcher bias.

The post achievement test and the engagement survey were given at the conclusion of the four week study to both groups. The researcher compiled the data and analyzed to examine the effects of using SRSs on achievement and engagement.

Results

The researcher completed an independent samples t-test on the pretest data from the experimental and control groups to compare the pre-algebra pretest scores between the experimental group and the control group. The purpose of the t-test was to determine group equivalency. Table 1 displays the data from the independent samples t-test for the pretest scores. There was no significant difference in pretest scores for the Student Response System Group ($M=5.88$, $SD=1.93$) and the No Student Response System Group ($M=5.88$, $SD=2.13$), $t(30)=.00$, $p>.05$.

Measures	Student Response System (n = 16)		No Student Response System (n = 16)		t (30)
	M	SD	M	SD	
Pre-Algebra pretest	5.88**	1.93	5.88	2.13	.00

** Possible maximum score: 10

Table 1. t-test for the eighth grade pre-algebra pretest score

Since students' prior knowledge was found not significantly different between the two groups, another one-tailed independent samples t-test was conducted to compare the pre-algebra post achievement test scores between the experimental group and the control group at the alpha level of 0.025. Table 2 shows the results of the one-tailed t-test. Homogeneity of variance assumption was met at 0.05 level. There was a statistically significant difference in the posttest scores for the Student Response System Group ($M=17.88$, $SD=2.70$) and the No Student Response System Group ($M=14.06$, $SD=4.01$), $t(30)=3.15$, $p<.01$. The effect size (Cohen's d) was 1.12 indicating a large effect.

Measures	Student Response System (n = 16)		No Student Response System (n = 16)		t (30)
	M	SD	M	SD	
Pre-Algebra posttest	17.88**	2.70	14.06	4.01	3.15*

* $p < .01$
** Possible maximum score: 20

Table 2. *t*-test for the eighth grade pre-algebra posttest score

Finally, the perception of engagement measured using an engagement survey from both the experimental group and the control group was examined by using a one-tailed independent samples *t*-test at the alpha level of 0.025. Table 3 shows a statistically significant difference in students' perceived engagement for the Student Response System Group ($M=3.89$, $SD=.46$) and the No Student Response System Group ($M=2.85$, $SD=.67$), $t(30)=5.13$, $p<.01$. The effect size (Cohen's d) was 1.81 indicating a very large effect.

Measures	Student Response System (n = 16)		No Student Response System (n = 16)		$t(30)$
	M	SD	M	SD	
Engagement survey	3.89**	.46	2.85	.67	5.13*

*p < .05
** Possible maximum mean score: 5

Table 3. *t*-test for the engagement survey score

Based on two one-tailed *t*-test results, the null hypotheses were rejected. And it was concluded that the use of SRSs in a pre-algebra classroom improves students' posttest achievement scores and also their perceived level of engagement.

Discussion

We concluded that the use of SRSs in pre-algebra class helps eight grade students be more engaged and score higher than students who did not use SRSs in the same class. The experimental group used the SRSs during their four week unit to review the skills. The teacher was able to use the student response system data immediately to assess the students understanding as they answered each question. The control group was taught the same skills, but the teacher used hand written answers to questions by students. The study supports the positive effects of SRSs in eight grade pre-algebra classes. An incidental finding that was noted during the study was the researcher noticed the experimental group had a slightly higher level of retention than the control group. They seemed to remember more from the previous day's lesson than the group that did not use the SRSs. This might be due to the fact the teacher was able to use the SRS questions as a tool to continuously check for students understanding. If there was a lack of understanding, the teacher could go back and review with the students. The teacher checked for understanding with the control group as well, but the SRSs made it easier for the teacher to notice the misunderstandings. The immediate feedback from the students allowed the teacher more time to promote deeper understanding of the content through discussions that were not available in the other classroom.

The results also showed a statistically significant difference in learning engagement between the experimental group and the control group. This difference supports the idea that engagement and achievement are closely tied to one another. This study provides concrete evidence that students who used the SRSs were more engaged than the students who did not use the technology. Students in the experimental group were more verbally excited about learning. They would ask the teacher about when they would get to use the SRSs again. On the days where the systems were used, the students showed excitement and a more willing attitude towards learning. The only limitation that may have affected the validity of the study is student absenteeism. On several occasions, a student or two were absent from the pre-algebra lesson. The researcher was diligent in making sure the absent students were caught up on the material they missed. The students came to the researcher during their lunch recess to make up the lesson. The students from the experimental group were given the opportunity during their lunch break to use the SRSs to answer the same questions the other students answered the previous day. The teacher had saved the questions each time in the computer so that any absent students had access to them.

The implications of the study are positive. Technology and engagement are currently two prominent topics in the education field. This study's findings support the idea that SRSs, when used by the students, can have a positive impact on learning. It also provides credence to the notion that when students are engaged, the potential for profound learning can take place. The findings from this study could assist educators in making decisions about what types of technology they should purchase and implement. School districts and administrators usually have a limited technology budget. This study supports the concept that student response systems can have a positive impact on student learning and engagement.

Rreferences

Carnaghan, C., & Webb, A. (2006). Investigating the effects of group response systems on student satisfaction, learning and engagement in accounting education. *Social Science Research Network*, 1-42.

Crossgrove, K., & Curran, K. (2008). Using clickers in nonmajors and majors level biology courses: Student opinion, learning, and long-term retention of course material. *The American Society for Cell Biology, 7*, 146-154.

Dangel, H., & Wang, C. (2008). Student response systems in higher education: Moving beyond linear teaching and surface learning. *Journal of Educational Technology Development and Exchange, 1*(1), 93-104.

Freeman, S., O'Connor, E., Parks, J., Cunningham, M., Hurley, D., Haak, D., Dirks, C., & Wenderoth, M. (2007). Prescribed active learning increases performance in introductory biology. *Life Sciences Education, 6*(1), 132-139.

Gauci, S., Dantas, A., Williams, D., & Kemm, R. (2009). Promoting student-centered active learning in lectures with a personal response system. *Advances in Physiology Education, 33*(1), 60-71.

Greer, L., & Heaney, P. (2004). Real time analysis of student comprehension: An assessment of electronic student response technology in an introductory earth science course. *Journal of Geoscience Education, 52* (4), 345-351.

Gutherie, R., & Carlin, A. (2004). Waking the dead: Using interactive technology to engage passive listeners in the classroom. *Tenth Americas Conference of Information Systems*, 1-8.

Kaleta, R., & Joosten, T. (2007). Student response systems: A University of Wisconsin system study of clickers. *Educause, 10*, 1-12.

Lincoln, D. (2007). *Using student response pads ("clickers") in the principles of marketing classroom.* Presented at the Australian and New Zealand Marketing Academy Conference, Dunedin, New Zealand.

Penuel, W. R., Boscardin, C. K., Masyn, K., & Crawford, V. M. (2007). Teaching with student response systems in elementary and secondary education settings: A survey study, *Educational Technology Research & Development, 55*, 315-346. DOI 10.1007/s11423-006-9023-4.

Poulis, J., & Massen, C. (1998). Physics lecturing with audience paced feedback. *American Association of Physics Teachers*, 1-6.

Preszler, R., Dawe, A., Shuster, C., & Shuster, M. (2007). Assessment of the effects of student response systems on student learning and attitudes over a broad range of biology courses. *Life Sciences Education, 6*, 29-41.

Purchase, H., Mitchell, C., & Ounis, I. (2003). Gauging students' understanding through interactive lectures. *Department of Computing Science*, 1-10.

Do Gender and ADHD Affect Media Multitasking Attitudes and Behaviors?

Lin Lin
University of North Texas, U.S.A.
Lin.Lin@unt.edu

David Bonner
University of Mary Hardin-Baylor U.S.A.
dmbonner@umhb.edu

Kim Nimon
University of North Texas, U.S.A.
Kim.Nimon@unt.edu

Abstract: The purpose of this study was to investigate the effect of gender and attention deficit / hyperactivity disorder (ADHD) factors on adolescents' media multitasking attitudes, self-efficacy, and activity levels. Data was collected from 120 adolescents between 10 and 14 years old. Among the participants, half (61 out of 121), divided by 43 boys and 18 girls, had ADHD. Results from three survey instruments showed different gender and ADHD interactions on media multitasking self-efficacy, attitude, and activity levels among the participants. This paper discusses the results.

Introduction

There has been an increase in the use of media and technologies, especially in the use of multiple media and technologies at the same time, a phenomenon called media multitasking, task-switching, or dual-tasking. Rideout, Foehr, and Roberts (2010) reported that on average, children 8-18 years old in the U.S. spent 7.38 hours on media daily, and that they packed a total of 10 hours and 45 minutes worth of media content into the 7.38 hours of media use. In a typical week, 81% of young people spend some of their media time using more than one medium at a time. Girls are more likely to media multitask than boys. Carr (2010) stated that our brains change in response to our experiences and that the technologies we use to find, store, and share information can literally reroute our neural pathways. Are young people growing up with digital technologies developing different capabilities in organizing and processing information? The implications of understanding the possible differences are critical for understanding cognition and behaviors of youth in the 21st century.

Whether it is coincidental or not, it is reported that an increasing number of children are diagnosed as having the attention deficit / hyperactivity disorder (ADHD). Nearly 5% of American children between ages 6 and 17 — about 4.5 million children — are diagnosed with the attention deficit / hyperactivity disorder (ADHD), and this number continues to increase (Diller, 2012). The relationship between ADHD and media multitasking, although not established, is an interesting phenomenon. The purpose of this paper is to report a study that investigated the effect of gender and ADHD factors on adolescents' media multitasking attitudes, self-efficacy, and activity levels.

Theoretical Framework

Research on aspects of multitasking such as dual tasking, task switching, and sequential actions has revealed that people experience severe interference when tasks are performed simultaneously, and that multitaskers do not retain as much information as they would have, if they had focused on one task (Baddeley, Chincotta, & Adlam, 2001; Burgess, et. al, 2000; Meyer & Kieras, 1997; Monsell, 2003; Poldrack & Foerde, 2007). Various studies also show that multitasking capacity depends on differences in gender, age, experience, cognitive load, tasks involved, automation, and expertise levels (Just et al., 2001; Lin, 2009; Lin, Lee, & Robertson, 2011; Lin, Robertson, & Lee, 2009; Sohn & Carlson, 2000; Spink & Park, 2005).

Several earlier studies have examined the different task-switching or multitasking abilities between children with or without ADHD. For instance, Cepeda, Cepeda, and Kramer (2000) examined the efficiency of executive control processes involved in task set inhibition and preparation to perform a new task in ADHD and non-ADHD children. They found that ADHD children showed substantially larger switch cost than non-ADHD children. Siklos and Kerns (2003) investigated whether children with ADHD would demonstrate a deficit in multitasking. They reported that children with ADHD attempted significantly fewer tasks than the control group, indicating that the children with ADHD were significantly worse in their ability to plan, organize their behavior, and monitor their ongoing performance to complete all tasks as compared to age-matched controls. Another study conducted by Chan, Guo, Zou, Li, Hu, and Yang (2006) explored multitasking skills in children with ADHD compared with healthy controls matched by gender, age, and IQ. They suggested that children with ADHD performed significantly worse than the healthy controls in almost all the domains, particularly in goal-directed planning, flexible strategy generation, and self-monitoring (2006). Hwang, Gau, Hsu, and Wu (2010) looked at adolescents 10-17 years-old with and without ADHD and discovered that the adolescents with ADHD encountered difficulties in estimating time duration due to the increased attentional load, subsequently leading to disorganization and poor time management. As a result, they suggested that a structured environment could help children with ADHD in reducing attention load. They also suggested that children with ADHD should focus on and carry out one task at a time before moving to the next and that it is important to set a suitable time schedule so that children with ADHD could get sufficient rest to regain their attentional resource for the next task, and that they could use extra assistance and educational intervention when they are assigned to finish complex tasks within a limited time.

Most studies on media multitasking, however, have been conducted in lab settings, which do not often represent a complete picture of what happens in real life (Lin, 2009). Media multi-taskers in real life often have more control over the tasks that they switch or conduct at the same time. Their attitudes, for instance, their likes, comfort, or excitement levels towards multitasking, can affect their task efficiency and capacity. Their self-efficacies, that is, their belief or confidence in their own ability to carry out the multiple tasks at the same time or switch between the tasks can affect their ability in multitasking abilities. Last but not the least, the frequency of their daily multitasking activities can affect their long-term multitasking abilities.

Methods and Data Source

In an earlier paper, we reported the parental influence on adolescent children's media multitasking attitudes and behaviors (Lin, Nimon, & Bonner, 2012). With this paper, we will report gender and attention deficit / hyperactivity disorder (ADHD) factors that may affect adolescents' media multitasking attitudes, self-efficacy, and activity levels. Therefore, our research questions are: In adolescent children aged 10 to 14, do measures of media multitasking self-efficacy (MMSE), attitude (MMA) or activity (MMI) differ by the factors of Gender or ADHD, and is there an interaction between these factors?

Procedure and Participants

The adolescent children were recruited from a medical office in the U.S. The participants and their parents signed consent forms and received a thank-you gift of $5 in cash for their participation. A total of 120 adolescents between 10 and 14 years old participated in the study. They averaged 12 years old. 58% of the children were white, although all races were represented. 62% came from a household income below $50,000, and 62% had parents with college and above education levels. Among the adolescent participants, there were 78 boys and 42 girls. About half (61) of the participants were indicated as having ADHD, including 43 boys and 18 girls. Please see Table 1.

Total No. of Participants	ADHD (61)		w/o ADHD (60)	
	Boys	Girls	Boys	Girls
120	43	18	35	24

Table 1: Number of Participants by Gender and ADHD factor

Instruments

In addition to demographics, three surveys were filled out by the adolescent children. They were the Media Multitasking Self Efficacy survey (MMSE), the Media Multitasking Attitude (MMA) survey, and the Media Multitasking Index (MMI) survey.

MMSE. The MMSE survey was developed to measure perceptions of one's ability to multitask based on the self-efficacy literature (Bandura, 1986, 1997). The MMSE used five items modified from Jones' (1986) measure. Items were rated on a 7-point scale with 1 indicated strongly disagree and 7 strongly agree. One item was negatively worded and reverse coded, and it caused the MMSE to have poor reliability when tested with the adolescent population. For this reason, the MMSE employed in the remainder of the study consisted of the four positively worded items.

MMA. The MMA survey was adopted using the ten items from the affective subscale of the Computer Attitude Measure (Kay, 1993), a semantic differential instrument originally designed to measure teachers' attitudes towards computers (Kay, 1993; Miyashita & Knezek, 1992; Christensen & Knezek, 2002). The items were measured on a 7-point scale (*extremely, moderately, slightly, neither, slightly, moderately, extremely*).

MMI. The MMI was adopted from a recent seminal work by Ophir, Nass and Wagner (2009) and it was designed to measure media multitasking activities including time spent and media involved. The MMI addressed 12 different media forms: print media, television, computer-based video, music, non-music audio, video or computer games, telephone and mobile phone calls, instant messaging on a computer, SMS text messaging, email, web surfing, and other computer-based applications (such as word processing). For each medium, participants reported the total number of hours per week they spent using the medium. In addition, they filled out a media-multitasking matrix, indicating whether, while using this primary medium, they concurrently used each of the other media *Most of the time*, *Some of the time*, *A little of the time*, or *Never*. Numeric values to each of the matrix responses were assigned and the responses were summed (see details in Ophir, Nass and Wagner, 2009).

Results

Two-way ANOVA analyses were used to evaluate the effects of the Gender and ADHD factors on media multitasking self-efficacy, attitude, and activity separately as measured by the three survey instruments: MMSE, MMA, and MMI. Table 2 summarizes the effects of Gender and ADHD factors of the three areas.

Survey Instruments	ADHD		Gender		Interactions btw ADHD and Gender			
	ADHD	w/o ADHD	Boys	Girls	ADHD Boys	w/o ADHD Boys	ADHD Girls	w/o ADHD Girls
MMSE	*4.8365**	*5.6968**	5.2583	5.2244	4.8143	5.8800	4.8824	5.4886
MMA	*4.8392**	*5.5919**	5.0938	5.3414	*4.6310**	*5.7973**	5.3046	5.3686
MMI	4.7609	5.7333	*4.7249**	*6.0291**	*3.9771**	5.8779	*6.6941**	5.5756

*Note: MMSE (ADHD) p=.005; MMA (ADHD) p=.036; MMA (Gender x ADHD) p=.06; MMI (Gender) p=.050; MMI (Gender x ADHD) p=.015

Table 2: Effects of ADHD and gender factors on adolescents' MMSE, MMA, and MMI

The first part of the research question asked whether media multitasking self-efficacy (MMSE) differed by Gender or ADHD, and whether there was an interaction between these two factors. In this case, there was a statistically and practically significant ADHD main effect (**ES = .078**). The mean MMSE for children without ADHD (5.6968) was significantly different from the mean MMSE for those with ADHD (4.8365) with $p = .005$. There was not, however, a significant Gender effect, nor was there a significant interaction effect between the factors of Gender and ADHD.

For the second part of the research question which addressed media multitasking attitude (MMA), there was also an ADHD main effect (**ES = .044**). The mean MMA measure for children without ADHD (5.5919) was significantly different from the mean MMA measure for those with ADHD (4.8392) with $p = .036$. As with MMSE, for MMA there was not a significant Gender effect. There was, however, a practically significant interaction effect (Gender x ADHD) with $p = .06$. This was exhibited in the difference between the mean MMA measure for boys with ADHD (4.6310) and boys without ADHD (5.7973). The mean MMA measures for girls with and without ADHD were similar (5.3046 and 5.3686 respectively). These relationships are illustrated in Figure 1.

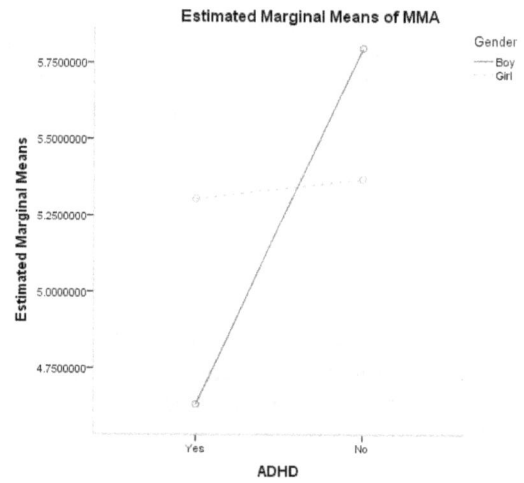

Figure 1: MMA Interaction Plot

The third part of the research question addressed media multitasking activity level as measured by MMI. In this case, there was no ADHD main effect as seen with both MMSE and MMA, but there was a statistically and practically significant Gender main effect (**ES = .040**) and a statistically and practically significant interaction effect (**ES = .061**). The mean MMI measure for girls (6.0291) was significantly different from the mean MMI measure for boys (4.7249) with $p = .050$. In addition, the interaction effect (Gender x ADHD) with $p = .015$ indicates that there is a large difference between the mean MMI for boys with ADHD (3.9771) as compared with the mean MMI for girls with ADHD (6.6941). It is also interesting to note that for children without ADHD there was not much difference in level of media multitasking activity (mean MMI for boys without ADHD = 5.8779; mean MMI for girls without ADHD = 5.5756). These relationships are illustrated in Figure 2.

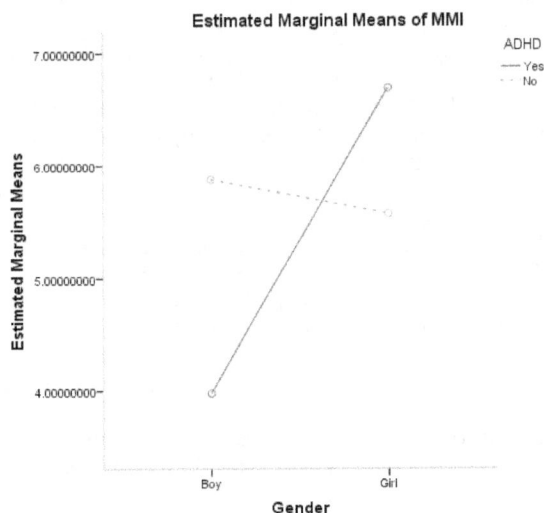

Figure 2: MMI Interaction Plot

Discussion and Scholarly Significance

The results showed that 1) the adolescent children with ADHD had lower self-efficacy towards media multitasking than those without ADHD; 2) the adolescents with ADHD, in particular, the boys with ADHD were less favorable towards media multitasking than those without ADHD; 3) The boys, in particular, the boys with ADHD, reported to have conducted fewer multitasking activities than girls did. In fact, the boys with ADHD reported the lowest media multitasking activities, the girls with ADHD reported the highest media multitasking activities, while the non-ADHD adolescents reported moderate media multitasking activities.

These findings were consistent with results of earlier studies in that the adolescent children with ADHD were less capable of various aspects of multitasking, task-switching or dual-tasking activities than children without ADHD. What was intriguing and perhaps most noteworthy of this study was that there were significant interaction factors between gender and ADHD in media multitasking attitudes and media multitasking activity levels. This study serves as a foundation for future studies since little research has been found examining different aspects of media multitasking of the adolescent children such as their self-efficacy, attitude and activity levels in real lives.

With more school children being diagnosed as having ADHD and other mental and physical differences or challenges, it is important for educators and parents to understand factors that attribute to the differences between their students and children. Only then will they be able to find solutions and work effectively with individual students. New media and technologies can help students learn, but they can also overload students or distract students from their learning. Teachers need to understand why they use technologies in the classrooms and need to be mindful when they incorporate technologies in their classrooms and curricula.

Reference

Baddeley, A., Chincotta, D., & Adlam, A. (2001). Working memory and the control of action: evidence from task switching. *Journal of Experimental Psychology: General, 130*(4), 641-657.
Bandura, A. (1986). *Social foundations of thought and action: A social cognitive theory*. NJ: Prentice-Hall/Englewood Cliffs.

Bandura, A. (1997). Self-efficacy: The exercise of control. NY: W. H. Freeman.

Burgess, P. W., Veithc, E., De Lacy Costello, A., & Shallice, T. (2000). The cognitive and neuroanatomical correlates of multitasking. *Neurosychologia, 38*(6), 848-863.

Carr, N. (2010). *The Shallows: What the Internet Is Doing to Our Brains*. NYC: W.W. Norton & Company.

Cepeda, N., Cepeda, M., & Kramer, A. (2000). Task switching and attention deficit hyperactivity disorder. *Journal of Abnormal Child Psychology, 28*(3), pp. 213-226.

Chan, R., Guo, M., Zou, X., Li, D., Hu Z., & Yang, B. (2006). Multitasking performance of Chinese children with ADHD. *Journal of the International Neuropsychological Society*, 12 , pp. 575-579.

Christensen, R., & Knezek, G. (2002). Instruments for Assessing the Impact of Technology in Education. In Assessment/Evaluation in Educational Information Technology, **Computers in the Schools, 18**(2/3/4), 5-25.

Diller, L. (2012). Remembering Ritalin: A doctor and generation Rx reflect on life and psychiatric drugs. NY: Perigee Trade.

Foehr, U. G. (2006). *Media multitasking among American youth: Prevalence, predictors and pairings*. Washington, D.C.: The Henry J. Kaiser Family Foundation.

Kay, R. H. (1993). An exploration of theoretical and practical foundations for assessing attitudes toward computers: The computer attitude measure (CAM). *Computers in Human Behavior, 9*, 371-386.

Hwang, S., Gau, S., Hsu, W., & Wu, Y. (2010). Deficits in interval timing measured by the dual-task paradigm among children and adolescents with attention-deficit hyperactivity disorder. *Journal of Child Psychology and Psychiatry, 51*(3): pp. 223-232.

Jones, G. R. (1986). Socialization tactics, self-efficacy, and newcomers adjustments to organizations. *Academy of Management Journal, 29*, 262–279.

Just, M., et al. (2001). Interdependence of non-overlapping cortical systems in dual cognitive tasks. *Neuroimage, 14*, 417-426

Lin, L. (2009). Breadth-biased versus focused cognitive control in media multitasking behaviors. *Proceedings of the National Academy of Sciences USA* 106: 15521-15522.

Lin, L., Lee, J., & Robertson, T. (2011). Reading while watching video: The effect of video content on reading comprehension and media multitasking ability. *Journal of Educational Computing Research, 45*(2), 183-201.

Lin, L., Robertson, T., & Lee, J. (2009). Reading performances between novices and experts in different media multitasking environments. *Computers in the Schools, 26:* 3, 169-186.

Lin, L., Nimon, K., & Bonner, D. (2012). Parents' influence on adolescent children' media-multitasking attitudes and behaviors. In Cleb Maddux & D. Gibson (Eds.). **Research Highlights in Technology and Teacher Education 2012. SITE. pp. 127-132.**

Meyer, D. E. & Kieras, D. E. (1997). A computational theory of executive cognitive processes and multiple-task performance: Part 1. Basic mechanisms. *Psychological Review, 104*, 3-65.

Miyashita, K., & Knezek, G. A. (1992). The Young Adolescent's Computer Inventory: A Likert scale for assessing attitudes related to computers in instruction. **Journal of Computing in Adolescenthood Education, 3**(1), 63-72.

Monsell, S. (2003). Task switching. *Trends in Cognitive Neuroscience, 7*(3), 134-140.

Ophir, E., Nass, C. I., & Wagner, A. D. (2009). Cognitive control in media multitaskers, *Proceedings of National Academy of Sciences USA* 106:15583–15587.

Oskamp, S. (1977). *Attitudes and opinions*. NJ: Prentice-Hall/Englewood Cliffs.

Poldrack, R. A., & Foerde, K. (2007). Category learning and the memory systems debate. *Neuroscience and Biobehavioral Reviews, 32*, 197-205.

Rideout, V.J., Foehr, U. G., and Roberts, D. F. (2010). *Generation M2 Media in the lives of 8 to 18 year-olds*. Menlo Park, CA: Kaiser Family Foundation.

Siklos S., Kerns K.A. (2004). Assessing multitasking in children with ADHD using a modified Six Elements Test. *Archives of Clinical Neuropsychology*, 19 (3), pp. 347-361.

Sohn, M. H., & Carlson, R. A. (2000). Effects of repetition and foreknowledge in task-set reconfiguration. *Journal of Experimental Psychology: Learning, Memory, and Cognition, 26*(6), 1445-1460.

Spink, A., & Park, M. (2005). Information and non-information multitasking interplay. *Journal of Documentation, 61*(4), 548-554.

Examining Factors Affecting Beginning Teachers' Transfer of Learning of ICT-Enhanced Learning Activities in Their Teaching Practice

Douglas D. Agyei
University of Cape Coast, Republic of Ghana
d.d.agyei@utwente.nl

Joke M. Voogt
University of Twente, The Netherlands
j.m.voogt@utwente.nl

Abstract. This study examined 100 beginning teachers' transfer of learning in utilizing Information Communication Technology-enhanced activity-based learning activities. The beginning teachers had participated in a professional development program characterized by 'learning technology by collaborative design' in their final year of their pre-service preparation program. Transfer of learning was postulated as characteristics of 1. the professional development program, 2. beginning teachers and 3. school environment. Beginning teachers held strong and positive pedagogical views about the professional development program, which was the strongest predictor in transfer of their learning. The study also showed that a significant amount of explained differences in the level of transfer of ICT-enhanced activity-based learning innovation could be attributed to range of factors across individual beginning teachers and school environment characteristics. Implications of these findings are discussed.

Keywords: pre-service teacher transfer of learning, ICT innovation, learner characteristics, school environment characteristics

Introduction

Formal training typically involves learning new knowledge, skills and attitudes in one environment (the training situation) that can be applied or used in another environment (the performance situation) (Goldstein & Ford 2002). However, several studies have shown that a common experience is that learning from a formal training program is often not or in a limited way applied on the job (e.g. Yamnill & McLean 2001; Saks 2002). Since Baldwin and Ford's (1988) highly recognized review of the "transfer problem" in training research, an outpouring of conceptual and research-based suggestions have focused on how to lessen the gap between learning and sustained workplace performance (Yamnill & McLean 2001; Goldstein & Ford 2002; Burke & Hutchins 2007). Baldwin and Ford (1988) define positive transfer of training "as the degree to which trainees effectively apply the knowledge, skills and attitudes gained in a training context to the job" (p. 63). To be able to bridge the gap between learning and sustained workplace performance, it is important to understand the dynamics of transfer in order to look for ways to minimize transfer losses while improving the yield from any training program. Baldwin and Ford (1988) identified a taxonomy of major conceptual factors influencing transfer. They divided these factors into three groups of characteristics which directly or indirectly influence trainees' learning and the transfer of training: trainee characteristics, training characteristics, and work environment characteristics. Trainee characteristics refer to internal factors (e.g. ability, personality, and motivation) whereas training characteristics involve training design factors (e.g. principles of learning, sequencing, and training content). Baldwin and Ford referred to work environment characteristics as external factors which directly and indirectly affect trainees' learning and the transfer of training. While the question of transferability of training has been present in various disciplines, there is not much evidence of comprehensive transfer studies in teacher education involving the transfer of learning of pre-service teachers. The purpose of this study is to attain understanding of factors that influence newly trained mathematics teachers' transfer of Information Communication Technology-enhanced (ICT) activity-based training which they received during their pre-service education.

The Professional development arrangement

This transfer study grew out of a program of research to introduce ICT as a tool to improve teaching and learning of mathematics in pre-service teacher education in Ghana. In two iterative studies (in 2009 and 2010), a professional development program was designed to prepare pre-service teachers to integrate ICT in teaching mathematics in a teacher education institute (Agyei, 2012; Agyei & Voogt, 2011). In early 2011, the approach was applied into a regular mathematics–specific instructional technology course of the teacher education institute (Agyei, 2012). The pre-service teachers involved in the arrangements were able to develop and demonstrate their competencies adequately in designing and enacting ICT-enhanced activity-based mathematics lessons as a result of the intervention in the three studies. Consequently, the arrangement enhanced their students' learning outcomes and motivation to learn mathematics (See Agyei, 2012). Approximately six, eighteen, and twenty-eight months after the third, second and first arrangements respectively, the pre-service mathematics teachers (hereafter referred to as beginning teachers) had been posted into various senior high schools and were pursuing their careers as mathematics teachers.

In this study the intervention, a professional development arrangement, adopted "Learning Technology by Collaborative Design" (LTCD) (Koehler & Mishra 2005) to provide opportunity for pre-service teachers to develop their competencies in ICT integration through collaborative design and enactment of ICT-based curriculum materials. Spreedsheets were used as a focal application because they are readily available on most computers and are an application that is relevant for developing mathematics pre-service teachers' integration competencies. Activity Based Learning (ABL) was applied as a pedagogical environment for use of spreadsheet. ABL assumes that students are actively involved in their learning process. It was expected that the combination of a specific pedagogy (ABL) and a specific technology (spreadsheets) would encourage the pre-service teachers to apply their knowledge and skills in designing and enacting lessons by employing a mix of direct instruction and hands-on activity to guide students through activities with spreadsheets to enhance student learning. The 14-week professional development program required for pre-service teachers to attend one-two hours lectures and one -two hours laboratory sessions per week. The lectures were meant to update the pre-service teachers by giving them the theoretical foundation/concepts (e.g. collaborative teacher design, ABL and other pedagogical tasks). Laboratory sessions included small group tasks in which design teams worked on their assignments and projects. Exemplary materials of spreadsheet-based demonstration lesson models designed by the researcher were a necessary component of the professional development arrangement. Based on their experiences, pre-service teachers were challenged in teams to select mathematics topics suitable for teaching with spreadsheets, and to make use of the affordances of the technology to design learning activities that foster higher order thinking. Pre-service teachers enacted their developed lessons in a micro or peer teaching experience and in some cases in real classroom situations at the secondary schools. Each lesson document comprised a teachers' guide to help set up the environment, a plan for lesson implementation and a student worksheet which promoted hands-on activities during the lesson implementation. The lessons were taught in a classroom with a computer and a LCD projector (for a more description of the professional development arrangement see Agyei, 2012; Agyei & Voogt, 2011). The researcher's role was demonstrative during the lecture sessions and consultative during lab sessions.

Factors influencing transfer of teacher learning

Of much relevance to this study is the potential of transfer of the ICT-enhanced activity-based learning in the teachers' professional and teaching practice. In this paper we used Baldwin and Ford's (1988) model to analyze the beginning teachers' transfer of learning. Based on Baldwin and Ford, one of the three factors influencing transfer of learning is the characteristics of the professional development program (LTCD). Burke and Hutchins (2007) indicated that the intervention design and delivery is an important factor that influences transfer directly or indirectly. Baldwin and Ford referred to the characteristics of this intervention design and delivery as "training characteristics". As reported earlier LTCD in this study was characterized by:

- Use of design teams to develop worksheets, spreadsheet techniques and lesson plans
- Use of exemplary materials (or resources from internet)

- Support from facilitator
- Learning by doing (by exploring spreadsheet techniques activities)
- Enactment of lesson plans in microteaching or classroom settings (cf. Agyei, 2012; Agyei & Voogt, 2011)

Ely (1990, 1999) formulated eight conditions for the implementation of an educational innovation. In the study we adapted Ely's conditions to postulate the other two factors of Baldwin and Ford's model. In particular, four of the conditions (*Dissatisfaction with the status quo, sufficient knowledge and skills, commitment and availability of time*) measured the characteristics of the learners or trainees whiles the other four (*Availability of resources, participation, Rewards or incentives and school culture*) measured work environment characteristics

Research Question and Instruments

The study examined the extent to which 100 beginning teachers were able to transfer knowledge and skills about designing and enacting ICT-enhanced activity-based learning activities (ICT-ABL) gained in the professional development program. The main research question that guided the study was: To what extent is beginning teachers' transfer of learning of ICT- ABL in their teaching practice influenced by learner characteristics, characteristics of the professional development program, and school environment characteristics? The study hypothesized transfer of ICT-ABL ($ICT\text{-}ABL_{transfer}$) (dependent variables) as a function of the independent variables: learner characteristics (LEC), school environment characteristics (SEC) and characteristics of the professional development ($LTCD_{perceptions}$) as were reported by the beginning teachers. Transfer of learning was reported in beginning teachers' actual use and observed enactment of the ICT-ABL.

In Table 1 an overview of the data collecting instruments measuring beginning teachers' perception of learning technology by collaborative design, learner characteristics, school environment characteristics, actual use and observed enactment of the ICT-ABL is presented.

	Instruments		
	Questionnaire	Semi-structured Interview	Observation checklist
Beginning teachers' learner characteristics	✓	✓	
Beginning teachers' school environment characteristics	✓	✓	✓
Beginning teachers' professional development program characteristics.	✓	✓	
Beginning teachers' demonstrated (transfer) ICT- ABL	✓	✓	✓

Table 1: Data collection instruments and relation to the model of transfer.

One hundred participants responded and completed the questionnaire survey which was administered through their emails. A random sample of 20 participants was interviewed and 6 of them were voluntarily observed to provide an authentic depiction of the way in which beginning teachers used ICT-ABL in their naturalistic classroom.

Results

Transfer of learning of ICT-ABL in beginning teachers' teaching practices.

Beginners' teachers reported use of ICT-ABL

A major question dealt with in the study was whether beginning teachers were able to transfer their knowledge and skill in enacting ICT-ABL in their current lessons and teaching practices. Table 2 presents the results of their reported use of ICT-ABL. Beginning teachers reported being able to transfer various aspects: use of teamwork among their students (*M*= 4.53, *SD*= 0.489), use of lesson notes in guiding lessons *(M*= 4.63, *SD*= 0.489) and use of activity-based pedagogical approach (*M*= 4.50, *SD*= 0.50) during instructions while other aspects: use of "interactive demonstration" of spreadsheet techniques (*M*= 3.06, *SD*= 0.653) and spreadsheet techniques to support mathematical concepts formation (*M*=3.18, *SD*= 0.599) appeared to be a challenge. Lack of ICT infrastructure might have been the strongest barrier constraining the teachers in their transfer; successful transfer of ICT-ABL requires ICT facilities. Beginning teachers explained this in their interview data. Two of them indicated:

> In my school, there is only one computer lab which is used for teaching basic ICT for all the students from year 1 to year 4. And the only projector in the school is used by the ICT teachers (T14)
>
> ...but the major problem that hinder my use of the ICT-ABL has been lack of resources. There is no mathematics lab and the computer lab is used purposely for ICT teaching. The projection devices are used mainly for entertainment (T11).

Components	Mean	SD
Activity-driven pedagogical approach (through worksheet) to support student learning	4.50	0.500
Spreadsheet techniques to support mathematical concepts formation	3.18	0.599
Use of teamwork among students	4.53	0.489
Use of "interactive demonstration" of spreadsheet techniques in class	3.06	0.653
Use of lesson plan to guide lesson implementation	4.63	0.489

5=always, 4=often, 3=sometimes, 2=hardly.1=never

Table 2: Beginning teachers' reported use of ICT-ABL (*N*=100)

Beginners' teachers' observed enactment of ICT-ABL

Of the 6 beginning teachers, Felix, Joel, Mark, Gifty, Rene and Ike (pseudonyms used) who were observed, two (Mark & Gifty) were from deprived ICT environments (without any ICT infrastructure whatsoever); the other four were situated in modest ICT settings (with a minimum of one computer lab with at least 40 computers). Mark had just gained appointment in a regional secondary school. The school itself was remote comprising of largely indigenous population. In his lesson, he used components of the ICT-ABL (activities on a worksheet, students working in teams) that did not require ICT facilities. He sees himself as one of the leaders in the school in terms of his ICT knowledge and skills in teaching, but exhibited frustration with the lack of ICT and support. Gifty, who found herself in a similar environment as Mark, used lesson plans to guide her lesson, in which students worked in teams using the worksheet to do various activities but did not use ICT as an instructional tool. She expressed similar frustrations in what she termed as poor leadership in supporting ICT-ABL and remarked on becoming somewhat de-skilled because of her lack of access to ICT facilities. Felix, Rene, Joel and Ike had some kind of ICT infrastructure in their school but had struggles accessing them for use in their classrooms. For example Rene conducted her lesson without any computer available to her (nor her students) in the classroom. She emphasized the possibility of having access to the computer lab once a week, but was hampered by what she sees as an apathetic school culture; in which timetabling was strictly adhered to leaving little or no room for changes. Felix admitted having his own laptop computer which he could use in class but explained that with the current class size of forty-five students, it was impossible to use the computer meaningfully for any student-directed activity without any projection device. Joel and Ike on the other hand were able to implement all components of ICT-ABL for teaching their lessons, yet were not without struggles. In observing Joel, he used his own laptop to enact his lesson (by rotating groups of students around his computer) to explore the potential of spreadsheets giving students' opportunity to discover mathematics concepts and perform authentic tasks because he did not have access to a projector. Ike's students also turned up in groups around his computer but had a difficult time in his lesson because the class size was large, 50. Table 3 shows the ICT-ABL components that the teachers used as were assessed by the researcher.

ICT-ABL components	Felix	Joel	Mark	Gifty	Rene	Ike
Activity-driven pedagogical approach to support student	✔	✔	✔	✔	✔	✔
Spreadsheet techniques to support mathematical concepts formation		✔				✔
Use of teamwork among students	✔	✔	✔	✔	✔	✔
Use of "interactive demonstration"		✔				✔
Use of lesson plan to guide lesson implementation	✔	✔		✔	✔	✔

Table 3: Observation of beginning teachers' use of the ICT-ABL ($n=6$)

Factors influencing beginning teachers' transfer of learning of ICT-ABL

Beginning teachers' perception of "Learning technology by collaborative design"

The beginning teachers in the study reported their perceptions about continued use of LTCD within the existing support structures in their school settings. The results showed positive high perceptions of teachers to learn technology by collaborative design as reported in Table 4.

Learning technology by collaborative design (LTCD)	Mean	SD
Use of design teams to develop worksheets, spreadsheet techniques and lesson plans	4.63	0.489
Use (importance) of exemplary materials (or resources from internet)	4.75	0.439
Support from the facilitator is helpful in the design process	4.88	0.328
Learning by doing (by exploring spreadsheet techniques activities) is a useful strategy in learning to design the spreadsheet-supported activity based mathematics lessons	4.96	0.010
Enactment of lesson plans in microteaching or classroom settings	4.98	0.004

(5 = strongly agree, 1 = strongly disagree)
Table 4: Beginning teachers' perceptions of LCTD ($N=100$)

The overall perception of LTCD ($M=4.85$, $SD=0.191$) was highly valued by the beginning teachers indicating that approximately six, eighteen or twenty-eight months after the professional development program the beginning teachers held strong positive pedagogical views about the professional development program 'learning technology by collaborative design'(LTCD). This was evident that the preparatory program had impacted beginning teachers' views about LTCD and could be central in influencing their use of ICT-ABL in their professions or teaching practice.

Beginning teachers' reported learner characteristics (LEC) and School environmental characteristics (SEC)

Based on the Hierarchical cluster analysis, the eight factors that promoted or hindered transfer were distributed in two clusters (see Figure 1). They were learner characteristics (LEC) (personal factors related to teachers' knowledge and skill, commitment, availability of time and their dissatisfaction with the status quo) as cluster 1 and school environment characteristics (SEC) (school- related factors: school culture, availability of resources, rewards and incentives and participation in decision making) as cluster 2.

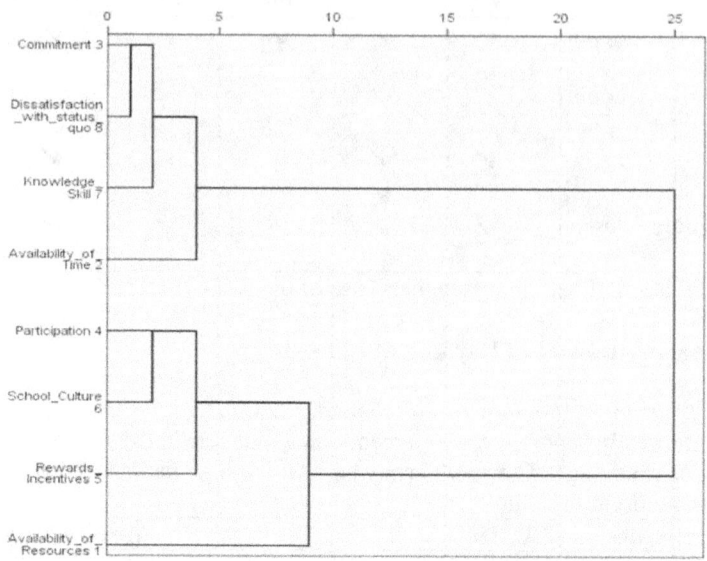

Figure 1: Hierarchical clustering dendrogram of conditions using Average Linkage

Cronbach's alpha for the items in each cluster: .71(LEC) and .79 (SEC) were acceptable according to guidelines provided by DeVellis(1991). Beginning teachers tended to agree strongly to LEC cluster ($M=4.20$, $SD=0.451$), while they tend to disagree on the SEC cluster ($M=2.48$, $SD=0.155$) indicating prevailing unfavourable school environment characteristics. In addition the standard deviation for SEC was relatively small, indicating that the beginning teachers did not differ much in their opinion about the SEC cluster. The differences between the mean scores of the clusters were statistically significant ($p < 0.001$) for both scale scores, with a large effect size ($d=3.17$). Table 5 shows the ranking of the factors with their means and standard deviations as reported by beginning teachers for each factor.

Conditions	Mean	Std Dev
LEC		
Knowledge and skills	4.57	.355
Dissatisfaction with status quo	4.48	.383
Commitment	4.21	.287
Availability of Time	3.75	.562
SEC		
Rewards and Incentives	3.17	.137
Participation	3.02	.103
School Culture	2.05	.292
Resources	1.71	.011

Table 5: Mean score and standard deviations for factors influencing beginning teachers transfer of learning ($N=100$)

Overall, *knowledge and skills* appeared to be the most valued factor followed by *dissatisfaction with status quo*. This seems to suggest that while the program might have impacted on the knowledge and skill acquisition, beginning teachers were dissatisfied with existing methods of instruction and reiterated the need for a change. Table 5 also indicates that the teachers' *commitment* and *availability of time* were important factors that contributed to their use of the ICT-enhanced activity-based activities. On the other hand existing conditions regarding *ICT resources, school culture* and *teachers participation* in decision-making appeared unfavourable and perhaps do not foster teachers' use of ICT-ABL. Lack of ICT resources and unfavourable school cultures especially were perceived as barriers to teachers' use of ICT-ABL. The teachers expressed their frustrations regarding these observations in the interview data in various ways:

> Very few resources are available. Apart from the problem with ICT resources, there are also problems with timetabling. The period for teaching mathematics with ICT is very short whereas the workload is huge (T03).
> The leadership of the school does not afford a high enough priority to ICT planning and implementation. As far as leadership goes in the school, use of ICT-based innovation is not a large focus so there is little I can do (T10).
> My school did not organise any in-service training and time table structure do not allow precise considerations to access computer labs for teaching (T04).

Predicting teachers' transfer of *ICT-ABL in their teaching practices*

The study postulates transfer of learning (ICT-ABL$_{transfer}$) as a function of beginning teachers reported learner characteristics (LEC), their existing (unfavorable) school environment characteristics (SEC) and their perceptions (LTCD$_{perceptions}$) about the professional development program. The exact weights of each parameter and relations between them were determined empirically (Table 6). The result indicates that the R^2 for transfer of learning regarding use of ICT-ABL predicted from the teachers' perception about LTCD showed that 19 % of the variance in the transfer of ICT-ABL in teaching practices was found to be attributable to the LTCD innovation characteristics. The F test ($F(1, 98) = 6.07, p < 0.01$) associated with the independent variable (LTCD$_{perceptions}$) was significant indicating that the independent variable predicted the dependent variable if only the "LTCD$_{perceptions}$" scale was considered in the model. Adding the LEC measure increased the predictability for ICT-ABL$_{transfer}$ from approximately 19% to approximately 21%. Although the LEC measure did not appear as strong as the LTCD$_{perceptions}$ measure, R^2 change =.02, the F test ($F(2, 97) = 3.06, p = 0.047$) was significant (at 0.05) for the model. The existing unfavorable SEC measure when added, increased the predictability significantly, R^2 change =.10, F test ($F = (3, 96) = 4.69, p < .01$) was significant.

ICT-ABL$_{transfer}$	*R*	*R*-square	*F* (Sig)	Standardized coefficients	Sig
Impact of LTCD$_{perceptions}$	0.44	0.19	6.07 (0.001)*	0.27 (*p*)	0.002*
Impact of LTCD$_{perceptions}$ and LEC	0.46	0.21	3.06 (0.047)**	0.25 (*p*)	0.003*
				0.08 (*t*)	0.033**
Impact of LTCD$_{perceptions}$, LEC and SEC	0.56	0.31	4.69 (0.001)*	0.26 (*p*)	0.002*
				0.09 (*t*)	0.036**
				-0.13(*s*)	0.011

Note: ** $p < 0.05$; * $p < 0.01$; p=perception of beginning teachers, t=TEC, s=SEC
Table 6: Coefficients of Predictors: School environment characteristics (SEC), learner characteristics (LEC) and perception about the ICT-enhanced activity-based activities ($N=100$).

Discussions

This study sought to attain an understanding of how characteristics of a professional development arrangement, existing school environment characteristics and beginning teacher's learner characteristics, influenced transfer of learning to utilize an ICT-enhanced activity-based learning in the teachers' professional and teaching practices. Results of the study showed that beginning teachers continued to employ aspects of the ICT-enhanced activity-based learning in their professional and teaching practice within the existing support structures of their respective schools.

The most influential factor reported, which facilitated teachers' transfer and use of the ICT-enhanced activity-based learning activities was the strong pedagogical views about the professional development program the beginning teachers still hold several months after the preparation at the teacher education program. Results from the regression analysis also showed that a significant amount of variance attributed to the teachers' learner characteristics explained differences in the level of transfer of the ICT-enhanced activity-based learning innovation. The most critical learner characteristics reported were knowledge and skills. It was encouraging to note that most beginning teacher's reported having sufficient knowledge and skills, which indicates how well the preparatory program contributed to teachers' professional learning.

The second most critical condition: teachers' dissatisfaction with the status quo shows that the teachers saw the need to change existing teaching approaches towards approaches which support ICT-enhanced activity-based learning activities. Furthermore, the beginning teachers' commitment factor was also reported to have promoted transfer of learning. Riel and Becker (2008) indicated that, teachers who are motivated and have strong commitments to their pupils' learning and their own professional development as teachers will evidently integrate ICT-based innovations, such as ICT-enhanced activity-based learning more easily during their teaching.

Conditions regarding existing school-related factors did not seem to differ much across schools and though were perceived as unfavorable or hindrances, the regression analysis indicated that they were significant in determining transfer of learning for beginning teachers' use of the ICT-enhanced activity-based activities. This is in agreement with studies conducted in the western world (Bate 2010; Benson & Palaskas 2006; Snoeyink & Ertmer 2002; Mumtaz 2000) that have identified school-related factors as important in implementing an ICT-based innovation.

The lesson observations confirmed that participants faced a complex mix of school-related constraints that when combined, contributed to a lack of creativity in using certain components of the ICT-enhanced activity-based learning activities. Particularly, lack of access to the ICT infrastructure and an unenthusiastic school culture were pronounced. In most schools, ICT facilities were not accessible in classrooms. This impacted on the creative use of ICT-enhanced activity-based learning, particularly in large classes. Often, even the most enthusiastic teachers could do little more than rotate students through teachers' personal computers in their classrooms. In situations where a centralized computer laboratory was available, participants struggled to gain appropriate and timely access. This state of affairs is also common in the literature (Groff & Mouza 2008) and also supports the contention that the specific positioning of computers in the school can foster or hinder ICT-based innovation use in teaching and learning (Tondeur, Valcke, & van Braak 2008).

Practical implications

The study showed that a significant amount of variation in the transfer of learning and the utilization of ICT-enhanced activity-based learning activities was attributed to a range of factors across individual beginning teachers' learner characteristics, characteristics of the ICT-enhanced activity-based learning innovation and existing school environment characteristics. The findings reported here therefore highlight areas that require further attention to move the goal of transforming teaching and learning through ICT-enhanced activity-based innovations beyond rhetoric.

Parent Teachers' Association, School Management and Boards must join forces and put priority on the provision of ICT facilities in Ghanaian schools (e.g. mathematics laboratories, computers and projection devices in classrooms) to facilitate and increase access to ICT of teachers. Easy access to ICT facilities will certainly contribute to teachers' use of ICT innovations in schools.

The study found that transfer of ICT-enhanced activity-based learning from the teacher preparation program to the real classroom setting was problematic especially with respect to unfavorable school environment. Consequently, there is an urgent need to resolve difficult dilemmas in the terrain of ICT and innovative school culture such as: school-based in-service education opportunities, flexibility of classroom timetable and willingness to change existing traditional approaches. The study therefore recommends that the Ghana Education Service (GES) strengthen and enforce policies regarding the practical use of ICT for educational practices in the curriculum. A clear articulation of policy within the framework of the teacher education institution and GES could ensure better grounding of learning and transfer of ICT-enhanced activity-based learning in education in Ghana.

Another practice that could smoothen the transition from the teacher preparation program to the schools is an advocate for a collaborative program between providers of pre-service education and schools. In this way principals and school leaders will be supported to provide the type of pedagogical leadership in ICT integration that will inspire new teachers to push the boundaries of using ICT-enhanced activity-based learning innovation. Apart from providing support for school leadership, such a "symbiotic" partnership will help in addressing the realities of specific teaching context; provide a forum for school- and pre-service providers to think together about the learning needs and challenges of beginning teachers' use of ICT in their practices and teaching professions.

The study also unveiled that lack of support in the face of a wide range of responsibilities was a compelling challenge for beginning teachers' use of the ICT-enhanced activity-based learning activities in their practice. For instance while ensuring that the curriculum was covered was particularly important to the beginning teachers in this study, questions like: *how teachers could balance the demands of a crowded curriculum by providing students with opportunities to explore mathematical concepts using ICT in ways that embrace the principles of lifelong learning* and *how effective models of ICT use that cut across curricula and timetable constraints could be addressed* were some concerns raised by the beginning teachers. According to Feiman-Nemser (2011) these multiple challenges of teaching alone for the first time can discourage new teachers from trying ambitious pedagogies and that good induction support could keep novices from abandoning these approaches in favor of what they may perceive as safer, less complex activities. The study has implications in this direction, to advocate for the introduction of induction programs for beginning teachers in Ghana and similar contexts. Such a program will serve as a short term support to ease new teachers' entry into the teaching profession and to help them cope with their first year on the job.

In conclusion the study draws attention to the importance of transfer of learning particularly in the situation of the development and implementation of educational innovations in developing countries to help lessen the gap between learning and sustained work performance for the reason that many innovations in this context are very vulnerable and fail to be transferred.

References

Agyei, D. D. (2012). *Preparation of Pre-service teachers in Ghana to integrate Information and Communication Technology in teaching mathematics.* Doctoral dissertation. Enschede: University of Twente.

Agyei, D. D. & Voogt, J. (2011). Determining Teachers' TPACK through observations and self-report data. In *Proceedings of Society for Information Technology & Teacher Education International Conference 2011* (pp. 2314-2319). Chesapeake, VA: AACE. Available http://www.editlib.org/p/36652

Baldwin, T. T., & Ford, J. K. (1988). Transfer of training: A review and directions for future research. *Personnel Psychology, 41*, 63–105.

Bate, F. (2010) A bridge too far? Exploring beginning teachers' use of ICT in Australian schools. *Australian Journal of Educational Technology, 26*(27), 1042-1061.

Benson, R., & Palaskas, T. (2006). Introducing a new learning management system: An institutional case study. *Australasian Journal of Educational Technology 22*(4), 548-567.

Burke, L. A., & Hutchins, H. M. (2007). Training Transfer: An Integrative Literature ReviewHuman Resource Development ReviewSeptember *Sage Journals, 6* (3), 263-296. doi: DOI: 10.1177/1534484307303035

Ely, D. P. (1990). Conditions that facilitate the implementation of educational technology innovations. *Journal of Research on Computing in Education,* 23(2), 298-305.

Ely, D. P. (1999). Conditions that facilitate the implementation of educational technology innovations. *Educational Technology,* 39, 23-27.

Feiman-Nemser, S. (2011) From preparation to practice: Designing a continuum to strengthen and sustain teaching. *Reachers College Record, 103*(6), 1013-1055.

Goldstein, IL, and Ford, J. K. (2002). *Training in organizations.* Belmont, CA: Wadsworth.

Groff, J., & Mouza, C. (2008) A framework for addressing challenges to classroom technology use. . *AACE Journal, 16*(1), 21-46.

Koehler, M., & Mishra, P. (2005). What happens when teachers design educational technology? The development of technological pedagogical content knowledge. *Journal of Educational Computing Research, 32*(2), 131-152.

Mumtaz, S. (2000). Factors affecting teachers' use of information and communications technology: a review of the literature. *Information Technology for Teacher Education, 9*(3), 319–342.

Riel, M., & Becker, H. J. (2008). Characteristics of teacher leaders for Information and Communication Technology. In J. Voogt & G. Knezek (Eds.). *International handbook of information technology in primary and secondary education* (pp. 397-417). New York: Springer.

Saks, A. M. (2002). So what is a good transfer of training estimate? A reply to Fitzpatrick. *The Industrial-Organizational Psychologist, 39*, 29–30.

Snoeyink, R., & Ertmer, P. A. (2002). Thrust into technology: how veteran teachers respond. Journal of *Educational Technology Systems, 30*(10), 85-111.

Yamnill, S. & McLean, G. N. (2001). Theories supporting transfer of training. *Human Resource Development Quarterly, 12*(2), 195–208.

How People, Tools and Rules Enhance or Inhibit Technology Use in the K-12 Classroom: A Design-Based Activity Systems Analysis

John Cowan
Mayra Daniel

Northern Illinois University

jcowan@niu.edu
mcdaniel@niu.edu

Abstract: This study explored a group of teachers' viewpoints of factors that support or inhibit the integration of digital media into the lessons of K-12 English language learners. The study was conducted using a design-based approach and data were gathered and analyzed using elements of Engeström's (1987) activity systems analysis. A review of participants' reflections on the activity systems elements of rules, tools, people and division of labor yielded two significant findings. First that schools range from low functioning to high functioning in regard to their capacity to support technology use by teachers. Secondly, the most significant determinant in the functioning level of technology use at a school is not the school's location, socio-economics, or ethnic makeup of a school, but rather the administrative rules that govern technology use of a school.

Introduction

The transition from the 20th to 21st century brought with it a new educational call to arms. The call was to assure that K-12 education results in graduates equipped with "21st century" thinking, process and technology skills. Groups designing 21st century standards widely aligned in identifying the need for fewer and more universal standards, such as students using technology and digital media strategically and capably (Common Core, 2010) and students exhibiting a range of functional and critical thinking skills related to information, media and technology (Partnership for 21st Century Skills, 2002). The International Society for Technology in Education (ISTE, 2011) standards, widely used either directly or in adapted form for state standards, call for student skills in using technology to:

- Be creative and innovative;
- Communicate and collaborate;
- Develop research and information fluency;
- Develop and use critical thinking, problem solving, and decision making skills;
- Become good digital citizens;
- Develop a broad base of technology operations and concepts.

In addition, the National Educational Technology Plan (United States Department of Education, 2010) called for the creation a model of learning powered by technology that engages and empowers learners. There are many positives regarding these bodies of 21st century technology standards. The inclusion of terms such as collaboration, analysis and critical thinking signal a return to a broader notion of what constitutes a quality education. Having these skills called for by standards opens the door for their inclusion in instruction. These standards also produce an alignment with the development a 21st century workforce, as identified in proposals such as that of the Ford Motor Company (2010) that calls for the re-design of education to include the development of skills such as problem-solving, critical thinking, communication and creativity and innovation.

The potential trouble with these new standards is that technology has a history of not living up to its promise. The history of technological innovation in classrooms has been described as repetitive cycles of innovation, frustration, failure and blame – with teachers most commonly placed at fault (Cuban, 1986; 1993, Erhmann, 2000). It is worth considering what factors will determine whether a new push for higher-order skills and technology use will create change or result in another cycle of innovation, frustration, failure and blame.

To interrupt these cycles, it is important to examine the challenges confronting teachers who attempt to integrate technology into their curriculum. Research has been done in regard to this issue, yielding a variety of identified characteristics that lead to technology use or non-use. Findings from these studies include barriers of system constraints and belief systems (Ertmer, 1999), the type of staff development employed (Schrum, 1999) and teachers' pedagogical expertise (Pierson, 2001).

This study emerged as a result of two colleagues, one with a background in English language learner instruction (ELs) and one with a background in education technology and technology integration discussing how more technology might be integrated into ELs coursework. This initial conversation ultimately led to a plan for the technologist to come into the ELs course classroom to teach a lesson on digital video production. Students in the course, most of whom were classroom teachers would then be assigned the task of producing a short digital video and integrating the video into a lesson. We hoped that having teachers initially produce a video themselves would provide them with the knowledge and skills that could lead to them helping students to produce movies of their own.

We were aware as we collaborated to design this lesson that our participants would return to their schools with the goal of using technology. We assumed that some would find success and engage students with video and that others might not be as successful. Though we felt there would likely be mixed results, we did not know how participants would be inhibited or supported in using digital video. We also wondered how the experience would vary between schools.

Our study attempted to learn what transpired by using a design-based research approach. This approach included engaging our participants in the process by introducing them to the definitions of the activity systems analysis terms, rules, tools, people and division of labor. We shared with participants that we would gather again at the end of the semester and at that time we would ask them to write reflectively about their experiences of rules, tools, people and division of labor as they integrated their digital movies into their instruction. This article shares the design, implementation and results of the study.

Design-Based Research

Design-based research is identified as a research method well suited to environments that are facing rapid changes, such as the rapid emergence of new technologies in schools. Wang and Hannifin (2007) define design-based research as:

> A systematic but flexible methodology aimed to improve educational practices through iterative
> analysis, design, development, and implementation, based on collaboration among researchers
> and practitioners in real-world settings, and leading to contextually-sensitive design principles
> and theories (p. 7).

They go on to describe design-based research as consisting of 5 main components. The design-based approach is: (a) pragmatic; (b) grounded; (c) interactive, iterative, and flexible; (d) integrative; and (e) contextual. Design-based research (DBR) involves the concurrent application of design, research and practice. Design-based research is one of a variety of approaches that have emerged and/or gained popularity in response to rapidly changing conditions, diverse and complex technical or social dynamics and the significant needs of areas ranging from technology hardware and software development to public school reform. Examples of these models include design based research (Wang and Hannefin, 2005), action research (Lewin, 1948), practitioner research (Anderson, Herr and Nihlen, 1994) and experiential learning (Kolb, 1985). Of one the common features of this model is that they all share a common process that is cyclic and moves through phases of problem identification, question formation/research focus, intervention and analysis. At the conclusion of the analysis, the cycle begins again - drawing upon what was learned in the previous cycle to improve the next iteration of the cycle. In addition, these processes involve direct, active and collaborative participation with stakeholders in the research environment.

The power of this research model is its capacity to bridge between theory and practice to generate solutions in both a timely and effective manner. Design-based research is driven by a disposition toward connecting design interventions with existing theory (Barab and Squire, 2004). In this case, the DBR process led to the applied use of an activity systems analysis approach to understand what happened when teachers attempted to create digital media with their students.

Activity Systems Analysis

Activity systems analysis (ASA) has been shown to be a reliable method to analyze data gathered in investigations that occur in complex social situations (Yamagata-Lynch, 2010). ASA grew out of the field of Cultural, Historical Activity Theory as it evolved from Vygotsky's work on mediated action (Cole, 1996; Cole & Engstrom, 1993). Vygotsky (1986) defined learning from both a developmental and a sociocultural perspective that joined the learner to his/her environment and the people in it. Engestrom extended Vygotsky's work by visualizing groups of individuals interacting as they pursued a goal as an activity system, which he represents with triangle diagrams.

ASA can be used to examine how the components within a system interact based on Vygotsky's preliminary work. In ASA activity systems are diagrammed using triangles to model the main components of an activity system and their potential interactions (see figure 1). Yamagata-Lynch (2010, p. 139) used Engstrom's triangle elements to define the components of an activity system as:

- Rules: Formal or informal regulations that can effect activity in varying degrees;
- Tools: Social others and artifacts (objects) that can act as resources for the subject in the activity;
- Division of Labor: The determination of how tasks are shared in an activity;
- Subject: The individual or groups involved in an activity;
- Object: The goal, motive or reason for subjects to take part in an activity;
- Outcome: The end result of an activity;
- Community: The social group members belong to during the activity.

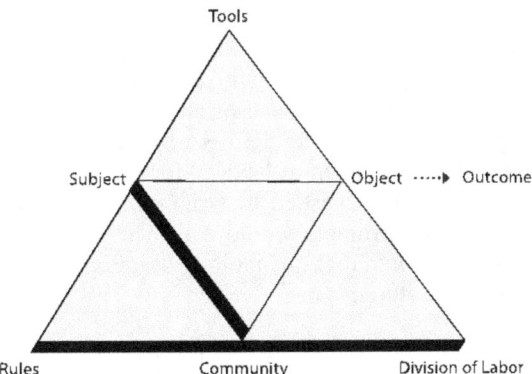

Figure 1: Engestrom's (1993) Activity Systems Triangle with its components.

The explicit identification of the system's components allows for the interactions between components to become accessible for examination. Each component in the system "represents specific, transactional aspects of human activity" (Yamagata-Lynch & Haudenschild, 2009, p. 508). An interaction between any of the components of an activity system has the potential to support or inhibit progress toward an outcome. For instance if a school (system) wants to improve technology use (object), things such as lab policies (rules), checkout systems, hardware and software (tools), and support personnel (people) should work in a manner that supports progress toward improved technology use at the school.

Making an activity system explicit allows for the system to be analyzed. The analysis then leads to potential for changes to the system to support growth and the movement toward the achievement of the object. Using ASA in this study allowed for the examination of the various factors that interacted within the activity system of participants creating and integrating digital movies into their practices.

Methodology

Yamagata-Lynch and Smaldino (2007) used activity systems analysis as a visual tool to capture the current state of a system of staff development in a school setting. They then shared the results of their analysis with the study's stakeholders and used the triangle representations of the system to represent the current dynamics of the staff development (system). This proved helpful in collaborating with participants to improve their staff development. The visual representation of the activity system and its conflicts helped participants to identify and resolve tensions in the activity system. Instead of sharing the process with the participants after the analysis (as in the Yamagata Lynch and Smaldino study), we chose to involve our participants from the onset of the research. This meant that study participants were introduced to the research plan, to activity systems analysis and to ASA terminology. Participants were told that they would be asked to reflect what roles rules, tools and people played in their efforts to integrate digital videos at a future class session. Providing these terms and instructions in advance proved to be effective in helping participants reflect on their experiences.

Participants

There were 26 participants in the study. All were in-service educators, either administrators or teachers, taking the course to fulfill requirements for certification in English Language Learner (ELs) instruction. Their experience ranged from 3 to 20+ years. Because this was a class in ELs endorsement, the participants worked in environments with large numbers of ELs students. The participants' schools were located in a mix of predominantly low and middle-class socio-economic communities, with a few wealthier communities represented as well.

Procedure

The study was introduced to participants at an initial 3-hour class session at the start of term in January of 2012. Students were introduced to and explored the Moviemaker application. They were then assigned the task of integrating a digital movie into an ELs lesson by the end of the semester. Next, the participants were introduced to activity systems analysis – its purpose, how it worked, the ASA triangle model and, most importantly, definitions for the ASA terms rules, tools and people and division of labor. After being introduced to ASA and ASA terminology, participants were informed that they would be asked to write narrative reflections on their experiences the last session for the course and that reflection prompts would ask them to write about how rules, tools, people and division of labor (work) supported or inhibited their technology use. Figure 2 shows the activity system dynamics of the teachers' schools prior to entering the study.

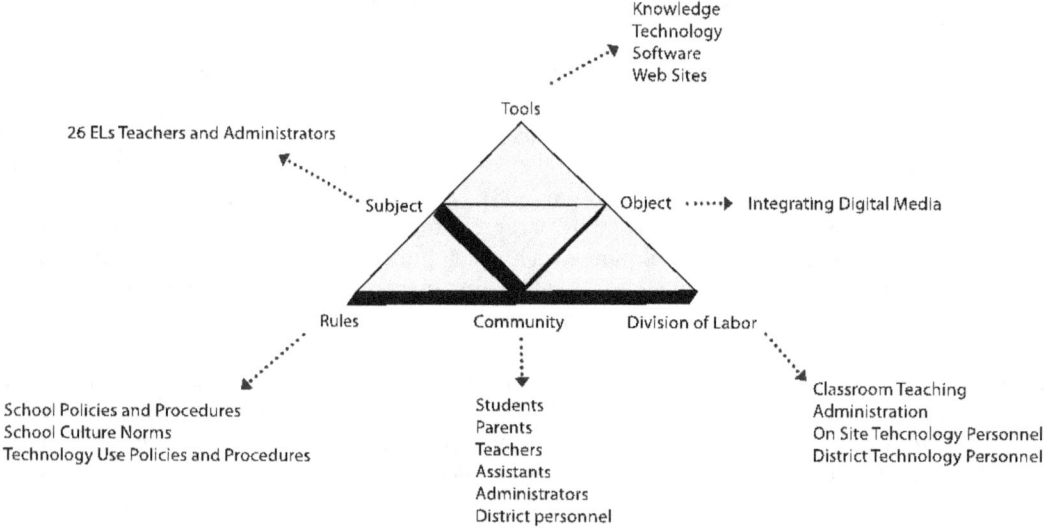

Figure 2: Participants school settings as activity systems.

Research Questions

The main focus of our research focused on two questions:
1. What was the outcome of ELs teachers creating and integrating digital movies into their lessons?
2. How did the experience vary between school sites?

We arrived at our findings by exploring the answers to the following ASA-based questions:
1. What roles did rules play in the outcomes?
2. What roles did tools play in the outcomes?
3. What roles did people play in the outcome?
4. What roles did division of labor (work) play in the outcome?
5. What do the outcomes tell us about schools as activity systems in regard to using technology in the classroom?

Data Collection

The final class session of the term took place in May of 2012. At this session students were presented with the following prompts. Each ASA reflection component re-shared the definitions that were provided at the initial session and then asked the participants to write reflectively about their experiences with digital video via an ASA lens.

Part 1: Rules

Rules can be formal rules such as legal regulations, program rules, established curricular expectations such as how equipment is checked out, or informal rules such as "everybody knows you don't bother Mr. "X" before he has his coffee".

When thinking about experiences working with technology in your teaching:
A. What types of rules (or absences of rules) can you think of that support you using technology with students?
B. What types of rules (or absences of rules) can you think of that inhibit, frustrate or block your use of technology?
C. Are questions "A" and "B" above more or less noticeable, enhanced or pronounced with ELL populations? Please explain.

Part 2: Tools

Tools can be anything that helps you to perform work. Tools can be hardware (computers, video cameras, etc.), software (graphics, word processing, digital video editing applications, etc.), knowledge (knowing the content of a topic) or skills (knowing how to do something).

When thinking about experiences in working with tools to teach with technology:
A. What types of tools (or absences of tools) can you think of that support you using technology with students?
B. What types of tools (or absences of tools) can you think of that inhibit, frustrate or block your use of technology?
C. Are questions "A" and "B" above more or less noticeable, enhanced or pronounced with ELL populations? Please explain.

Part 3: People

People are involved when you teach with technology. For the purposes of this exercise people are considered to be anyone who is in the environment while you are using technology or play some role in setting up the lesson, providing equipment, providing access to technology, etc. In interacting with people for a lesson that uses technology you may collaborate with peers, share equipment, coordinate with administrators, tech people, librarians, media specialists etc.

When thinking about experiences interacting with others in your teaching with technology:
A. What types of people (or absences of people) can you think of that support you using technology with students?

B. What types of people (or absences of people) can you think of that inhibit, frustrate or block your use of technology?
C. Are questions "A" and "B" above more or less noticeable, enhanced or pronounced with ELL populations? Please explain.

Part 4: Work

Work refers to any physical or mental effort expended to create and teach a technology-based lesson. To conduct a lesson that uses technology you may need to plan the lesson, learn new skills, schedule equipment, etc.

When thinking about experiences working with technology in your teaching:
A. What types of work can you think of that support you using technology with students?
B. What types of work can you think of that inhibit, frustrate or block your use of technology?
C. Are questions "A" and "B" above more or less noticeable, enhanced or pronounced with ELL populations? Please explain.

After the participants completed their written reflections, we held a 45-minute group discussion regarding their experiences attempting to create and use digital media in their classroom. Having this discussion just after their writing reflections prompted a thoughtful discussion.

Data Analysis

Our data collection resulted in a pool of data that consisted of the participants written reflections and notes from the group discussion that occurred just after the students completed their written reflections. For the first phase of data analysis we independently coded all data to achieve a measure of interrater reliability. Using a modified axial coding process (Strauss & Corbin, 1990), we read through data and identified statements made by participants. Statements began to cluster as recurring themes in the data as we progressed. Because we had preemptively introduced participants to ASA, we also looked for items in the narrative that reflected the role of people, rules, tools and division of labor. In addition to this process, we also engaged in the ASA approach of situating our findings on the triangle model (see Figures 3 and 4). In the next phase of analysis, we compared our analysis and derived findings from those items that showed up as themes in both of our analyses. This process led to the emergence of two key findings.

Findings

Finding 1: The schools in our study displayed varying levels of functioning in technology use.

The application of Engstrom's ASA applied in our study led to a finding the schools where our participants work (their activity systems) range from being from low functioning to high functioning as it relates to activity that supports teachers using technology in the classroom.

Finding 2: Administrators and administrative policies emerged as the primary determinants of functioning level.

Our analysis of the data revealed that the primary determinant of whether a school was low functioning or high functioning as it relates to technology use was not the community in which the school was located, the socioeconomic status of the school, or by its ethnic make-up – all of which have been identified as potential causes or identifiers of schools at risk for a lack of technology use in the classroom. Instead, the common factor that determined the degree of functioning was the schools' administration and the administrative policies that established the rules, tools and division of labor in the system.

High functioning schools.

The high functioning systems displayed low levels and numbers of tensions. The rules, tools, people and division of labor in high functioning schools served to encourage innovation. Up-to-date tools were available to teachers and students and there was an overall sense of openness to doing what needs to be done to support technology users (as indicated in Figure 3).

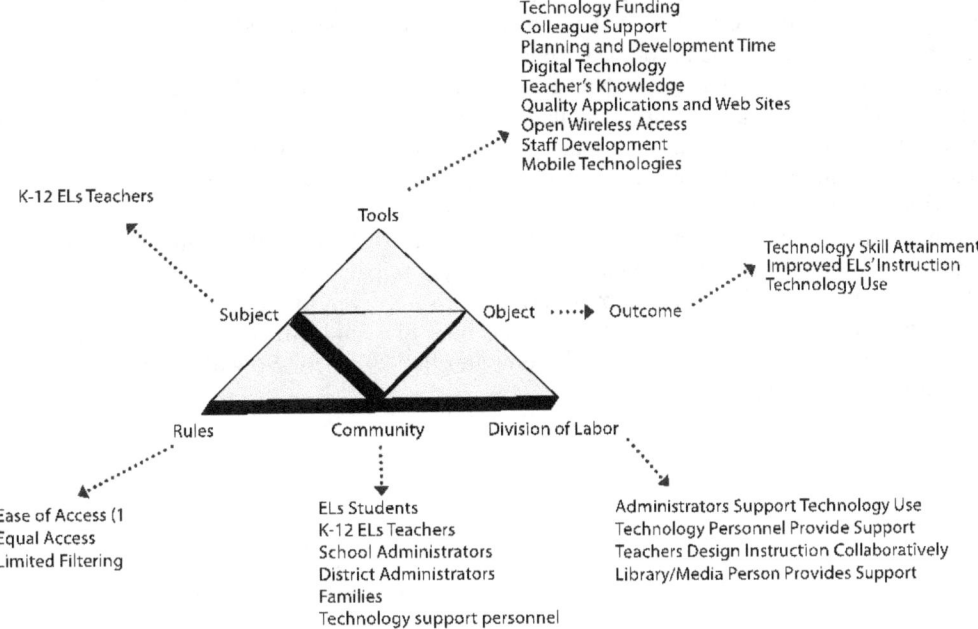

Figure 3: Computer use activity system in a high functioning (low tension) school.

Teachers in high functioning systems report that their districts provided tools that ranged from professional development to the availability of current technologies such as digital cameras, Smartboards, and document cameras. In poorer school districts, teachers in high functioning schools stated that grants were financing some of the new technologies to which they had access. Some reported receiving equipment and training through grants and stated that they were confident that their administrations would continue to seek and find support for their technology programs.

The rules in high functioning schools supported access, collaboration and the sharing of information. Teachers in high functioning schools felt supported in their efforts to use technology. They reported feeling supported by their district, school administration, parents and peers. Teachers in high functioning systems are more likely to be allowed to visit educational web sites of their choice and to have at least minimal access to download software and manage their computers and devices.

The people and division of labor in these systems placed teachers in the role of content experts and the technology staff in the role of supporting the educational process. The technology staff in high functioning schools tended to support teachers by helping them to resolve constraints they encountered when attempting to use technology.

Low functioning schools.

Our data revealed that teachers in low functioning schools must overcome higher numbers of challenges and resolve a variety of tensions if they are to integrate technology into their classrooms (see Figure 4). In low functioning systems top-down rules/controls tend to discourage innovation. Budgets in low functioning schools are inadequate to support current technologies, and creative expression can be discouraged, not only by the system itself, but by teachers' peer groups as well.

In regard to tools, teachers in low functioning systems highlighted issues such as broken equipment and low student to computer ratios. One district was reported to have one mobile laboratory for 1500 students. Two teacher administrators who were part of the teacher cohort of participants shared revealing information about technology budgets in schools during our discussion. One said, "There's nothing built into school budgets about how many computers a school should have." The other administrator shrugged his shoulders and shook his head before sharing the timeline for replacing outdated equipment in his district. He said, "There's typically a 10 year cycle for replacing computers in budgets." Not a single participant from a low functioning school noted that teachers' technological expertise and ability to collaborate with colleagues were tools, which was not the case for teachers in high functioning systems. In fact, some participants from low functioning schools identified a friction between colleagues who attempt to innovate with technology and those oppose technology infusion. They attributed the negative stances of their coworkers to the perception that many teachers feel they lack the time needed to develop technology expertise and did not want others to make the effort. The rules in low functioning schools tended to favor equipment protection over equipment use. Many participants reported having their access to software blocked and their access to web sites stopped by filtering software. Even in the repair of systems tensions emerged. One teacher's statement captures the tenor of these tensions. She said "In my school we are required to email problems to the tech staff. How can we email if our computer breaks down? So we have to go to another classroom to email them. And then they don't come."

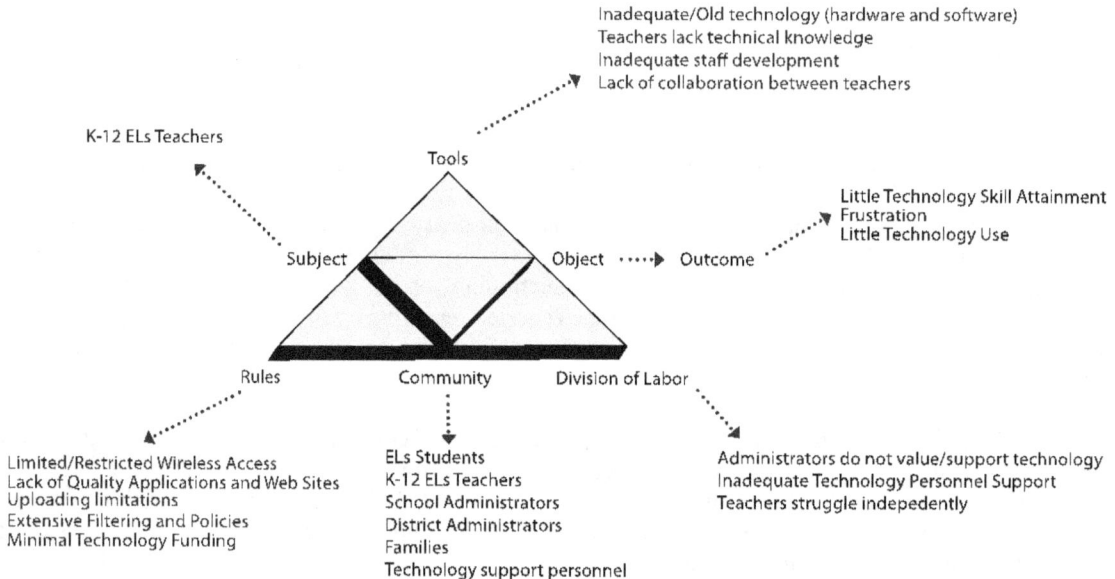

Figure 4: Computer use activity system in a low functioning (high tension) school.

Low functioning schools also demonstrated high degrees of tension in the division of labor. The division of labor in low functioning schools often included an imbalance of power. Teachers who were the content experts, and primarily responsible for instruction, were often denied access by personnel with less education and training. Teachers in low functioning schools reported that decisions about what tools, materials and facilities were accessible and when were taken out of the hands of the teachers and made by others such as educational assistants – who were usually carrying out school and district policies. These policies often created additional constraints, making it more difficult to integrate technology into teaching and learning. This represented a division of labor where personnel who should support technology use actually impeded progress.

Limitations of Study

While we feel the results of this study have merit, the very nature of design-based research means that context is key and therefore we make no claims is it relates to generalizability. It may be that others will find similar results, but we were after answers for our particular context and we will feel encouraged by our findings and plan to engage in further research on this topic.

Conclusions

This study led us to understand that teachers who learn how to use technology to enhance instruction have access to technology and are supported by the rules and people in a system that provides support for innovation and technology use. This finding leads us to believe that educational administrators might need to be more heavily targeted for inclusion in technology skill and technology program development. Based upon our analysis of the experiences our participants shared with us in their reflections, some administrators, schools and districts - regardless of location, economics or ethic makeup - have found a way to support teachers using technology. Other administrators, schools and districts have not. If 21st century learning standards and skills are to be achieved, then teachers will need to be supported by their administrators in their efforts to be innovative and to use technology – not just at some schools – but at all schools. It may well be that a key to reaching the goal of students graduating with 21st century skills is the development of administrators technology skills and knowledge. Shuldman (2004) found that administrative support played a key role in integrating technology into the classroom. The current technology standards from the International Society for Information technology in Education (ISTE) National Educational Technology Standards (NETS) now includes a skill set for administrators (NETS-A). These standards call for digital age leadership, which includes, "Transforming schools into digital age places of learning requires leadership from people who can accept new challenges and embrace new opportunities" (ISTE, 2012, ¶ 1).
Administrators, armed with a better understanding of technology use and technology program development, might be the difference between a K-12 education system yielding students with 21st century skills, or yet another cycle of innovation, frustration, failure and blame – with teachers placed at fault.

References

Anderson, G., Herr, K. & Nihlen, A (1994). Studying your own school: An educators guide to qualitative practitioner research. Thousand Oaks: Corwin Press.
Barab, S. and Squire, K. (2004). Design-based research: Putting a stake in the ground. The journal of the learning sciences, 13(1), 1–14.
Cole, M. (1996). Cultural psychology: A once and future discipline. Cambridge: Harvard University Press.
Cole, M., & Engeström, Y. (1993). A cultural-historical approach to distributed cognition. In G. Salomon (Ed.), Distributed cognitions: Psychological and educational considerations (pp. 1-46). New York: Cambridge University Press.
Common Core (2010). Common core state standards initiative: Preparing America's students for college and career. Retrieved September 3, 2012, from http://www.corestandards.org/.
Cuban, L. (1986). Teachers and machines: The classroom use of technology since 1920. New York: Teachers College Press.
Cuban, L. (1993). Computers meet classrooms: Classroom wind. The Teachers College Record, 95(2), 185-210.
Engeström, Y. (1987). Learning by expanding: An activity theoretical approach to developmental research. Helsinki: OrientaKonsultit.
Ehrmann, S. C. (2000) Technology and educational revolution: Ending the cycle of failure. Retrieved 08/24/12, from www.tltgroup.org/resources/V_Cycle_of_Failure.html.
Ertmer, P. (1999). Addressing first and second order barriers to change: Strategies for technology integration. Educational Technology research and Development, 47(4), 47-61.
Ford Motor Company Fund (2010). PAS next generation learning framework. Ford Motor Company.
International Society for Technology in Education (2011). National educational technology standards for students. Retrieved 08/12/12, from http://www.iste.org/standards/nets-for-students.
International Society for Information Technology In Education (ISTE). (2012). National educational technology standards for administrators. Retrieved 10/15/2012, from http://www.iste.org/standards/nets-for-administrators.
Partnership for 21st Century Skills (2002). The partnership for 21st century skills. Retrieved 08/4/12, from http://www.p21.org.
Kolb, D. A. (with J. Osland and I. Rubin) (1995) Organizational Behavior: An Experiential Approach to Human Behavior in Organizations 6e, Englewood Cliffs, NJ: Prentice Hall.

Lewin, K. (1948) Resolving social conflicts; selected papers on group dynamics. Gertrude W. Lewin (ed.). New York: Harper & Row, 1948.

Pierson, M. (2001). Technology integration practice as a function of pedagogical expertise. Journal of research on technology in education. 33(4).

Schrum, L. (1999). Technology professional development for teachers. Educational Technology, Research and Development. 47(4), 83-90.

Shuldman, M. (2004). Superintendent conceptions of institutional conditions that impact teacher technology integration. Journal of Research on Technology in Education, 36(4), 319-343.

Strauss, A., & Corbin, J. (1990). Basics of qualitative research: Grounded theory procedures and techniques. Newbury Park, CA: Sage Publications, Inc.

United States Department of Education (2010). Transforming American education - Learning powered by technology: The national educational technology plan 2010. Retrieved 09/4/12, from http://www.ed.gov/blog/topic/national-education-technology-plan/.

Vygotsky, L. S. (1986). Thought and Language. Cambridge, MA: MIT Press.

Yamagata-Lynch, L. (2010). Activity systems analysis: Understanding complex learning Environments. New York: Springer.

Yamagata-Lynch, L., & Smaldino, S. (2007). Using activity theory to evaluate and improve K-12 school and community partnerships. Evaluation and Program Planning, 30_4), 364-380.

Yamagata-Lynch, L. & Haudenschild, M. T. (2009). Using activity systems analysis to identify inner contradictions in teacher professional development, Teacher and Teacher Education, 25, 507-517.TESOL-NCATE Standards for P-12

Wang, F. & Hannafin, M. (2005). Design-based research and technology-enhanced learning environments. Educational Technology, Research and Development. 53(4), 5-23.

The Challenges and Supports of Teaching Geometry in a 1:1 Classroom

Anthony Dove
Radford University, U.S.A.
adove3@radford.edu

Abstract: While schools are integrating more technology, research suggests that professional development is needed to help teachers implement technology-enhanced lessons. This study examined the challenges and supports that influenced teachers' instructional practices and technology integration while participating in a long-term professional development program that focused on teaching Geometry with *The Geometer's Sketchpad*. Cross-case analysis suggested that teachers faced challenges of time to complete activities and cover the curriculum, learn the affordances and constraints of *GSP*, and managing student discourse. In addition, teachers found support through success in using *GSP*, participation in professional development, and the building of a colleague support system. The findings of this study suggest that professional development can provide the support needed for teachers to overcome challenges and integrate more technology-enhanced student-centered practices into their lessons.

Introduction

Educating our digitally-active students is becoming increasingly important to prepare graduates for STEM-related careers. However, current trends show that the number of students graduating in STEM-related areas has been declining (Friedman, 2005). To alter this current trend, changes need to occur within the classroom to help engage and motivate students to pursue careers in STEM-related areas.

One promising strategy for altering this trend may be to integrate technology into the mathematics classroom. Studies which have investigated the influence of technology integration into mathematics classrooms have suggested that students were often more engaged in classroom activities, showed greater motivation for learning, and had significantly greater growth in learning (e.g. - Dove, 2011; Ysseldyke et al., 2004). Additionally, mathematical programs such as dynamic geometry environments (DGEs) (e.g.- *The Geometer's Sketchpad* (*GSP*)) offer students opportunities to explore, conjecture, discover, and experiment in ways that are not possible with pencil and paper (Jones, 2000; Marrades & Guittierez, 2000). DGEs incorporate features that allow "students to see as many examples as necessary in a few seconds, and provide them with immediate feedback that cannot be obtained from paper-and-pencil teaching" (Marrades & Guittierez, 2000, p. 119). These features can also help students improve their deductive reasoning skills (Jones, 2000).

Research suggests that digital tools are best integrated through inquiry-based student-centered practices that incorporate opportunities for active discourse (Borko et al., 2005; Piburn et al., 2000). However, access to digital tools does not ensure teachers will shift their instruction or incorporate the available tools (Warschauer, 2006). Such change requires professional development that is content-specific, provides an active learning environment, and integrates similar technologies that the participants have available in their classrooms (Darling-Hammond et al., 2009; Penuel et al. 2007). When such professional development has been provided, teachers in technology-enhanced environments begin to transition towards more inquiry-based learning and collaborative learning opportunities (Fairman, 2004).

Currently, there is limited research on teaching Geometry in 1:1 classrooms. In a 1:1 classroom, every child and teacher have a laptop throughout the entire year. The purpose of this study was to examine challenges and supports that influence Geometry teachers' instructional practices and integration of technology while participating in long-term face-to-face and online professional development that focused on teaching Geometry with *GSP*. Specifically, this study examined the following question: What challenges and supports influence Geometry teachers' pedagogical practices in a technology-enhanced learning environment?

Methods
Participants

This study used a collective case study design (Creswell, 2007) of four Geometry teachers from the same school district (Table 1). During the study, the teachers participated in a larger professional development program that focused on integrating *GSP* into the 1:1 Geometry classroom. As part of the program, the teachers participated in two 5-day face-to-face summer institutes in 2010 and 2011 and completed six online modules during the 2010-2011 school year. This study took place during the fall semester of 2010, following the first face-to-face institute and during the completion of the first three online modules.

Teacher	Years Teaching	School	School Size
Reese	5	School A	741
Rob	3	School B	977
Sean	12	School B	977
Sarah	22	School C	457

Table 1: Participants of the Study

Data Gathering Methods

Multiple qualitative methods were used to gather data, including observations, interviews, and lesson artifacts such as worksheets, *GSP* files, and websites. All teachers were observed during four 90-minute classes throughout the fall semester of 2010. Since all schools were on a semester-based schedule, this allowed the researcher to observe the entire Geometry curriculum. During each observation, the researcher took field notes that included descriptions of activities, questions posed, perceived engagement of students, and any information related to the teacher's instructional practices and integration of technology during the observation. Post-observation interviews occurred at a convenient time for the teacher. All interviews were semi-structured and audio recorded. Questions probed lesson creation, perception of the lesson, reasoning for any technology use, challenges that occurred, and future changes. The participants were also able to contact the researcher via email between observations for any additional help they may need in planning lessons as he was involved in facilitating the professional development. These emails were saved with all other collected data.

Data Analysis Procedures

To perform the cross-case analysis, the four observations, interviews, and artifacts of each individual case were first analyzed (Creswell, 2007). Each case was examined at each observation point using the Levels of Technology Integration (LoTi) (Moersch, 2002). LoTi was utilized because "primary emphasis is given to the degree that technology is used to support a constructivist orientation to classroom pedagogy based on the available hardware and software at the school site" (Moersch, 1996, pp. 52 – 53). For each observation, the most appropriate LoTi level was used to characterize the teacher's Technology Integration and Instructional Practices. Data from the field notes and interviews were integrated to support each characterization. A summary was then created to examine each participant's potential changes throughout semester, as well as factors that may have enhanced or limited such changes. Finally, interview analyses were used to provide the participants' view on the professional development's possible influence on their instructional practices.

The cross-case analysis followed the suggestions of Yin (2003) who stated that for cross-case analysis, one must first identify issues within the individual cases and then examine these issues to identify themes that emerge from multiple participants. While completing this task, the researcher noted any topics that continually appeared or were considered possibly cross-cutting with other participants. Several topics directly appeared in at least two cases such as colleague collaboration, student discourse, use of *GSP* (both supports and struggles), and support from the professional development. All other topics were reexamined to determine if they may be combined into a single theme or if they only appeared for one teacher. The analysis revealed three themes around the challenges and three supports of teaching technology-enhanced student-centered lessons. Challenges included general issues of time, learning *GSP* and its limitations, and handling student discourse. Supports included success in implementing *GSP* activities, time spent in the on-going professional development, and creation of a colleague support system. Each observation and interview was re-analyzed to find supporting data for each theme.

Findings
Challenge 1: Time

Time served as a challenge in that additional time was needed to teach *GSP*, activities using *GSP* often took longer, and there was an underlying pressure to cover the broad curriculum. This challenge was most prevalent early in the semester. Initially, all four teachers stated that *GSP* activities were slowed by students struggling to learn the capabilities of *GSP* such as measuring, constructing, and dragging. The teachers mentioned that this made them rethink the time needed for upcoming lessons and activities. For example, in Sarah's first observation, several students did not complete a *GSP* quiz in class and had to return during lunch. Sarah reflected that some students "are not comfortable and not quick with [*GSP*]. They can find it, if the time is there." (Sarah, Interview 1). However, this challenge decreased such that by the end of the semester, most students were using *GSP* proficiently during observations.

In contrast, the challenge of time to complete activities and cover the curriculum influenced each teacher differently. The lack of a state exam alleviated some of Sarah's concerns as she suggested, "If I'd have had a state exam hanging over my head, I don't know if I would have done it as much" (Sarah, Interview 4). Conversely, Sean did not worry that his *GSP* activities took longer because he felt it was important to provide opportunities for construction and discussion.

I like them just experimenting, though it's always like this trade off. I have to make this instructional decision... You're investing time in something where you're saying, "Hey, if they can make it." Then at some point in the future whether it's tonight's homework or EOC or things like that, if they're being asked to recall facts about the rhombus, they might be able to tie that to the time we spent doing that. (Sean, Interview 4)

Challenge 2: Learning GSP and its limitations

Teachers also faced challenges in learning the capabilities and restrictions of teaching with *GSP*. During his second observation, Rob did not consider that the "Distance" measurement in *GSP* would always be positive. This became a problem when he asked students to find the slope of the line by dividing the "Rise" measurement by the "Run" measurement. He reflected on this afterward, "I didn't even think about it until I came in about how there wouldn't be any negative slope because the lengths were always positive" (Rob, Interview 2).

Sarah also encountered restrictions that she did not anticipate. While teaching the relationship between the central angle, inscribed angle, and corresponding arc, the inscribed angle could be dragged to open the opposite direction of the central angle. Sarah reflected:

I didn't know how to keep it from going past the original vertex so that it was always true... But I don't think that was a big problem because once I said, "Don't cross over that vertex", they stopped doing that and then they could see the relationship. (Sarah, Interview 3)

The teachers also mentioned specific topics that they struggled in finding ways to use *GSP*. Both Sarah and Reese struggled at the end of the semester trying to create *GSP* activities for more complex topics like surface area and volume. Reese reflected:

> I don't know how to do the volume in there. I don't know what its capabilities are, so I just went with something that was fairly easy to use to put problems up on the board and just have them plug in their calculators. (Reese, Interview 4)

Sean and Rob struggled considering if and how *GSP* could be integrated into teaching logic. Sean stated, "Up until this time, I mean, you talk about things like 'What's the converse of this if-then statement?' I mean that's a little harder to do on Sketchpad" (Sean, Interview 2). Sean decided to utilize a *GSP* activity that allowed students to collaborate and conjecture while meeting his objectives for that specific lesson in the logic unit. In contrast, Rob did not feel comfortable with the *GSP* activity he created and instead used direct instruction to teach topics of logic.

Even with issues in learning *GSP* and its restrictions, all four mentioned they used *GSP* whenever possible. Reese's final reflection best summarized how most dealt with this challenge.

> I think that, as the semester progressed, we used it more and more until I got to the point where I don't know how to do, you know, certain things in it… [E]verything that I could find something for, I think that we used Sketchpad for it. (Reese, Interview 4)

Challenge 3: Classroom Discourse

A final challenge that the teachers encountered was deciding when and how to integrate student discourse. This was especially important as active student discourse is a primary component of learner-centered practices. Two major challenges of discourse arose: how to manage on-task discussions; and how to enhance student discourse.

Managing in-class discussions was a concern of Reese, Sarah, and Rob. Sarah was the most anxious about student discourse. After one observation, Sarah stated, "They're a social class, so I try to do discovery with them, but then sometimes I have to pull back because they get off task very easily" (Sarah, Interview 3). However, Sarah recognized that many students were participating in on-task discussions. During the same interview, she also reflected, "I saw them sharing their pictures and looking and talking. So I felt like they were already talking about it, a lot of them" (Sarah, Interview 3).

While Sarah worried about off-task discussions, Reese struggled to keep students on-task. During her four observations, there were times when students did not complete *GSP* or paper-based activities and instead sat talking off-task. Reese believed this occurred because students did not feel confident in each other to effectively collaborate. Reese reflected:

> As long as it's an activity that is fairly straightforward, I don't think there's too much of a challenge in getting this crew to talk about it. If it becomes a little bit more involved, the more frustrated they get with it… the less likely they tend to talk about stuff. They tend to then go, you know, "Me, me! Help me! Help me!" instead of helping each other more. (Reese, Interview 3)

In contrast, Rob and Sean found ways to make discourse become more effective, such as having students use partners during *GSP* activities. Rob was originally against using partners. However, by the final observation, Rob used partners regularly, stating, "When I use Sketchpad, I definitely almost always use pairs or small groups" (Rob, Interview 4). He felt that the use of partners helped both with *GSP* technical issues and activity collaboration. Comparably Sean found partners to be beneficial in building student confidence.

> They're adding value when they're together. I mean, I saw that today… I'd even make a list of nine different interactions that I had with at least one or two students that were maybe working together on something that I

thought were very valuable and I, I can individually remember those things and so I know that there was value that was there. (Sean, Interview 2)

Support 1: Success with GSP

Although the teachers faced multiple challenges, the positive learning opportunities created when *GSP* activities were used served to support and enhance the use of *GSP* throughout the semester. Even when facing challenges, the teachers still spoke positively about how *GSP* activities were able to push student understanding and improve student engagement. The improved engagement was also observed by the researcher as students were more often on task during *GSP* activities than at any time during the observations. Rob observed, "I think something about Sketchpad kind of gets them to work on things a little bit more" (Rob, Interview 3).

Teachers believed this occurred because *GSP* provided unique capabilities in exploring various topics. Reese and Sarah both reflected that *GSP* had been helpful for their visual learners. Reese shared, "I think that they did well using the Sketchpad to actually explore it and then be able to kind of see the relationship and then discuss that relationship" (Reese, Interview 3). Sarah stated:

I think that [*GSP*] has really helped my visual learner. Where before I would try to do things visually by using models and things, but this allows them really to play and fool around with it and really be able to look at it in different ways. (Sarah, Interview 4)

The teachers also suggested that the dragging was one of the most relevant features as it provided a method to create multiple representations efficiently. "Sketchpad lets you look at so many cases all at once" (Rob, Interview 2). Reese suggested the ease of dragging also improved student engagement.

If they just had a pencil and paper, I'm not going to get about half of them to actually play with it and to work with it as you do with the technology because it is fairly accessible to them. They're able to get in there and manipulate it. (Reese, Interview 1)

The four teachers also integrated constructing and measuring when using *GSP* activities. In his fourth observation, Sean had students work to construct the rhombus and square using only their basic properties. One pair of girls measured, dragged, and revised their construction until they created a dynamic square. In their excitement, they asked Sean to come and manipulate their square. In his third observation, Rob stated that he used *GSP* specifically because of its ability to provide accurate measurements and calculations of ratios in similar triangles. He stated, "[*GSP*] basically let them see that the ratios were the same without the error of measuring with the ruler" (Rob, Interview 3).

Finally, the teachers believed that *GSP* provided students improved opportunities to explore geometrical relationships, build their deductive reasoning, and enhance their conceptual understanding. Sarah summarized:

I've been trying to use a lot of Sketchpad, hoping that, with them creating... that they're going to take more ownership in it... In six weeks, they're going to remember that. Or, if they don't remember that, they understand how to recreate it and figure it out. So, I'm hoping that, in the long run, that they are going to become that independent learner (Sarah, Interview 3).

Support 2: Ongoing Professional Development

One of the reasons the teachers felt that they were able to handle the various challenges and be successful when teaching with *GSP* activities was the continuous professional development. This support provided teachers opportunities to build their own understanding of *GSP*, activities that were ready to be used in class, and an active learning environment that focused on student-centered instructional practices. The most mentioned component of the professional development was the opportunities provided to increase one's ability in creating *GSP*-based activities. Sarah reflected that *GSP* gave her a desire to teach topics in a new way.

> The Summer Institute really helped me feel like I can use Sketchpad. Those items I don't know, I am now willing to figure it out. I really feel Sketchpad has really helped my students grasp concepts and think for themselves better. And they seem to enjoy it! (Sarah, Interview 3)

Reese suggested the professional development had improved her ability to use *GSP*. "I knew how to do some pretty simplistic stuff, but I know how to do a lot more now and a lot more connected-type stuff instead of just simple basics" (Reese, Interview 4).

The teachers also mentioned they were using or modifying activities from the professional development. Reese mentioned that she had incorporated several activities throughout the semester such as a project to determine the optimal location for an amusement park between three cities (Summer Institute) and an activity for constructing an animated Ferris wheel (online module). Sean and Rob incorporated the animated Ferris wheel as a project in their classes as well. Sean also modified a triangle construction activity (online module) that was used during the second observation.

One unique idea that was gleaned from the professional development was Sean's concept to build an online repository for *GSP* files. The larger professional development program provided a website in which participants could post *GSP* activities. Sean decided to make a similar site for the math teachers at his school.

> And that's been kind of an idea that I got from the Summer Institute. I really encouraged our math teachers to, I said to them, "Don't we want like, a repository for all of our Sketchpad things. Then if I like something, Rob can access it and, so kids can access it very quickly. And that's why we have the [schoolBmath.com] website… The other teachers can open up things and go, "Oh, I could use some of that in class, I don't know about all of it, though." And then they can modify and post their own things. (Sean, Interview 2)

Finally, the professional development provided continuous learning throughout the semester. Sarah reflected, "Going to the Summer Institute and doing the staff development online, it has kind of kept me going with [using *GSP*]. I think that if I had just stopped, I would have forgotten things" (Sarah, Interview 4). Rob also felt that the continued professional development's methods had given him the confidence needed to enhance his own teaching. "I feel much more confident in my ability to bring in things like Sketchpad. And I think it's helpful. I think it allows me to do a lot of investigating that I haven't been able to do in the past" (Rob, Interview 4).

Support 3: Colleague Support

As Rob and Sean worked at the same school, they both discussed how colleague support helped them handle challenges they faced in creating and implementing technology-enhanced lessons. At Rob and Sean's school, the teachers often collaborated on creating *GSP* activities. The creation of the repository by Sean greatly assisted with this collaboration. In his first observation, Sean reflected that his colleagues helped him improve his *GSP* deductive reasoning activity.

> I came up with it. I sent it to [the other teachers], and they gave me some comments on it… Rob had given me this suggestion, about what if you said, rather than just make a conjecture, what if you actually said, "Such and such student makes the conjecture about this picture, blah, blah, blah" and have the students evaluate somebody else's conjecture. I think that's a really valuable thing for them to disprove somebody else. (Sean, Interview 1)

Both believed that the teacher collaboration had helped them significantly improve their *GSP* files and activities. Rob stated, "When tricky things do come up, between [the four teachers], we're always able to knock it out or trick it into doing what we want" (Rob, Interview 4). Sean agreed and suggested the professional development opportunities had made this possible.

We've got at least two other teachers here that are doing the same things. I think that's really important for us to be able to share those things and debrief at the end of a lesson or at the end of semester. To just say, "Hey, if we tweak this sketch or that sketch, we might be able to combine these ideas or save us an extra day"... So those types of things are happening that I think the past haven't, you know, haven't happened. That's been a really good outcome [of the professional development]. (Sean, Interview 4)

Discussion

The purpose of this study was to explore the challenges and supports that influence Geometry teachers' instructional practices and integration of technology while participating in face-to-face and online professional development. The teachers faced challenges of time management, learning the affordances and restrictions of *GSP*, and how to appropriately manage student discourse in class. However, teachers found support in the continued success of utilizing *GSP* activities, the continual increase in their skills and confidence by participating in the professional development, and opportunities to collaborate with colleagues to create and refine *GSP* activities. Through these challenges and supports, teachers believed they were using technology more in their lessons and activities than in prior years. In addition, the teachers were observed incorporating more learner-centered practices when *GSP* activities were used.

The themes that emerged from this study resonate with findings from prior research. For example, time is a consistent challenge when technology is used. Pierce and Ball (2009) found that while a majority of the teachers believed that using technology motivated students, made learning more enjoyable, provided opportunities for in-depth learning and real-world problems, there were also significant concerns with the amount of time needed for technology-enhanced activities and covering the curriculum.

Research has also suggested that the challenge of learning new technology often limits or inhibits teachers from integrating technology-based activities into their lessons (Manoucherhi, 1999). Part of this problem is that teachers are often expected to participate in professional development and learn these new technologies beyond the school day or during the summer. "The consequence of this practice is obvious... the use of technology becomes yet another addition to an already crowded daily schedule" (p. 38). In addition, the available professional development opportunities often do not follow researched-based best practices (Darling-Hammond et al., 2009).

The challenge of incorporating student discourse is a challenge that many teachers face as they include more student-centered practices. McDougall (1996) found that teachers who believed their role was to serve as the authority figure struggled the most with allowing student discourse. McDougall concluded, "Students need to communicate with each other. This communication could cause anxiety for teachers who feel that classrooms should be quiet, or that only one person should be talking at a time" (para. 48).

The support themes are also validated, especially that long-term research-based professional development can influence teachers' instructional practices (Darling-Hammond et al., 2009; Penuel et al., 2007). Within this study, the teachers stated that they believed the ongoing professional development had improved their skills, their confidence, and their instructional practices. Kor and Lim (2009) similarly found that the teachers who participated in year-long professional development improved their confidence and skills in *GSP*, created more *GSP* activities, and utilized more learner-centered instructional practices.

This study observed how various challenges and supports influenced four teachers' technology integration and instructional practices while participating in on-going professional development. While this study supports the need for content-specific long-term professional development opportunities, it also suggests that there exist challenges that may limit teacher implementation of such instructional practices. Professional development may need to address how to overcome these challenges when integrating technology-enhanced learner-centered activities. Continued research in how professional development can assist in mitigating such challenges is needed.

This study also suggests that opportunities for collaboration both during the workshop and beyond can provide long-term support for teachers. Having multiple teachers from the same school participate in the same professional development may provide the time needed for the teachers to collaborate, refine, and create new technology-enhanced learner-centered lessons. It may also provide the opportunity need to begin a PLC that can be continued beyond the professional development. In this study, opportunity for collaboration appeared to have a positive influence on both Rob, a new teacher, and Sean, an experienced teacher. More research should be conducted to explore how learning communities can influence instructional practices and technology integration as well as how teachers at small schools may be able to find similar support through online PLCs.

Professional development provides the opportunity for teachers to experience, critique, create, and collaborate on utilizing new innovations within their classrooms. Teachers in this study were able to participate in long-term professional development around utilizing *GSP* to make teaching and learning Geometry dynamic and engaging. Although the teachers are still learning and working to improve their lessons, considerable transitions towards more student-centered technology-enhanced practices were observed. As Rob reflected at the end of the first semester:

I think the Institute [and online professional development] has shown me that it is a lot easier than what I might think it may be… I feel much more confident in my abilities to come up with worthwhile sketches to use in the classroom. (Rob, Interview 4)

References

Borko, H. et al. (2005). Artifact packages for characterizing classroom practice: A pilot study. *Educational Assessment,* 10 (2), 73-104.

Creswell, J. W. (2007). *Qualitative inquiry & research design: Choosing among five approaches* (2nd ed.). Thousand Oaks, CA: Sage.

Darling-Hammond, L. et al. (2009). *Professional learning in the learning profession.* Washington, DC: National Staff Development Council.

Dove, A. (2011). The influence of 1:1 school environments on geometry achievement of economically disadvantaged students. *Society for Information Technology & Teacher Education International Conference, 2011,* AACE, Nashville, TN.

Fairman, J. (2004). *Trading roles: Teachers and students learn with technology Maine Learning Technology Initiative.* (Research Report #3). Maine Education Policy Research Institute, The University of Maine Office, Gorham, Maine. Retrieved from http://usm.maine.edu/cepare/Reports/MLTI_Report3.pdf.

Friedman, T. L. (2005). *The world is flat: A brief history of the twenty-first century.* New York: Farrar, Straus and Giroux.

Jones, K. (2000). Providing a foundation for deductive reasoning: Students' interpretations when using dynamic geometry software and their evolving mathematical explanations. *Educational Studies in Mathematics,* 44, 55 - 85.

Kor, L. K., & Lim, C. S. (2009). Lesson study: A potential driving force behind the innovative use of Geometer's Sketchpad. *Journal of Mathematics Education,* 2 (1), 66 – 82.

Manoucherhri, A. (1999). Computers and school mathematics reform implications for math teacher educators. *Journal of Computers in Mathematics and Science Teaching,* 18 (1), 31-48.

Marrades, R., & Gutierrez, A. (2000). Proofs produced by secondary school students learning geometry in a dynamic computer environment. *Educational Studies in Mathematics,* 44 (1/2), 87-125.

McDougall, D. E. (1996). Mathematics teachers' needs in computer-based geometric environments. *8th International Congress on Mathematics Education.* 1996, ICME, Seville, Spain. Retrieved from http://mathforum.org/mathed/seville/mcdougall.html.

Moersch, C. (1996). Computer efficiency: Measuring the instructional use of technology. *Learning and Leading with Technology,* 52 – 56.

Moersch, C. (2002). *Beyond hardware: Using existing technology to promote higher-level thinking.* Eugene, Oregon: International Society for Technology in Education.

Penuel, W. R. et al. (2007). What makes professional development effective? Strategies that foster curriculum implementation. *American Educational Research Journal,* 44 (4), 921-958.

Piburn, M. et al. (2000). *Reformed teaching observation protocol (RTOP): Reference manual* (ACEPT Technical Report No. IN00-3). Tempe, AZ: Arizona Collaborative for Excellence in the Preparation of Teachers.

Pierce, R., & Ball, L. (2009). Perceptions that may affect teachers. *Educational Studies in Mathematics, 71*(3), 299 – 317.

Warschauer, M. (2006). Going one-to-one: The experiences of cutting-edge schools suggest the whys, the why nots, and the hows of laptop learning programs. *Learning in the Digital Age,* 63 (4), 34-38.

Yin, R. K. (2003). *Case study research: design and methods* (3rd ed.). Los Angeles, California: Sage Publications.

Ysseldyke, J. et al. (2007). Use of a progress monitoring system to enable teachers to differentiate mathematics instruction. *Journal of Applied School Psychology,* 24 (1), 1-28.

Teachers Teaching Teachers Technology:
An Innovative PK-12 Professional Development Program

Mark W. Simpson
Florida Gulf Coast University, United States
msimpson@fgcu.edu

Sheila Bolduc-Simpson
Florida Gulf Coast University, United States
sbolduc@fgcu.edu

Abstract: This action research study involved the design, development, implementation and assessment of a professional development program for the training of PK-12 educators in the use of Web 2.0 technologies for the teaching of writing in their content areas. Twenty-two educators from the five counties served by Florida Gulf Coast University (FGCU) in Southwest Florida participated in the **Spring 2012 Technology Workshop Series**. They received instruction in the use of Web 2.0 technologies, used them in their classes, reported on their use to their fellow workshop participants, and held Web 2.0 technology training sessions with their school colleagues. Data was collected using pre-Series, formative, summative and post-Series tools, and on-site class visits. Findings indicated that the Series was effective but that involvement by stakeholder school districts was necessary. Components of an effective professional development program model are suggested. An iterative PK-12 professional development program is also outlined.

Introduction

Picture this all too familiar scenario that takes place in PK-12 public schools in America. It's the third Tuesday of the month. The bell rings at 11 a.m. Students stream out of class in orderly lines out the door and onto the yellow school buses. It's early dismissal day and time for professional development. Teachers lumber off to the media center for the mandatory in-service half day or half hour of less than action-packed learning on the integration of technology across the curriculum. Huber (2010) refers to this reluctant learning as "polite learning." Except for a few first-year teachers, the rest stare fixedly over the head of the outside expert who drones on about something that may or may not be related to what the teachers are doing in their classrooms or should be doing in their classrooms. Meanwhile, the teachers are in another world thinking about how they will get through the 175 papers that sit on their desks ready to be graded. This top-down model of delivering professional development in which information is dispensed to unwilling participants has questionably worked even in the industrial age of education where learning was about input and output. Information goes into the empty vessels and knowledge comes out. Traditional models of professional development often give the allusion of collaboration and conversation because teachers are together in one room, but often the reality is that this conversation becomes a Q&A session at the end of the workshop or in-service session.

There are many problems with the typical PK-12 professional development model that result in not meeting the needs of teachers. These problems include lack of stakeholder involvement, the one-stop shopping approach vs. the ongoing professional development approach, direct teaching vs. practice and follow up, and short-term and shallow assessment procedures. These are not the healthiest ingredients in a recipe for a positive professional learning experience for PK-12 teachers who are already overburdened during their teaching day - with the actual work of teaching!

This action research project addresses these problems and the need for Florida's teachers to integrate technology comfortably and skillfully into their content areas. The need to teach Florida's students technology skills is woven throughout Florida's Sunshine State Standards. Florida's Department of Education technology standards state, "Students must learn to use technology effectively to be prepared to live and work in our complex, information-rich world (Technology and the Florida Sunshine State Standards, 2012). In order for students to learn these skills, educators must learn them.

As PK-12 school districts in Florida move closer to adopting and implementing the national Common Core Curriculum standards, technology integration will be highlighted. In the Next Generation Sunshine State Standards (2010), there is a vision outlined for what it means to be a literate person in the 21st century. The Common Core Curriculum standards describe the information literacy and technology skills that are needed to help students meet the challenges of living in a complex digital world.

According to the IESD (2011) National Survey Report titled, *Digital Districts: Web 2.0 and Collaborative Technologies in U.S. Schools*, in spite of a national upward trend in the acceptance and use of online technologies in K-12 school districts, only 25% of teachers make use of teacher and/or student-generated content. In contrast, most respondents reported positive attitudes in their districts toward both teacher and student-generated online content. Regarding Web 2.0 technologies, recommendations in the report call for increased and/or improved professional development opportunities, the development of professional learning communities, and simple and user-friendly ways for educators to integrate Web 2.0 technologies with instruction.

An additional need for the professional development of educators in the five counties of Southwest Florida served by FGCU – Lee, Collier, Charlotte, Hendry and Glades - who participated in the **Spring 2012 Technology Workshop Series** was identified. At the beginning of the Series, ninety-four percent of the participants indicated that their proficiency level of Web 2.0 technologies was at the beginner or intermediate level. All indicated an interest in incorporating Web 2.0 technologies into their lessons. One respondent stated, "I would like a thorough understanding of using the technology before introducing it in my classroom. It is difficult to participate in professional development that is offered before school for half an hour. We just get started and we have to leave. I would like 'hands on training' to help me retain the information." (Spring 2012 NWP @ FGCU Technology Workshop Series Information and Application).

The primary research question posed by the researchers was, "Is there a professional development model that will prepare PK-12 educators to increase their proficiency in the use of technology to support their teaching and engage their digital learners?"

Literature Review

Today's educators are expected to use technology in their classrooms to optimize student learning. Professional development programs that train teachers how to be more proficient in the integration of technology into their classroom teaching must involve all stakeholders: school district IT personnel, school media specialists, professional development staff, school administrators, and the teachers themselves. All of these stakeholders must be a part of the decision making process and have an investment in the outcome of the training program. Workshops or in-service activities that have made an impact in teaching and student learning are ones that are focused on improving student learning and are connected to student learning outcomes (Jensen, 2009).

Yeung, Taylor, Hui, Chiany & Low (2011) found in their study of the mandatory use of technology in teaching that when policy makers require teachers to apply digital technology in teaching, the more competent teachers are less likely to be compliant and those who were competent may not actually implement technology in their teaching. They suggest that a more productive approach to training teachers in the integration of technology in their classrooms is to increase the competence of the teachers so that they perceive the value of technology as a tool for instruction and learning and apply it in their teaching. Instead of requiring people to adhere to directives, a better approach to professional development would be to increase teachers' self-perception of their technology competence so they see the value of technology.

Mandatory workshops and in-service activities that require teachers to attend may not always lead to positive professional learning experiences. Valuable workshops and in-service activities are those that are interactive and based on teachers working as a collaborative community of inquiry. They are not one-stop shopping events but instead are teachers coaching one another, sharing best practices and discussing the challenges of meeting the needs of learners and improving student learning (Laurel et al., 2001).

Providing teachers with opportunities to attend technology development workshops on a voluntary basis has merit. These workshops would offer both intrinsic and extrinsic motivators, be non-threatening and focus on the incremental development of skills and knowledge in the use of new technologies. When teachers have positive experiences in learning these technologies, they will more likely have more positive attitudes towards using them.

Research by Garet, Porter, Desimone, Birman and Yoon (2001) support professional development activities that focus on content knowledge, active learning opportunities, ongoing collaboration of teachers, and professional learning that includes experiences that are consistent with teachers' goals and are tied to state standards and assessments. Their study demonstrated that sustained professional development provides more opportunities for in-depth discussion of content and teaching strategies. A second benefit of sustained professional development is that teachers are more likely to experiment with new learning activities in their classrooms and obtain feedback on their teaching.

Inherent in the definition of "professional development" is the idea of ongoing formative and summative evaluation. Training programs must be regularly assessed for their effectiveness, efficiency, and impact in achieving identified learning goals, improving teaching, and assisting all students in meeting the goals (Learning forward - professional learning for student results). In Don Kirkpatrick's four levels of evaluation (The Kirkpatrick Philosophy) behavior change on the job is necessary before results demonstrating the value of training can be possible. This provides "strong evidence that effective training led to targeted learning, which contributed to critical on-the-job behaviors" (Kirkpatrick, 2007). An effective professional development program includes these concepts in its design.

An area of knowledge that is explored in the TPACK (Technological Pedagogical Content Knowledge) framework focuses on the development of technological and instructional knowledge and skills (Technological Pedagogical Knowledge – TPK). Activity types that actualize this, at K-6 grades, for example, include the use of Web 2.0 applications (K-6 Literacy Learning Activity Types).

Methodology

Sponsored by mini-grants from the FGCU Chapter of the National Writing Project (NWP) and the FGCU Whitaker Center for STEM Education, the **Spring 2012 Technology Workshop Series** was held on six alternate Saturday afternoons on the university campus. PK-12 educators in the five counties served by FGCU were invited to submit applications online (see Figure 1). From approximately thirty applications, a select group of eighteen PK-12 educators was chosen (four in higher education).

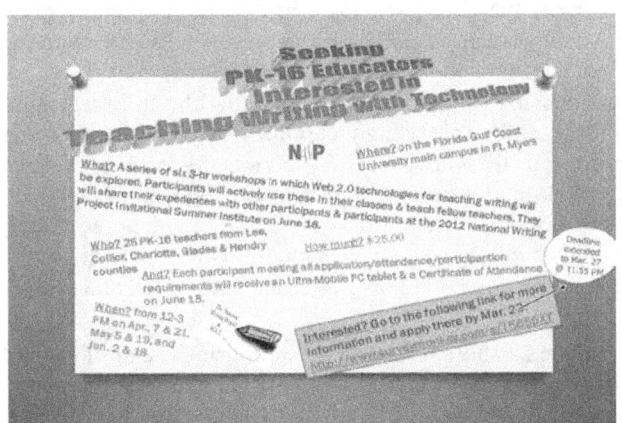

Figure 1: Advertisement for the Spring 2012 Technology Workshop Series

The Series focused on the instruction and use of sixteen Web 2.0 technologies in the teaching of writing in their courses. Each three-hour workshop targeted a different functional category: presentation (SlideRocket, StoryBird, TimeToast), communication (Schoology, Voki, GoAnimate, VoiceThread), collaboration (Scribblar, bubbl.us, Google Docs Drawing), assessment (QuizStar, Polleverywhere, Lino), and productivity (Weebly, Youblisher, LiveBinders) tools.

A multifunctional, interactive website was developed and continues to serve as a resource for the professional learning community that has evolved from the Series. The website houses materials developed by facilitators and participants (e.g., Web 2.0 tutorial handouts, participant reflective writing, surveys, blog posts, Web 2.0 resources) and was developed using Weebly.

Workshop format included a period in which participants shared how they and/or their students used the Web 2.0 tools presented in the previous workshop. Following this, participants learned and practiced three new Web 2.0 tools. Finally, participants shared what they produced with the group and how they planned to use the tools in their teaching before the next workshop.

As an added benefit, each Series participant received a state-of-the-art Android tablet for meeting program requirements:
1. attendance at each of the six workshops
2. one presentation and/or workshop on these technologies at their schools attended by fellow educators at the schools and to which the Series facilitators were invited and attended.
3. a presentation/workshop at the 2012 Invitational Summer Institute sponsored by the FGCU chapter of the NWP on the FGCU campus on June 18, 2012.

Pre-Series, formative, summative and post-Series/follow up assessment tools and visits to participants' classes have been used to evaluate the effectiveness of the Series.

Findings

Thirty-one pre-workshop surveys were completed by PK-12 educators in the five counties served by FGCU who were interested in attending the **Spring 2012 Technology Workshop Series**. Their feedback provided, among other information, their grade level, school, and knowledge of various Web 2.0 tools for each of the five functional categories noted earlier. Asked to comment on why they felt that they should be selected to participate in the Series, responses varied from wanting to incorporate technology into their lessons for the benefit of their students to having the knowledge and skills necessary to train the trainers. One applicant noted, "Technology has the opportunity to be an equalizer in the lives of the children I teach. Web 2.0 tools can give children opportunities to express themselves and their knowledge and abilities in ways that may better suit their learning styles and abilities." Another stated:

> I believe that I should be selected to participate in this Technology Workshop Series because I believe that technology is a critical piece of the teaching puzzle. There are many pieces that work together to make learning fun and build successful adults, but if we are not teaching with technology then we are missing something and not getting the full picture that our puzzle creates. Our students need to feel comfortable using technology outside of their social lives. They need to be able to use technology in the classroom...By taking this series I would not only be able to further my technological skills, I would be a great role model to my students: showing them that as technology advances so do I. That I too am a lifelong learner. Lastly, I would have the opportunity to help fellow colleagues advance their skills. I am an FGCU alumni and know firsthand as a student and a professional how important team work and collaboration are.

Series participants completed a short six-response survey at the end of each of the five Web 2.0 workshops. The formative feedback consistently indicated that all participants strongly agreed or agreed that the sessions were clear and to the point, well organized and that the level of difficulty was appropriate. They also reported that they would use what they had learned in their teaching. Commenting on what they liked most about the second workshop, for example, one participant stated, "I like that we share ideas on how to use these tools in our classroom. Ideas were shared that I had not even thought of, and I can implement these ideas for my summer classes." In this same survey, in comments for improving the workshops, participants suggested shortening the initial 'show and tell' presentations so that more Web 2.0 instruction and practice time was available. A follow up survey indicated that nine (64.3%) of the 14 participants who completed it preferred the workshop format as it was: 30 minutes for show and tell , 120 minutes of Web 2.0 presentation and practice, and 15 minutes of invitation to write and evaluate.

Sixteen participants of the Series completed the summative survey administered on the last day of the workshops. In self-describing their level of Web 2.0 technology expertise before completing the Series, 9 (56%) described themselves as beginner while 7 (44%) noted that they considered themselves intermediate. After the Series, 10 (62%) described themselves as having intermediate Web 2.0 technology expertise and 6 (38%) as advanced. The Web 2.0 technology most used in classes after workshop presentations by the participants was Voki (14 participants or 87.5%) followed by SlideRocket (12 participants or 75%). Nine participants (56.3%) reported never using VoiceThread after the workshops. Twelve (75%) participants planned to use YouBlisher as a productive tool in the following academic year. Six (37.5%) participants felt that VoiceThread was the least useful Web 2.0 tool for their teaching whereas StoryBird was noted as the most useful (10 participants or 62.5%).

Participants noted different ways in which their students used the Web 2.0 tools. Some examples were the following:

1. A kindergarten teacher used Scribblar. The children designed a room. They had to add a picture of their sea life creature, add three facts about their sea creature, and ask a question for their friends to respond.
2. A Media Specialist demonstrated Scribblar in her school with other teachers in remote buildings chiming in.
3. A college math teacher had his students use TimeToast to present the history of math at Research Day at Florida Gulf Coast University.
4. A second grade teacher had her students create StoryBird books at home with their parents.
5. An eighth grade teacher used Polleverywhere to check comprehension of English concepts (http://www.polleverywhere.com/free_text_polls/LTIxMzQzMTY4NjQ).
6. A fourth grade teacher had her students create a GoAnimate movie.
7. A ninth grade teacher used Linoit as a virtual poster board to brainstorm ideas for a group project and post questions on readings.
8. A college Colloquium professor had her students use SlideRocket for their Colloquium projects.
9. A kindergarten teacher used Polleverywhere for question of the day, favorite part of the day, history of the day review.
10. A third grade teacher introduced Bubbl.us to students and they brainstormed what they learned about ocean life creatures.
11. A fifth grade teacher used Voki to introduce a social studies lesson on the three branches of the government.
12. A ninth grade teacher used Schoology for a group research project.
13. A chemistry teacher used TimeToast for her calendar on the learning management system to remind students of assignment due dates. Scribblar was used by this same teacher for online weekly office hours.

Participants likewise were employing the tools in creative ways such as using Weebly as a class website, LiveBinders as a collaborative tool with the teachers on a team, and Polleverywhere in class or before class to seek student responses to service learning and field trip experiences.

In describing their experiences teaching their colleagues about one or more of these Web 2.0 tools (during the professional development workshop/presentation required by all participants in the Series), comments such as the following were typical

My colleagues are so excited about using these tools. I presented everyone of these to all of our teachers and admins, plus outside vendors when appropriate. Everyone connected with at least one application and several teachers are using many. The feedback and desire to learn more is overwhelming.

Since this was an integral part of the Series, the facilitators produced MP4 video clips of each participant's professional development session, posted these on the Series website, and shared them with all participants. The following are sample clips:

1. Elementary School in Ft. Myers, Florida (http://youtu.be/zWcXajWiIzs)
2. Elementary School in Charlotte, Florida (http://youtu.be/H4IxYFQesww)
3. Elementary School in Clewiston, Florida (http://youtu.be/lCTld2bH5JI)
4. Elementary-Middle School in Sanibel, Florida (http://youtu.be/J3IsDvJz2yg)
5. High School in LaBelle, Florida (http://youtu.be/kVGMjPFWHWU)
6. State College in Ft. Myers, Florida (http://youtu.be/WwTPAd2qUJg)
7. University in Ft. Myers, Florida (http://youtu.be/CPZEo7TjwIk)
8. The presentation/workshop at the 2012 Invitational Summer Institute sponsored by the FGCU chapter of the NWP on the FGCU campus on June 18, 2012 (http://youtu.be/D58RxVT3vYM).

When queried about receiving a mobile tablet upon completion of all requirements of the Series, 9 (60%) of the participants noted that it was a secondary motivator, two (13.3%) that it was the main motivator, 1 (6.7%) that it was the only motivator, and 3 (20%) that they would have completed all requirements of the Series if no tablet were offered.

A follow-up survey in the fall of 2012 assessed the Series participants' current use of the sixteen Web 2.0 tools in their classes. Table 1 summarizes the responses from the 15 respondents.

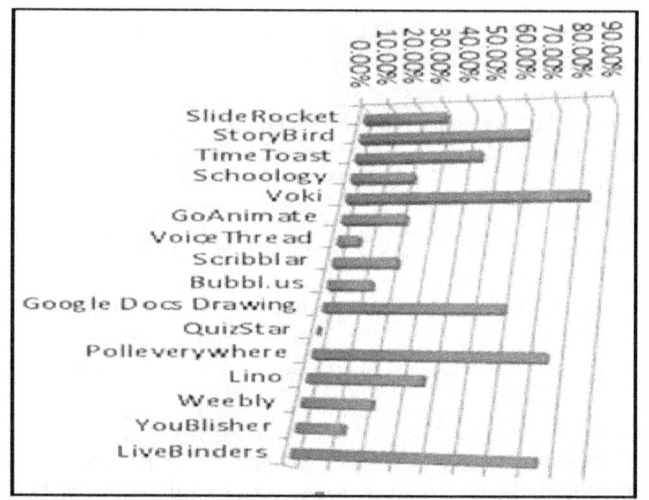

Table 1: Use of Web 2.0 Tools: Post Technology Workshop Series

One participant commented on the use of one of the presentation tools: "I created a Voki for my website. As the year progresses with my 2nd graders, I plan on having them create their own Voki's as well. This tech workshop introduced me to Schoology. From there, I learned about a similar site called Edmodo and I prefer that one and use it with my class."

More than three-fourths of the participants responded that the colleagues to whom they had presented a workshop on a few of the tools in the spring were also using them in the fall. The Series participants were requested to estimate how many students had been exposed to the tools as a result of these collegial workshops. Some of their comments follow:

1. The Secondary AVID students used the web 2.0 tools. 4 Educators - 150 students

2. 7 Colleagues 22 students per class
3. I have presented to both teachers in my school and the district media specialists. By anecdotal evidence only, within my school, approximately 300 students would have been exposed to several of the tools at this point. I expect to go over them again in the spring so they can be integrated into end of the year projects. I have no way to know about the media specialists, but there are 32 elementary schools and many of them told me they showed it to their teachers. So the potential would be perhaps hundreds of students introduced to the tools.
4. I estimate that at least 5 teachers at my school now use Voki with their class. That would be about 100 students.

When asked to comment on the level of student engagement with the Web 2.0 tools that participants have used in their classes, all respondents stated that students were either engaged (23.1%) or highly engaged (76.9%). A typical comment was "Students ask to use them daily!"

Conclusions and Recommendations

There is an ongoing need for today's teachers to be equipped with the latest skills in and knowledge of new and emerging technologies in order to meet the ever demanding needs of their learners and the increasing focus on these technologies by local, state and national oversight organizations. This action research project focused on a professional development model that emphasized various components for success. One shortcoming was the exclusion of all stakeholders in its design, development and execution, that is, local school district personnel involved in the professional development of their teachers were not consulted. Their contribution to the Series would have positively impacted the significance of the project to all of their teachers, ensured that initial applications reached all district teachers, and provided valuable expertise on the technologies that might have been offered.

Notwithstanding, feedback from the Series participants and follow up visits to their classes by the authors clearly suggest that there is a professional development model that can effectively prepare PK-12 educators to become more proficient in the use of technologies to support their teaching and engage their learners. Components of an effective professional development program model include building teachers' confidence through incremental training sessions with varied active and collaborative learning activities over an extended period of time. Equally important factors are offering voluntary program participation by appealing to both intrinsic and extrinsic motivators, focusing on meeting the real needs of teachers often expressed in meeting required student outcomes, and including multiple assessment tools involving participant self-reporting and on-site visits.

What's Next?

There is a need for the professional development of PK-12 educators in the use of existing and emerging technologies. The 2012 *NMC Horizon Report* identifies mobile devices and their applications, and tablet computing as technologies expected to enter mainstream (P)K-12 classrooms in one year or less. Game-based learning is predicted to come into use in two to three years.

Further evidence of the need to prepare PK-12 educators to teach existing and emerging technologies to their digital learners is noted in the *School Principals and Social Networking in Education: Practices, Policies, and Realities in 2010* in which, "ironically, students and many teachers are now using online, collaborative technology at home, on the go, and even sometimes in the school hallways - but typically *not* in the classroom" (p. 3).

Building on the success of the Spring 2012 Technology Workshop Series, the authors propose An Iterative Professional Development Program: Teachers Teaching Teachers Technology which focuses on current and emerging technologies. This program addresses the ongoing need for instruction in existing and emerging online technologies in PK-12 schools in the five counties served by FGCU. This program can be successfully implemented annually as both the reach is extended and the scope is broadened. It will engage students to become more effective digital learners and increase the proficiency of PK-12 educators in the use of existing and emerging online technologies to support their teaching.

The proposed program will target not only existing (Web 2.0) but also emerging (mobile devices and applications, tablet computing, and game-based learning) online technologies broadening the scope of the original program. Furthermore, it will involve active collaboration with PK-12 stakeholders (school district technology and professional development units), thereby, extending the reach of the original program. A benefit of this collaboration will be the possibility for participants to receive continuing education units. The program will further develop the fundamental principle of teachers teaching teachers by progressively involving more and more program participants in the program and in its facilitation as it moves into the future. This iterative element will ensure that a new group of educators is trained annually and former program participants are involved as facilitators and also educated in emerging technologies and, hence, extend the reach of the original program.

In addition to the use of formative and summative evaluation metrics, stakeholder feedback (school districts) will be an important program design, development and evaluation tool. Additionally, follow up surveys and visits to participants will assess their use of the new technologies. Picture this new scenario: An iterative PK-12 professional development program in which teachers teach teachers technology.

References

2010 Next Generation Sunshine State Standards. Retrieved October 8, 2012, from http://www.fldoe.org/bii/curriculum/sss/.
A continuous improvement model for teacher development and evaluation. (2010). Retrieved October 8, 2012, from www.aft.org/pdfs/teachers/improvemodelwhitepaper011210.pdf.
Bolduc-Simpson, S., & Simpson, M. Spring 2012 Technology Workshop Series. *Spring 2012 Technology Workshop Series - Home.* Retrieved October 8, 2012, from http://nwpweb2.weebly.com.
Gable, E., & Burns, M. (2005). Models and best practices in teacher professional development. *Using technology to train teachers: Appropriate uses of ICT for teacher professional development in developing countries.* Washington, DC: infoDev/World Bank. Retrieved from http://www.infodev.org/en/Publication.294.html.
Garet, M. S., Andrew, C. P., Desimone, L., Beatrice, F. B., & Kwang, S. Y. (2001). What makes professional development effective? results from a national sample or teachers. *American Educational Research Journal, 38*(4), 915-915. Retrieved from http://search.proquest.com/docview/200450497?accountid=10919.
Huber, C. (2010). Professional Learning 2.0. *Educational Leadership, 67*(8). Retrieved October 25, 2010, from the Academic Search Complete database.
IESD, Inc. (2011). Digital Districts: Web 2.0 and Collaborative Technologies in U.S. Schools. *National Survey Report.* Retrieved October 24, 2012, from http://tinyurl.com/ceran6b.
Jensen, B. (2012). Focus PD on student learning. *Phi Delta Kappan.* Retrieved October 24, 2012, from http://www.kappanmagazine.org/content/94/2/76.short.
K-6 Literacy Learning Activity Types. Retrieved March 23, 2013, from http://activitytypes.wmwikis.net/K-6+Literacy.
Kirkpatrick, J. (2007). The hidden power of Kirkpatrick's four levels. *T&D Training & Development, 61*(8), 34-37. Retrieved October 25, 2012, from the Academic Search Complete database.
Laurel, E. J., Quatroke, R., Amy, J. S., Victoria, J. E., et al. (2001). What workshop or in-service activity has been most valuable to you in your teaching? *English Journal, 90*(5), 28-31. Retrieved from http://search.proquest.com/docview/237285294?accountid=10919.
Learning forward - professional learning for student results. Retrieved October 25, 2012, from http://www.learningforward.org/default.aspx.
National Survey Shows District Use of Web 2.0 Technologies on the Rise and Improves Learning. *Press Release Distribution - Submit Press Releases Online - PRWeb.* Retrieved October 25, 2012, from http://www.prweb.com/releases/2011/03/prweb5205194.htm.
NMC Horizon Report | 2012 Higher Ed Edition | The New Media Consortium. *The New Media Consortium | Sparking innovation, learning and creativity.* Retrieved October 8, 2012, from http://www.nmc.org/publications/horizon-report-2012-higher-ed-edition.
NMSU: Proposal Templates. *NMSU: College of Education Center for Research and Outreach.* Retrieved October 8, 2012, from http://cro.nmsu.edu/proposals.html.
School principals and social networking in education: Practices, policies, and realities in 2010. Retrieved October 8, 2012, from http://www.edweb.net/fimages/op/PrincipalsandSocialNetworkingReport.pdf.
Technology and the Florida Sunshine State Standards. Retrieved October 8, 2012, from www.paec.org/david/big/sssgl.pdf.

The Kirkpatrick Philosophy. *Kirkpatrick Partners*. Retrieved October 25, 2012, from www.kirkpatrickpartners.com/OurPhilosophy/tabid/66/Default.aspx.

Yeung, A. S., Taylor, P. G., Hui, C., Lam-Chiang, A. C. and Low, E.-L. (2012). *Mandatory use of technology in teaching: Who cares and so what?* British Journal of Educational Technology, 43: 859–870.

Acknowledgements

The authors would like to thank the participants of the Series, their students, colleagues, and administrators. In particular, Nan Akin, Marge Cox, and Andy Delgado were instrumental in helping facilitate the workshops. The Series would not have been possible without mini grants from the FGCU chapter of the National Writing Project and the Whitaker Center for STEM Education at FGCU.

Using Technology to Promote Mentoring and Reflection between Beginning and Experienced Math Teachers

Denise Johnson
Winston-Salem State University, United States
johnsondt@wssu.edu

Farrah M. Jackson
Elizabeth City State University, United States
fmjackson@mail.ecsu.edu

Nancy Ruppert
University of North Carolina Asheville, United States
nruppert@unca.edu

Abstract. This paper discusses how technology was used to promote reflection and mentoring in a beginning teacher support program for math teachers. Various technologies were tested and used to virtually connect mentees and mentors from various locations across the state. Data was collected by analyzing responses in online modules, blogs, surveys, and in professional growth feedback cycles. Results revealed that some technologies promoted reflection and mentoring interaction by providing convenience and programmatic integration while others challenged participants with technical specifications and a lack of ease of use.

Introduction

The Fostering Effective Teachers Through Support (FETTS) program was designed to connect beginning math teachers with experienced math teachers virtually. Oftentimes small districts and low-wealth schools have difficulty finding experienced teachers in the same content area to serve as mentors for beginning teachers. FETTS used technology to eliminate physical barriers that sometimes keep teachers from working collaboratively. Mentor teachers supported novice teachers by connecting with them virtually on several platforms. Project pairs traded lesson plans and video vignettes of teaching. Online professional development on Differentiated Instruction was offered to mentee and mentor teachers. Teachers also used virtual environments to get advice about classroom management, working with parents, and common challenges that beginning teachers face.

Review of Literature

New teachers develop their content and pedagogical knowledge to a great extent during the first three years of initial teaching and thus have the capability to improve their teaching tremendously very early on in their career (Darling et al., 2009; Ingersoll & Kralik, 2004). In order to facilitate the learning process novice teachers require support to understand and cope with the day to day instructional and non-instructional responsibilities that they face in schools (Feiman-Nemser, 2000). In the past 15 years induction programs have been at the forefront of efforts to serve beginning teachers (Darling-Hammond & Sclann, 1996). Ganser et al. (1998) provided a collection of papers that highlighted mentoring programs and found that teachers in induction programs improved various instructional practices including questioning techniques and classroom management (Ganser et al., 1998; Ingersoll & Strong, 2011). Smith and Evans (2008) worked with lateral entry teachers and found mentoring "teams" influenced teachers' morale and success in implementing instructional strategies. Furthermore, a study conducted by the National Commission on Mathematics and Science Teaching for the 21st century (2000) suggests that providing more training and professional development opportunities to teachers is the clearest way to increase the achievement level of students in mathematics: hence, the establishments of effective mentoring programs have the potential of having effects way beyond the benefits they provide to teachers.

There is a considerable amount of research on face-to-face mentoring programs; however, the increase in electronic communication and information technology has led researchers to study the effects of a new mentoring phenomenon called electronic mentoring or e-mentoring. E-mentoring is defined as mentoring which is carried out using technology such as the internet, computer-mediated communication, e-mail, electronic newsletter and/or discussion groups (de Janasz et al., 2008; Mueller, 2004). E-mentoring has been proven to be effective in providing beginning teachers with professional development, emotional support, and increased confidence (Ensher & Murphy, 1997). Bierema et al. list the fact that e-mentoring is "easier to manage, less costly, unconstrained by geography or time, faster, and more egalitarian than traditional mentoring" as features e-mentoring offers which cannot be found in traditional mentoring. Since oftentimes support for beginning teachers comes from the assignment of a mentor-teacher at the school or district level (Elliot & Calderhead, 1993) it is quite easy to see why e-mentoring may be particularly attractive for teachers in the current economic climate. Although the structure of mentoring programs can vary greatly between schools, the use of reflection is one of the most common characteristics of effective mentoring programs (Lopez-Real & Kwan, 2005). Allowing mentees to reflect on their teaching experiences both individually and with the input of their mentees is extremely useful in increasing the skills and confidence of new teachers (Feiman-Nemser, 2000; Gilbert 2005). The use of video recorders, online discussion forums, and online blogs in mentoring programs provides numerous opportunities for teachers to reflect on their teaching experiences. Furthermore, integrating technology into mentoring programs allows information to be preserved so that teachers can reflect on their teaching over time which allows them to see their growth and further develop their confidence.

Description of the Project

From 2009 to 2011 experienced and beginning teachers from three North Carolina counties participated in an e-mentoring project through two public universities that focused on teaching mathematics. The project, Fostering Effective Teaching Through Support (FETTS), focused on developing effective planning & teaching techniques in beginning teachers (mentees) as well as more effective teacher leaders in the experienced teachers (mentors). Program participants could independently apply to the program or be referred by their principal. Mentor/mentee pairs were made based on grade assignment only and each participant received a stipend for their participation. At the beginning of the project all mentors received training on effective mentoring techniques. Program participants engaged in a variety of activities in order to achieve the established goals. Mentors analyzed mentees' lesson plans, instructional videos, and provided advice on classroom issues. Mentors and Mentees both blogged about their experiences and shared details about their growth and development: mentors comments centered around the North Carolina Professional Teaching Standards 2 – 4 (Respectful Environment for Diverse Students, Teachers Know the Content they Teach, and Teachers Facilitate Learning respectively) while mentees used Standard 5 (self-reflection) as a self-assessment. Mentees participated in an online course and attended other professional development activities. All participants communicated using prescribed electronic mediums (i.e. email, video portal, blog, etc.) and were required to meet face-to-face at least two times during the academic year, at the opening program in August and the closing program in April. During the initial meeting mentors and mentees were introduced to the various technologies that they would be utilizing throughout the program.

Mentoring Through Lesson Plan Reflections and Video Observations

A major component of the interaction between mentor and mentees was the sharing of advice and tips on mathematics teaching strategies. Mentor and mentee pairs shared lesson plans, teaching strategies, and classroom videos with each other. Mentees were first tasked with developing lesson plans on a math topic that they planned to teach in the near future which they then submitted to their mentor via email. The mentee also uploaded an electronic version of the lesson plan on Survey Monkey using a lesson plan template based on the 5-E Learning Cycle. Once received, mentors were able to see how the novice teacher organized the teaching of a math concept and provided feedback to the mentee about ways the lesson could be improved. Mentors engaged in dialogue about ideas for lesson plan revisions directly with their mentee via email and/or phone (and in some cases face-to-face).

Once the lesson plan was finalized, the mentee teacher videotaped themselves teaching the lesson in their own classroom using an iPod or Flip camera and uploaded the video into the project's Vimeo account. Vimeo, an online video management tool, allowed participants to post sizable video clips of their teaching in a secure manner which allowed participants to review videos without concern for storing or sharing such large files via email. After reviewing their mentee's video, mentors completed a lesson observation summary on Survey Monkey (based on NC Professional Teaching Standards). In addition, mentors also shared video of them teaching a lesson in their own classroom that specifically addressed areas where their mentee needed improvement; providing mentees with immediate feedback on methods of addressing their deficiencies without any interruption to participants' school schedule.

Although communication between mentor and mentee is essential for any mentoring program the project team also felt that it was very important that there be dialogue exclusively among mentors and dialogue solely between mentees. To help facilitate the communication among mentors and mentees program participants used blogging to reflect on how their mathematics teaching practices were impacted over time. Initially, two WordPress accounts (one for mentees and one for mentors) were created to ensure confidentiality and promote open and honest feedback between the two groups. This component of the program was transitioned to Blackboard in year 2. Both mentors and mentees blogged at various intervals during the program period with the assistance of guided prompts designed to capture their reflections of the impact of the program on teaching and learning. Specifically, mentors were given opportunities to describe their observations of the growth of their mentee within and between multiple lesson plan developments and teaching videos. Mentees blogged about their experiences in the program; particularly, how they would characterize their strengths and areas of improvement based on the feedback from their mentors. Mentees also reflected on their teaching videos in the blog area.

Research Questions

1. How did participants use blogs and videos to reflect on their progress and experiences while teaching and working with a mentor/mentee?
2. In what ways did participants readily use electronic mediums to communicate with other participants and researchers?
3. In what ways was technology used to facilitate a continuous improvement model for the project?
4. What do participants view as the strengths and weaknesses about communicating with their mentee/mentor using email and other electronic means?

Methodology

Data was collected from all participants of the program at the beginning, midpoint, and end of each academic year. In this study, the data collected was used to determine (a) the participant's use of blogging and video for reflection, (b) the use of technology/virtual environments to facilitate mentoring, (c) the types of information shared/requested during mentoring events, and (d) the successes and challenges of new teachers and supporting them using electronic mediums. Input from mentee and mentor participants, principals, and advisory board members were used to guide the direction of the program. The information provided from the data analysis can be used by staff development coordinators, mathematics instructional coaches, principals, and teacher education programs that prepare teachers to teach mathematics to develop programs and resources for beginning teachers of mathematics and to support individuals that mentor them. Our method for determining the role technology plays in the mentoring process between mathematics teachers involved both descriptive and qualitative analyses. To answer our first two research questions about overall use of technology and how it promoted reflection, we began by reviewing feedback data given by participants at midterm and post-year events. These data were coded by the research team by first using open coding for patterns then axial coding techniques for categories because this method can illuminate interesting and important details that are worthy of attention (Creswell, 2007). We expected that teachers who were new to teaching (particularly younger teachers) would be more likely to engage in interactions via electronic media. We also expected participants to consider blogging as journaling, in reference to individuality and privacy, as a means to share fears and concerns with little ramifications.

We investigated the remaining two research questions by reviewing participants' responses on post-project surveys, built-in feedback opportunities at program symposia, and informal interviews and conversations with researchers. The program advisory board and researchers found this particular data quite interesting as it influenced how the program evolved over the two years. When possible, questions that yielded interesting or unclear ideas on post surveys were reworded and asked at symposia events.

Participant Sample, Recruitment, and Selection

FETTS focused on providing opportunities for novice and experienced teachers to engage in discourse and mentoring relationships focused on teaching mathematics. Program participants were novice math teachers in primarily Title I (low wealth) schools, student teachers in Title I schools, and experienced math teachers across North Carolina. There were a total of 12 mentors and 13 mentees involved in year 1 of the program. In year 2, there were 6 mentors and 7 mentees involved in the program. As consistent with current US demographics, 90% of program participants were female. About half of the participants taught elementary level mathematics and were teaching in rural school environments. The remaining half taught middle or high school mathematics with a split between rural and urban school districts. FETTS participants could self-nominate and apply for participation or be chosen at the district-level. Participant selection criteria were based on teacher's: classroom experience, value-added data, and recommendations (mentors) and classroom experience, school environment, and approval by building leadership (mentees). All participants had to be full-time classroom teachers with an interest in learning more about learning and teaching mathematics.

Findings

Blogs and Videos

During the mid-term and final symposia participants were asked to discuss their feelings towards blogging. Mentees noted that blogging was "informal" and they "felt comfortable" sharing their innermost details (i.e. reflections) about their perceptions of their teaching abilities. Some mentors also commented that they liked how Wordpress allowed them to "see everyone's responses and reflect". Both mentors and mentees commented about the ease of blogging stating things such as "Love blogging! Quick and easy way to reflect". Although it was clear that participants used blogging to reflect on their teaching they did comment that they would have liked to talk about more during their blogs. Specifically they wanted to use the blogs within their mentee/mentor group to share things such as innovative teaching strategies, teaching pitfalls and effective uses of technology in teaching mathematics.

Participants discussed several positive aspects about sharing videos, including how it "was easy to get quick videos" using the iPod. Participants also commented that using videos to share lessons meant that they did not have to lose any class time with their students which "allowed them to maintain their normal scheduled day". Several of the mentors commented that creating and watching videos was good for both mentors and mentees and that it provided experience for any teacher who was interested in seeking National Board certification. Every participant agreed that the use of videos allowed them to reflect on their teaching. One mentor, who was paired with a mentee who taught one grade higher, stated that "watching my mentee's video made me more aware of what I need to do to prepare my students for the higher grades." In another case, a mentor discussed how their "use of technology increased" after they observed their mentee using the SMART Board in an innovative way during her video observation. A minority of the participants commented that "at times it was difficult to see what the students" were doing and said they would rather observe in person.

Communication

The following tables give the results from the post survey given to both mentors and mentees, Y1 denotes the first year of the study and Y2 denotes year 2.

	Mentor Y1	Mentee Y1	Mentor Y2	Mentee Y2
Mostly via email	44%	80%	57%	50%
Email & Phone	11%	0%	28%	0%
Face to Face	44%	40%	28%	50%

Table 1: How did you communicate with the mentor/mentee?

	Mentor Y1	Mentee Y1	Mentor Y2	Mentee Y2
4-6 times	56%	60%	29%	25%
7-9 times	11%	20%	0%	0%
More than 9 times	33%	40%	71%	75%

Table 2: How many times did you initiate communication with your mentee/mentor?

	Mentor Y1	Mentee Y1	Mentor Y2	Mentee Y2
1-3 times	11%	0%	43%	25%
4-6 times	33%	40%	14%	0%
7-9 times	11%	20%	0%	0%
More than 9 times	33%	40%	43%	75%

Table 3: How many times has your mentor/mentee responded back to you?

Strengths and Weaknesses

The following results are from the mentor and mentee post surveys given in year 1 and 2 (unless indicated).

Describe 2 strengths about communicating with mentee/mentor using emails or other electronic means.
Mentor – (1) Convenient to reply on your time schedule / easy; (2) Allows you time to think about communication before you respond
Mentee – (1) Quick Response and (2) Ability to Share resources

Describe 2 weaknesses about communicating with mentee/mentor using emails or other electronic means
Mentor – (1) Impersonal/ Lack emotion; (2) Conversation not fluid; (3) Response not immediate (Year 2)
Mentee – (1) Response not immediate; (2) Things can be misinterpreted; (3) More face to face meetings

Recommendations for Improvement

Below you will find participants' responses to questions asked during the mid-term and closing symposia.

What recommendations do you have in terms of using blogs and videos?
Year 1 – (1) Clarify length of videos; (2) Work with schools to permit access to technology; (3) Reduce number of websites used/confusing structure
Year 2 – (1) See other participants' videos (mentors and mentees); (2) Work with schools to permit access to technology; (3) Sending email reminders of when the Blogs are due.

What recommendations do you have in terms of lesson plan sharing?
Year 1 – (1) Use a similar lesson plan template; (2) Eliminate lesson plans since not required by principal
Year 2 – (1) Provide more feedback on lesson plans

What recommendations do you have for improving the overall logistics of the program?
Year 1 – (1) Meet as a FETTS group once every 3 months; (2) Better understanding of websites/technology used; (3) Create one site for technology (hard to keep track of which site is affiliated with each technology)

Year 2 – (1) Set specific timelines for responding to emails; (2) Give all due dates at the beginning of the program; (3) Use Google docs for lesson plan sharing

Analysis

Research indicates that new teachers have the potential to improve greatly with support, professional development, and mentoring within the first three years (Darling et al., 2009; Ingersoll & Kralik, 2004). This study provided mentoring relationships for novice teacher's first two years in the profession and used technology to facilitate thoughtful reflection regarding the impact on instruction. It is clear that the use of blogging and video critiques are two powerful mechanisms for teachers to use to become reflective educators (Kerka, 2002; Schön, 1987). Consistent with Cyboran (2005) participants described their experiences with blogging as "easy", "personal" and "an intimate reflection time" and discussed ways in which mentoring has helped them become more thoughtful, confident teachers.

The use of technology provided an opportunity for the type and manner of instructional practices used to teach math to improve. Specifically, the mentors suggested that the opportunity to see other mentor's videos and read the experiences and feedback of other mentor's blogs allowed them to challenge and question their own professional and instructional beliefs; an experience consistent with studies that document the importance of reflection (Lopez-Real and Kwan, 2005). These experienced, well-established teachers reported finding a renewed commitment to more thoughtful considerations about the instructional techniques they were using in the classrooms. The technology and mentoring process combined provided opportunities for beginning and veteran teachers to examine their own practices, by observing one another, sharing lesson plans, and discussing common challenges about teaching. By sharing their views virtually to see so many different perspectives of successful implementations of the strategies, mentees were encouraged to build classrooms that addressed communication, assessment, instructional activities, and the needs of students; topics identified as essential components of successful classrooms (Ingersoll & Strong, 2011).

Not all teachers are able to be assigned to a veteran, passionate mentor in their school; especially in low-wealth or schools with high teacher turn-over. This research advocates for the development of more e-mentoring content-specific programs even within districts. This type of program can be used as a way to induct new teachers or support those who face professional challenges. In addition, LEAs (**Local Educational Agencies**) and universities can work collaboratively to build schools' capacity to offer professional development for teachers.

Strengths and Weaknesses of E-mentoring

Experienced teachers have many responsibilities both inside and outside of the classroom so the convenience and flexibility of e-mentoring is viewed as a clear strength. It is well documented in the 2011 MetLife Survey of the American Teacher that many teachers desire to collaborate, observe, and provide feedback to colleagues, but feel that typical school schedules are not conducive for them to do so, this study found that communicating electronically helped address this issue. This study also found that e-mentoring allowed for mentors to construct more thoughtful responses regarding their mentees teaching since they were not tasked with responding immediately and had time to carefully create their responses. Since participants were already communicating electronically the idea of mentors sharing resources developed organically which was viewed as extremely beneficial by mentees. Although participants had access to iPods and could talk using Face Time only three mentee/mentor pairs took advantage of this technology, which could explain why participants still viewed communicating electronically as impersonal. The lack of fluidity in conversations was another weakness of electronic communication cited by participants, however the use of Face Time or even chatting using an instant messenger system are both potential solutions to this problem.

Changes made based on Recommendations

As a result of the feedback from the Year 1 symposia and surveys, the project team realized that although the technology itself was not an issue for participants, the logistics of managing several pieces of technology was a definite barrier and needed to be addressed. Participants were concerned with how they accessed the technology and were requesting a central repository that was accessible to all participants. During year 2 of the program

CourseSites, a free online learning management system developed by Blackboard, was used to post and update program material in one central location. CourseSites consisted of two course shells, one for mentees and one for mentors, with an Assignments tab that housed: lesson plan submissions, self-reflections, video submissions, and blogs. Many participants stated that CourseSites provided them with an "ease of use" and commented about the "benefits of only having to remember one web address" to access their individual tasks.

Another concern of participants during the first year was their difficulty in uploading their videos because of the size of their file which "caused a lot of stress". The issue with uploading videos was reduced dramatically during the second year of the project when participants were instructed to reduce the size of their file and limit their videos to 20 minute increments. Although some participants remarked about having to submit lesson plans to their mentor/mentee, even though they were not required by their principal, the project team continued to require them during year 2 requiring everyone to use a lesson plan template based on the 5-E Learning Cycle to help with continuity. Feedback from the first year made it clear that participants wanted more face to face interaction therefore in year 2 mentee and mentor pairs met three times during the year, in August, December and April.

Implications for Teacher Educators

An e-mentoring program has many benefits to pre-service teachers, alumni, and the teacher education program as a whole. Using alumni to connect with pre-service and recent graduates can aid a university in expanding mentoring and support options. Some programs are challenged by providing adequate support for novice teachers once they have left academic programs and many LEAs are already overwhelmed with providing resources to new teachers. Connecting beginning teachers with experienced alumni already in the profession could supply the encouragement and assistance needed for them to have a successful first year.

Although pre-service teachers are not faced with the pressures of running a classroom all on their own, an e-mentoring program can offer additional methods of preparing prospective teachers. In a methods course, e-mentors can be used to mentor students on developing effective lesson plans or implementing classroom management techniques. In clinical experiences, e-mentors can be used as supplemental advisers to guide students. These mentors can serve in a non-evaluative manner when the clinical student (or student teacher) has so many people observing and evaluating his/her abilities (i.e. clinical supervisor, cooperating teacher, etc.). The mentor can assist the clinical student in interpreting feedback as well as serve as a resource when students want additional perspectives.

An e-mentoring program that utilizes alumni can be advantageous to teacher education faculty and administrators. Programs that use this structure as a continuous improvement model can build in opportunities to provide professional development to alumni as well as get feedback regarding how well the program prepared them to teach. Former students and current students can engage in dialogue about lessons learned that can be used to improve programs. In addition, connecting with alumni could stimulate opportunities for them to provide financial support to activities and programs.

Conclusion

The use of technology can be extremely helpful in a mentoring program, particularly in encouraging participants to reflect on their teaching experiences over time. Advances in technology now allow individuals to save large quantities of both written and visual data that can be evaluated months and even years after they were developed. Although the specific technology itself may not present a barrier, when developing an e-mentoring program it is essential to consider how the technology is organized and delivered to participants. Having access to the latest cutting edge technology is wonderful but can sometimes be overwhelming. The existence of one piece of technology that addresses all of the intricacies of a mentoring program unfortunately may never exist so the seamless integration of various systems should always be at the forefront of any program. Through continuous feedback between mentors, mentees and the project team the FETTS program was able to continue to utilize the wonderful features of various pieces of technologies while simultaneously addressing the technology overload felt from participants by consolidating to a centralized managing system. Recommendations for future e-mentoring programs include:

- Requiring participants to have virtual face-to-face communication once a month
- Using Google docs to share lesson plans as opposed to using email
- Allowing other participants to view videos
- Working with school districts to ensure that technology can be accessed from schools

Using Vimeo to collect videos of mentors and mentees over a two year period allowed the project to develop the beginnings of a video archive of recent and relevant mathematics teaching. This was not an original goal of the project, but served to be extremely helpful to the participants.

References

Bierema, L., & Hill, J. (2005).Virtual mentoring and HRD. *Advances in Developing Human Resources 7 (5)* 556-568.

Creswell, J. W. (2007). Qualitative inquiry and research design: Choosing among five approaches (2nd ed.). Thousand Oaks, CA: Sage

Cyboran, V. L. (2005). Fostering workplace learning through online journaling. *Performance Improvement 44*(7), 34-39.

Darling-Hammond, L., & Sclan, E. M. (1996). Who teaches and why. Dilemmas of building a profession for twenty-first century schools. In Handbook of Research on Teacher Education, second edition, J. Sikula, T. J. Buttery, & E. Guyton (Eds.), pp. 67- 101. New York: Macmillan.

Darling-Hammond, L., Wei, R., Andree, A., Richardson, N., & Orphanos, S. (2009). *Professional learning in the learning profession: A status report on teacher development in the U.S. and abroad.* Dallas: National Staff Development Council.

Elliot, B. & Calderheadl, J. (1993). Mentoring for teacher development, in: D.McIntyre, H. Hagger, and M. Wilkin (Eds) *Mentoring: perspectives in school-based education*, London: Kogan Page, 166-189.

Ensher, E. A., & Murphy, S. E. (1997). Effects of race, gender, perceived similarity, and contact on mentor relationships. *Journal of Vocational Behavior*, 50(3), 460-481.

Feiman-Nemser, S. (2000) Mentoring in schools: a handbook of good practice, London: Kogan Page.

Gilbert, L. (2005). What helps beginning teachers? *Educational Leadership, 62*(8), 36-39 SL W PD.

Ingersoll, R. & Kralik, J. (2004).*The impact of mentoring on teacher retention: What the research says.* Denver, CO: Education Commission of the States. Retrieved from http://www.ecs.org/clearinghouse/50/36/5036.htm

Ingersoll, R. and Strong, M. (2011). "The Impact of Induction and Mentoring Programs on Beginning Teachers: A Critical Review of the Research."Review of Education Research. Vol. 81(2), 201-233.

Kerka, S. (2002). *Journal writing as an adult learning tool.* Retrieved May 30, 2004 from: The Clearing House on Adult, Career, and Vocational Education (ACVE) Web site: http://www.cete.org/acve/docgen.asp?tbl=pab&ID-112

deJanasz, S. C., Ensher, E., & Heun, C. (2008). Virtual relationships and real benefits: using e-mentoring to connect business students with practicing managers. *Mentoring & Tutoring: Partnership in Learning*, 16(4), 394-411.

Lopez-Real, F., & Kwan T. (2005). Mentors' perceptions of their own professional development during mentoring.*Journal of Educationfor teaching*, 31.1, 15-24.

Mueller, S. (2004). Electronic mentoring as an example for the use of information and communications technology in engineering education. *European Journal of Engineering Education*, 29 (1), 53-63.

National Commission on Mathematics and Science Teaching for the 21st Century. (2000). *Before it's too late: A report to the Nation from the National Commission on Mathematics and Science Teaching for the 21st Century.* Washington, DC: Author.

Schön, D. A. (1987).*Educating the reflective practitioner.* San Francisco: Jossey-Bass.

Smith, E. R., & Evans, C. (2008). Providing effective mentoring for alternate route beginning teachers. The Teacher Educator, 43(4), 249-278.

The MetLife Survey of the American Teacher. (2011). *Teachers, Parents, and the Economy.* New York, NY: Harris Interactive.

www.ingramcontent.com/pod-product-compliance
Lightning Source LLC
Chambersburg PA
CBHW081842230426
43669CB00018B/2789